GeniusX

Business Intelligence

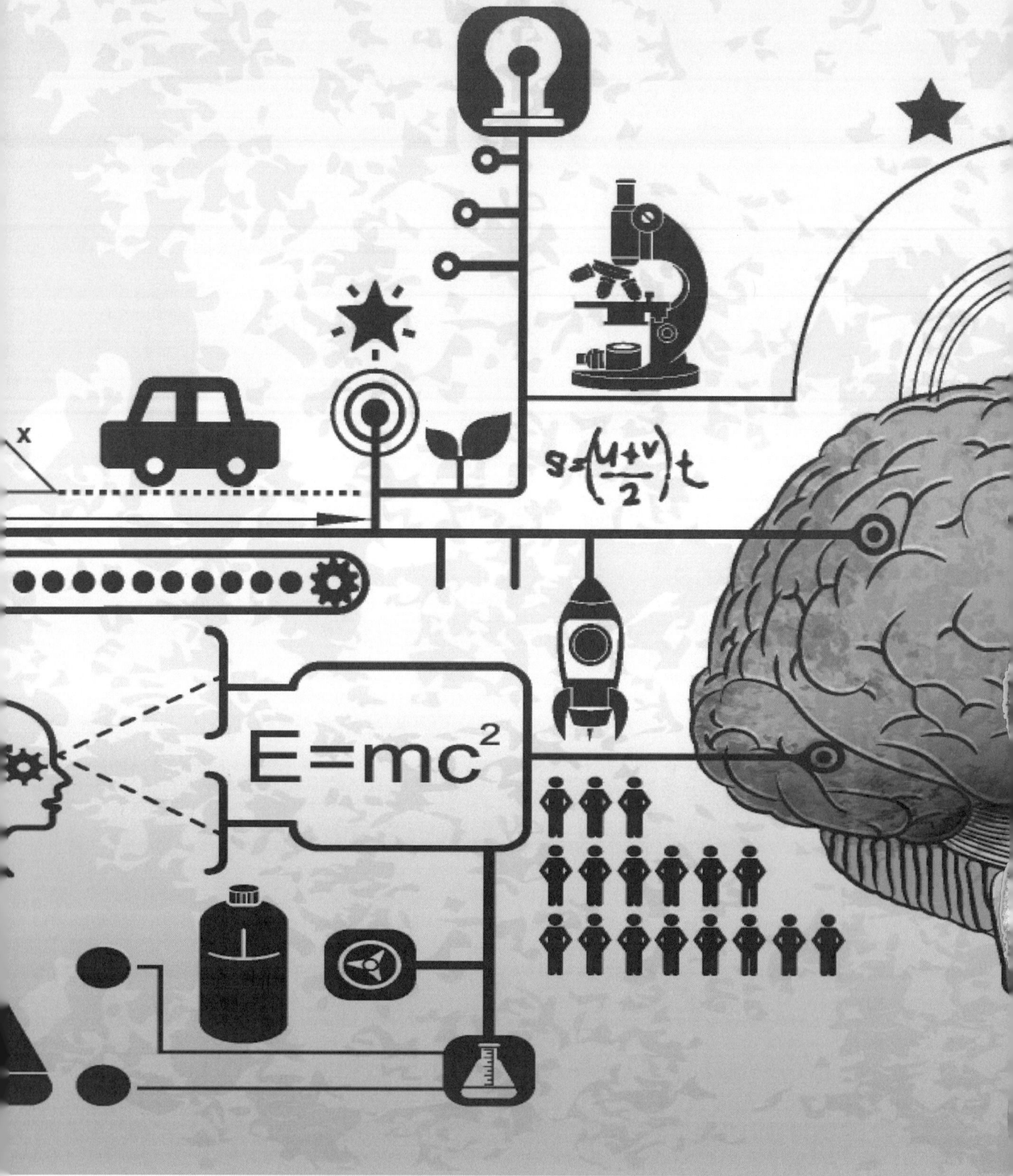

$$s=\left(\frac{u+v}{2}\right)t$$

$$E=mc^2$$

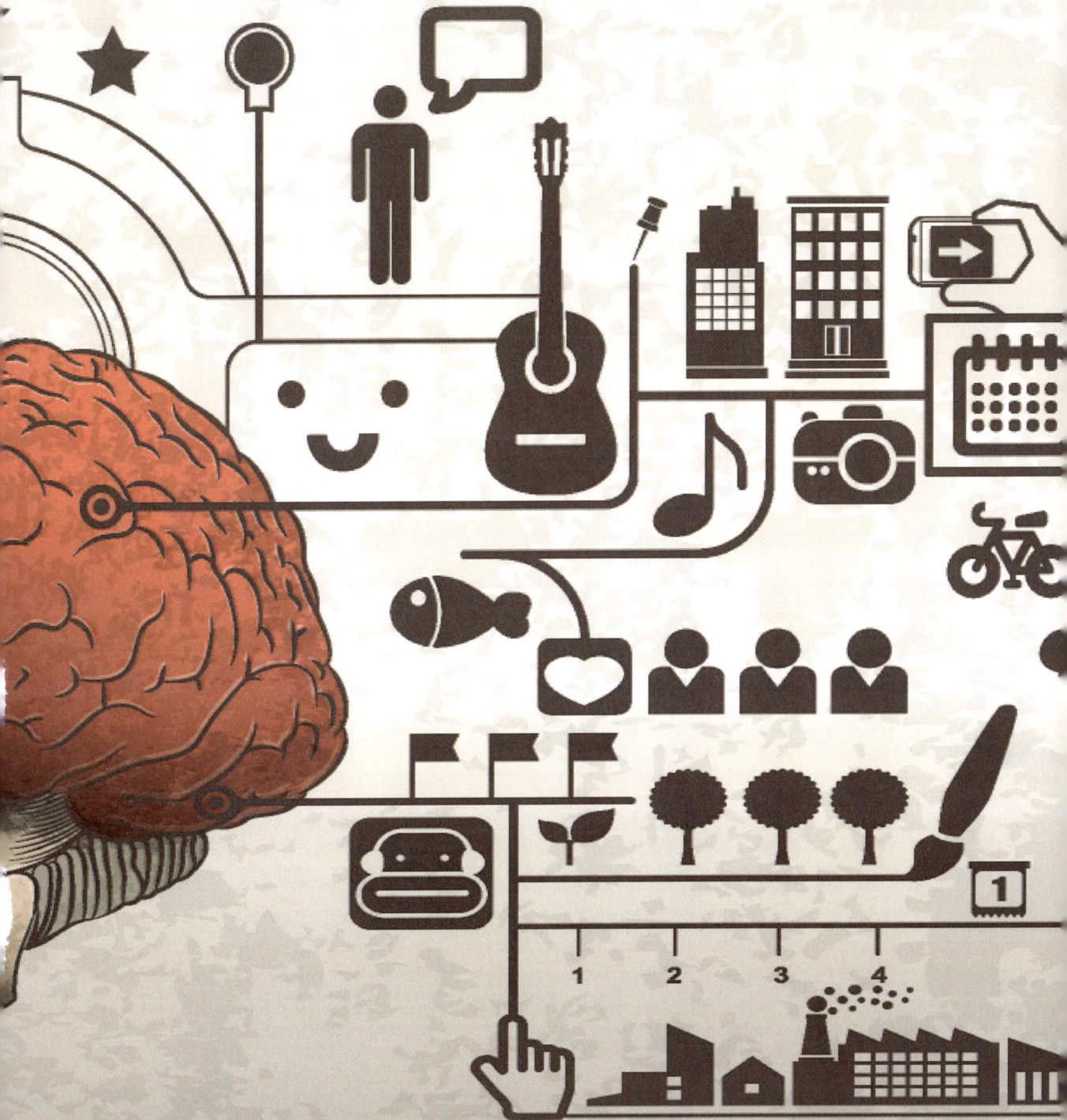

If you wish to know which type of person you are, I encourage you to try our online quiz at **www.neurogenius.com**

GeniusX
Business Intelligence

Filament Publishing

Writer:	Damrong Pinkoon
Editor:	Philip Hall
Graphic designer:	Napas Ittitanakam
Cover designer:	Napas Ittitanakam
Proofreader:	Pharitporn Aroonvivatkul
Editorial staff:	Sira Noithip
	Sunan Sasomsap
	Kamol Ruangsri
	Jiranan Waklang
	Wipapan Kongkow
	Sukanya Taphun

Damrong Pinkoon Company Limited
5th Floor, Gaysorn Plaza Building,
999 Ploenchit Rd. Lumpini,
Pathumwan, Bangkok 10330
Tel. +66 (0) 2255 3000
Fax. +66 (0) 2252 5888
email: pinkoon123@gmail.com
www.facebook.com / Damrong Pinkoon
Instagram: pinkoon123
Tax id: 0105561188975

1st edition: January 2020
This book is published by

Filament Publishing Ltd
16 Croydon Road, Beddington, Croydon,
Surrey, CR0 4PA, United Kingdom.
www.filamentpublishing.com
Telephone: +44 (0) 20 8688 2598

This time,

we will not read people by their faces.

We will not read people

by their handwriting.

But,

we will read them from their minds.

We will read them

from their thoughts,

and we will be able to

identify...the behaviours

identify...the actions

identify...the outcomes

of each person.

Prof. Dr. Sriroen Kaewkangwan, *Psychology of Personality Theory (Knowing Yourself and Other People),* (Bangkok: Moh-Chao-Ban Publishing House, 2008), 15th Edition.

Jessada Denduangboripant, *Evolution,* (Bangkok: Chulalongkorn University, 2012).

GeniusX Thinking System

It is said that **people only use 10% of their mental potential,** therefore by learning and understanding **the thought processes of the six personality types** at the subconscious level as we've discussed in this book, you not only get to **know your self better,** but you also **learn how you'll interact with other people** in an instant. With this skill, you'll be able to continue gaining new knowledge, because in life continually exercising the brain – as we do our bodies – will **make us richer** and increase our ability to **understand others better.**

GeniusX Business Intelligence

A) Six Personalities

1. Learn about the six types of people
   G = Game Changer
   E = Entrepreneur
   N = Networker
   I = Informationist
   U = Unique
   S = Sharer
2. Do the test
3. Know which type of person you are
4. Know which types of people your family members are
5. Know which types of people your team are

B) Skill Improvement

6. Beginning to apply each strategy appropriately
7. Improving skills, creating new strong points and trying to eliminate weak points
8. Adding new strategic skills to develop new personalities and rectify other weak points

C) Strategy (Study and Select)

9. Learn 48 models of self-development strategies
10. Select a strategy suitable for your personality
11. Willingly carry out a thorough study to get a profound understanding

D) Score (Evalution & Enjoy)

12. Score points for relationships and work outcomes in your organisation to evaluate and measure improvement by using figures
13. Record changes, both good and bad
14. Evaluate performance, both at work and in your personal life
15. Be happy with changes in life

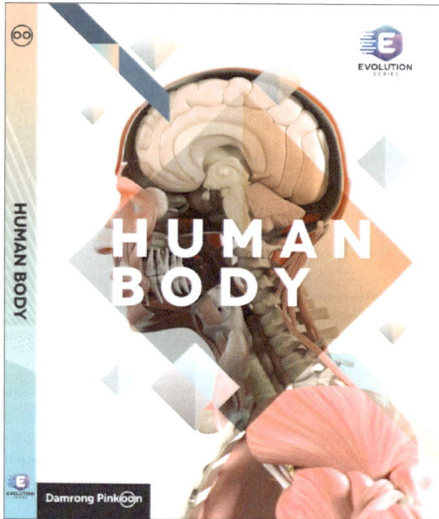

Human Body

The human body and its myriad of organs, tissues and muscles is one of Mother Nature's most miraculous creations. Humans not only have the ability to do all types of weird and wonderful things both consciously and unconsciously – but our body is also able to fight a wide range of infections and viruses and repair itself after major and minor injuries. In this book, you will learn about many of the diseases that affect the human body and its internal systems and various methods to keep in tip-top condition by eating healthily and staying in shape through exercise.

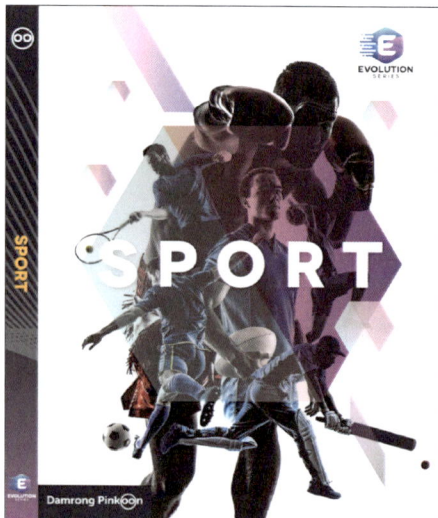

Sport

Since the dawn of time people have always found time to engage in some type of sporting activity. In fact, most of our modern day sports have a long history that more often than not came about through warfare. Today, sports are much less violent and the world of sport has mushroomed into a multitude of events with professional athletes earning vast sums of money. Furthermore, gender is no longer a barrier with all-female teams participating in sports that were once the domain of men only.

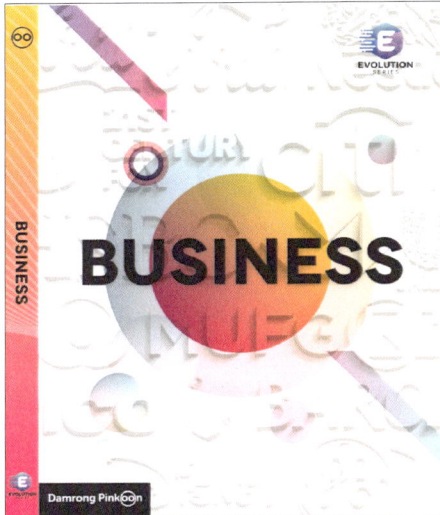

Business

Many of the biggest corporations in the world today began life as small ventures. By their very nature, businesses are all about making profits for their owners and shareholders. Corporate Social Responsibility (CSR) program are a great way for large companies to reinvest a portion of their profits back into the local communities. In this book, you will come to learn about more than 200 companies and the business segments they dominate as well as their annual turnover and profits and the people they employ.

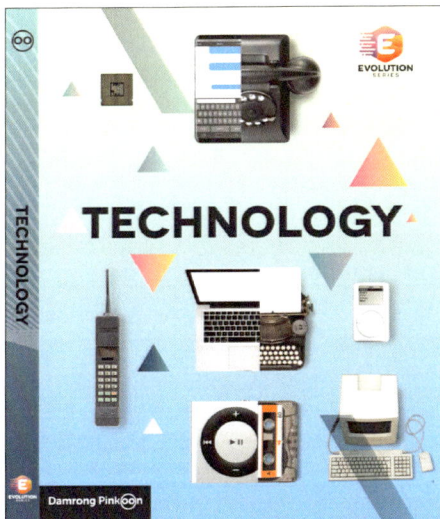

Technology

Just over a century ago, there were no planes flying in the skies, there were no cars speeding along the roads and long-distance communications were a hit and miss affair. However, thanks to our ability to create and control electricity, a plethora of inventions quickly became household products. The telephone, which uses a tiny amount of electricity, has changed our world while at the same time morphing into handheld devices and being the backbone of the Internet. Here, we present to you the men and women who worked tirelessly to bring the best technology to market.

Damrong Pinkoon's Books

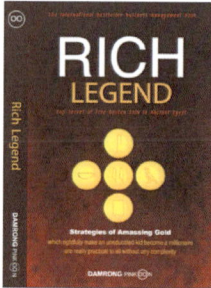

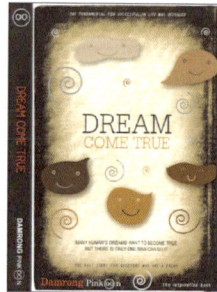

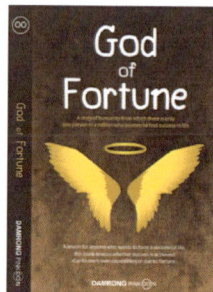

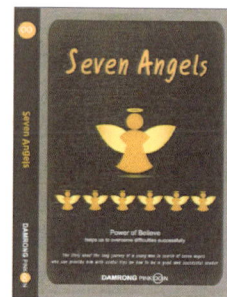

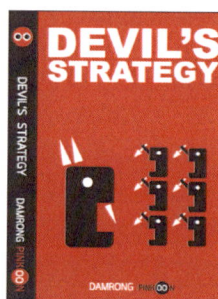

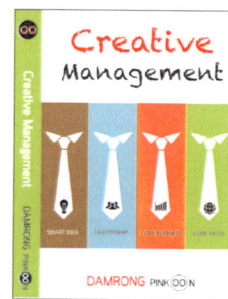

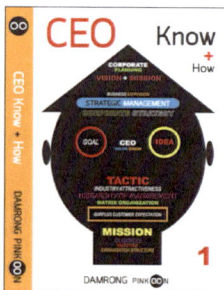

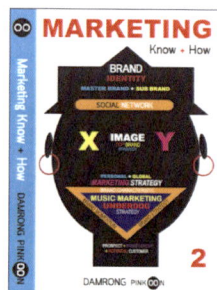

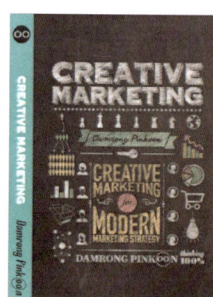

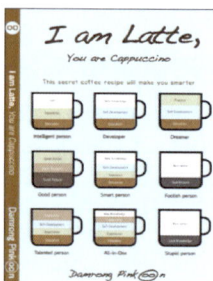

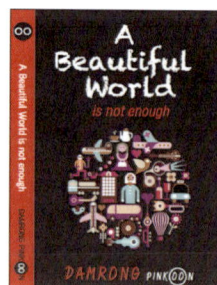

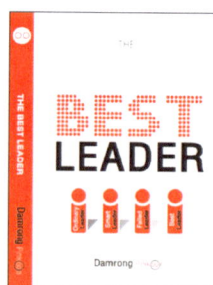

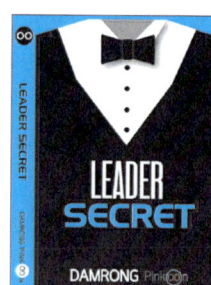

RICH LEGEND
Strategies of Amazing Gold
Rich Legend
DAMRONG PINKOON

DREAM COME TRUE
Dream Come True
DAMRONG PINKOON

God of Fortune
God of Fortune
DAMRONG PINKOON

Seven Angels
Seven Angels
Power of Believe
DAMRONG PINKOON

MARKETING idea
Marketing idea
DAMRONG PINKOON

STRATEGY + IDEA
Strategy + idea
DAMRONG PINKOON

DEVIL'S STRATEGY
DEVIL'S STRATEGY
DAMRONG PINKOON

Creative Management
Creative Management
DAMRONG PINKOON

CEO Know + How
CEO Know + How
DAMRONG PINKOON
1

MARKETING Know + How
Marketing Know + How
DAMRONG PINKOON
2

CREATIVE MARKETING
CREATIVE MARKETING
DAMRONG PINKOON

PRODUCT MARKETING
PRODUCT MARKETING
Damrong Pinkoon

I am Latte, You are Cappuccino
I am Latte, You are Cappuccino
Damrong Pinkoon

A Beautiful World *is not enough*
A Beautiful World is not enough
DAMRONG PINKOON

BEST LEADER
THE BEST LEADER
Damrong

LEADER SECRET
LEADER SECRET
DAMRONG PINKOON

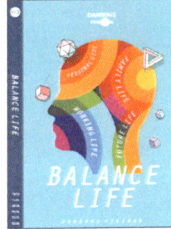

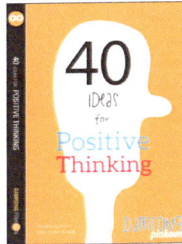

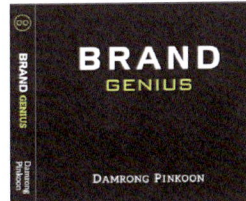

GENIUSX BUSINESS INTELLIGENCE

1st Edition in January 2020

Available in

United Kingdom	Brazil
India	Malaysia
South Korea	Czech Republic
Hong Kong	Singapore
Columbia	Turkey
The Philippines	Brunei
France	Hungary
Lebanon	Italy
Netherlands	Russia
Indonesia	Costa Rica
Mexico	Peru
Chile	Argentina
Germany	Canada
Paraguay	El Salvador
Guatemala	Ecuador

Kindle Application
ebook : Amazon Application
www.Amazon.com
search : *Damrong Pinkoon*

Nook Application
ebook:Barnes&NobleApplication
www.barnesandnoble.com
search : *Damrong Pinkoon*

Damrong Pinkoon Application
ebook : Damrong Pinkoon Application
iPad + iPhone + Google Play + Android
Search : *Damrong Pinkoon*

DAMRONG
PINK OO N

Contact **Damrong Pinkoon**
Email: pinkoon123@gmail.com
Email : pinkoon1@gmail.com
facebook / DamrongPinkoon_English

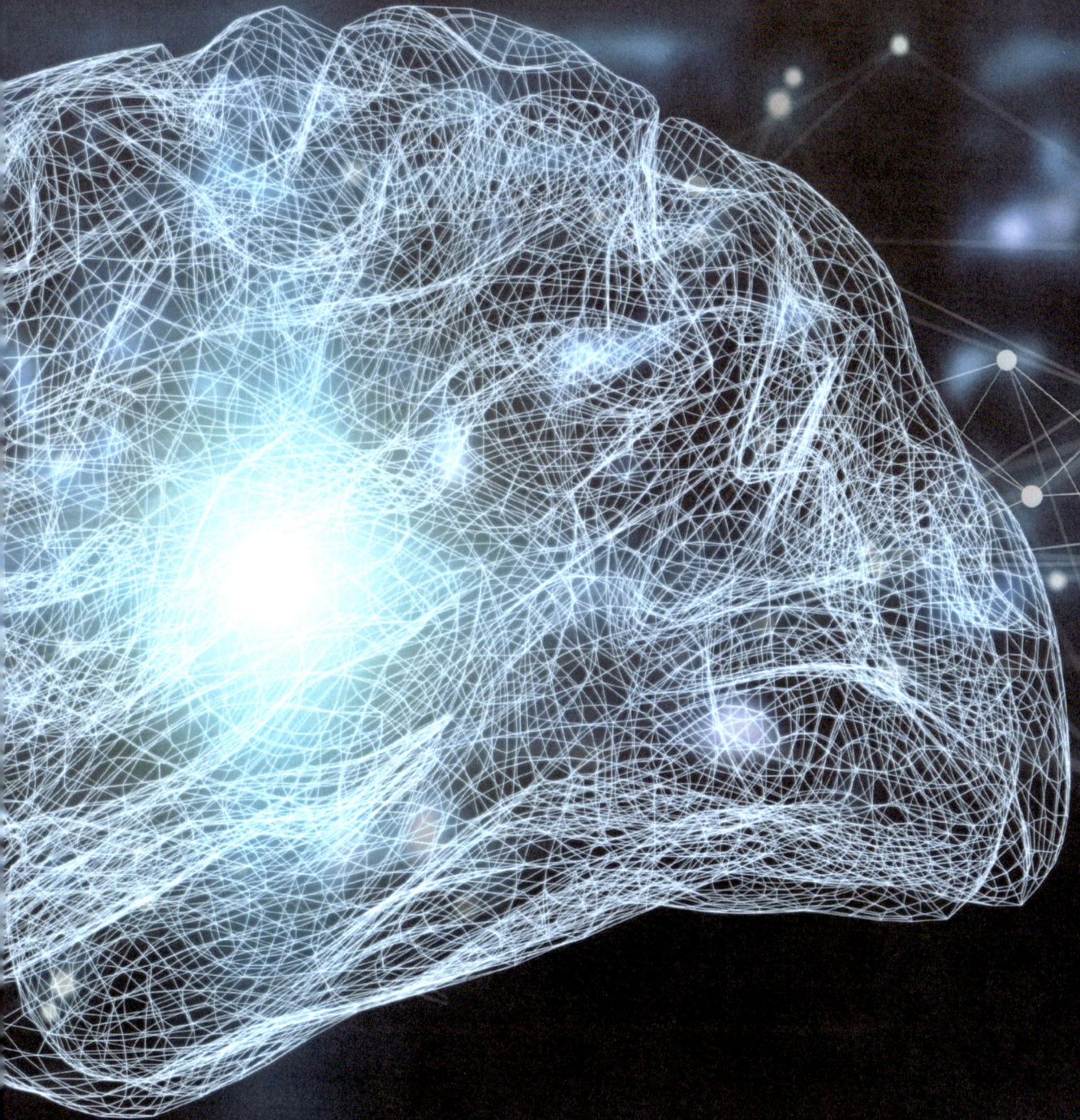

If you can't fly, run.
If you can't run, walk.
If you can't walk, crawl,
but by all means,
keep moving forward.

Martin Luther King Jr.

Minister and Civil Rights Activist

Your time is limited.
So, don't waste it living someone else's life.

Steve Jobs

Co-Founder of Apple Inc.

Swim upstream.
Go the other way.
Ignore the conventional wisdom.

Sam Walton

Founder of Wal-Mart

Genius is one percent inspiration,
Ninety-nine percent perspiration.

Thomas Edison

American Inventor

You were born to win,
but to be a winner you must plan to win,
prepare to win, and expect to win.

Zig Ziglar

American Author

Give me six hours to chop down a tree
and I will spend the first hour sharpening the axe.

Abraham Lincoln

16th American President

Business

Great things in business are never done by one person,
they're done by a team of people.

Steve Jobs

Co-Founder of Apple Inc.

There are no secrets to success.
It is the result of preparation, hard work,
and learning from failure.

Colin Powell

American Statesman

Making money is art and working is art
and good business is the best art.

Andy Warhol

American Artist

The true measure of the value of any business leader
and manager is performance.

Brian Tracy

Motivational Speaker

Intelligence

Intelligence is
the capacity to create works
that need intellect to make them fulfilled.

Edward Lee Thorndike

American Psychologist

Comprehension, inventiveness, direction and criticism:
intelligence is contained in these four words.

Alfred Binet

French Psychologist

Intelligence is the aggregate or global capacity
of the individual to act purposefully, to think rationally
and to deal effectively with his environment.

David Wechsler

Psychologist

There is nothing about an individual
as important as his IQ,
except possibly his morals.

Lewis Terman

American Psychologist

The use of our intelligence gives us pleasure.
In this respect, the brain is like a muscle.
When it is in use we feel very good.

Carl Sagan

American Astronomer and Author

The true sign of intelligence
is not knowledge
but imagination.

Albert Einstein

Eminent Physicist

Business Intelligence

Business intelligence
is a person's ability
to use the skills of thinking and decision-making
and apply them to business strategies
whereby you achieve success
and gain continual profits.

Damrong Pinkoon;

Thai Businessman, Author

and Motivational Speaker

Table of contents

Chapter 9 GeniusX Idea   258
Methods to Gain Success for Each Personality Type

Chapter 10 GeniusX Conclusion   286
Business Strategies

Bibliography   302
References   304
GeniusX Thinking System   306

Preface

It is not difficult to learn about "someone else"... when you put bias aside. However, it is not easy to learn who "we" are... without partiality and sympathy towards ourselves.

Intelligently learning about other people and understanding their point of view is the best way to resolve troubling issues.

Because...80% of our problems in life are due to people. If we learn to understand people, we could solve 100% of our problems.

Furthermore, if we learn about and better understand ourselves, it is also possible to let go of all our problems.

Here are some examples of our common problems:
What do I have to do for living, as I want to get rich?
How can someone else sell things for three times the price we can?
How do I encourage my employees so that they give 100% cooperation?
How can we reason with them when they never listen to the opinions of others?
Why do I feel frustrated every time I am rejected?
How can someone still smile and talk to other people without feeling guilty when they always arrive late for appointments?
How do I control my feelings when I have to deal with someone who always puts their own interests first?
Why doesn't she get angry when he speaks to her like that?
How can I find my place in society without being looked down on?

Why do I always care so much about how others feel, that it leaves me feeling like I can't carry on?

Why do some people still feel unhappy even though they have a lot of money?
How can people who struggle financially still find happiness?

If you have struggled with one or more of these **"questions"** *or* **"problems",** *then GENIUSX Business Intelligence can be of help to you.*

GENIUSX Business Intelligence
is a book that will help you understand yourself, your way of thinking, how to make important decisions, and learn about your way of life.

This includes how you run your own business so that you may become successful simply by learning. By understanding the internal workings of our brain, we can become knowledgeable and adapt to situations that may cause problems.

More importantly, when we understand that our brain is like a muscle that requires regular exercise, we will care little for the limitations others place on us. Knowing what we are capable of will allow us to employ the full potential of our brain and reach our goals.

The complexities of our brain – and the many different parts that vary in their functions – means that people have different thoughts that tend to result in different behaviours.

Consequently, when two people with a similar education and background make a decision, the outcome differs from one person to another.

David C. McClelland, the renowned American psychologist and proponent of the Iceberg Model, believes that people's behaviour can be classified as follows: Less than 10% of our behaviours are linked to the Iceberg that's visible above the water, or what we call consciousness – the way we lead our lives. More than 90% of our behaviours are caused by the Iceberg that is under the water, or what we call unconsciousness – those actions that drive us to subconsciously act and create both positive and negative actions.

These are acts based intuitively on instinct and we make them without thinking. Hence, this state of mind substantially affects our way of life and leads to outcomes that can result in success or failure in the future.

Today, the branch of scientific study called neuroscience is helping us understand the mechanism of changes that occur in the brain as people learn various subjects. Larry R. Squire, a Professor of Psychiatry, Neurosciences and Psychology at the University of California explained that neuroscience **applies many branches of scientific knowledge to analyse the nervous system,** leading to a basic understanding of biology that is the source of our behaviour patterns.

The field of neuroscience is helping us shed light on the various working processes of the brain. Specifically, **Cognitive Developmental Neuroscience** reveals that we will be able to learn and do things better if we understand factors relating to the brain's functionality. (Usha Goswami, 2006)

Neurocognitive Learning Theory is a mixture of three components of investigation; namely Neurophysiology which involves the biological state of the brain and by extension the nervous system's activities; Cognitive Science with a focus on information or data processing of personal experiences; and Learning Theory which explains how people interact and adapt to their environment.

According to the current cognitive theory, we know that **Sensory Input is received from the body's five senses which are transformed into electrical signals.** These signals are processed by the thalamus in parallel streams and instantaneously categorised as either a prior experience or a new experience. The cortex, stimulated by electrical signals, then sends the signals to the major sensory processing centres of the brain to form what we call **Sensation or Stimulation.**

The ongoing process that follows **Sensation** within the processing centres of the brain is referred to as **Perception.**

Perception occurs simultaneously with the categorisation of signals that are being processed by neurons at different positions along neural pathways. All signals between neurons occur via specialised connections called synapses and are instantaneously compared, grouped and defined. Our ability to **think creates a relation of information that over time yields new information, which in turn becomes more and more complex.**

A neural network that supports repetitive signal circulations will become steady, i.e. a pathway along which signals pass easily to form a **memory**. (Akrapoom Jarupakorn and Pornpilai Lerdwicha, B.E. 2550; Sousa, David A., 2006)

Therefore, the received information is imported into the brain's internal information management process *which corresponds to the stored information in the* Long Term Memory.

The incoming information is divided into two groups; **externally received information (sensory neurons) and internally received information (motor neurons).**

The information management process sends new information to the Working Memory (Anderson, O. Roger, 2009) as working memory affects our learning ability. The Short Term Store (STS) acts as a temporary stored memory that relates to something like a response or decision that needs to be made. It is a significant and complex component in our thought process whereby we establish an understanding of our environment by intellectual processes (mentally). The working memory's main duty is to help us think and solve problems and to enhance the acquirement of new knowledge which leads to achievement of activities' objectives. (Baddeley and Logic 1999, referred to in Price, Jodi et. al. 2007, Surang Koatrakool, B.E. 2550)

When a person's actions are not aligned with their thoughts, this will result in Cognitive Dissonance, which is used to deceive the brain. *For example, we know cigarettes are bad for our health, so we try to find reasons why we smoke; or gambling when we know the odds are not in our favour but we think we'll get lucky this time. When we partake in other bad habits such as drinking alcohol, lying, having an affair or even eating meat or an extra portion of dessert, we trick our brain into thinking what we are doing is justified.*

Conclusively, when we want to do something that is bad, unhealthy and produces adverse effects to life in the long term, our subconscious tries to find excuses. We are fooled into thinking that what we are doing has some kind of benefit or advantage. The subcortex produces a feeling of innocence for our actions so that we do not feel guilty.

Many people have said, "If we fail before we are 30, we will be lucky."

The answers to the question why we think like that are...
1) All things that have occurred...are good. (We cannot go back and fix the past)

2) We try to find positive reasons for our past failures.

Hence, the brain tries to find a contradictory answer *such as...* **"failure = good".** *(In fact, it cannot be good.)*

*This is...*the brain's thinking method in the form of Cognitive Dissonance.

...People can overcome problems if they are able to use their brain to its full potential. *Eminent scientist Albert Einstein put it this way:* **"We cannot solve our problems with the same thinking we used when we created them."**

When a person starts a business they want to be successful.
1.2 million Americans start a new business each year,
while 500,000 Koreans and 200,000 Thais do the same.
From this, 90% will fail within the first year, **while half of the rest are likely to shut their businesses within five years.**
Therefore, only 2-3 businesses have a chance to succeed and become successful.

GENIUSX Business Intelligence *will help you know yourself and other people through a means of different strategies, thought processing, decision-making, choice and selection, way of life and customised business methods through the* concept of the categorisation of people *into six types based on* Cognitive Neuroscience. *The way to success is to learn about people, diverse decision-making and to rectify problems as they arise. Learning to deal with all types of people, as well as understanding their working methods can only be achieved by fully utilising your brain. Making and sustaining links in order to achieve success in your work and personal life is only possible by actively using the power of your brain.*

Damrong Pinkoon

1		2		3
	**+**		**+**	

Limited time

Smart brain

Cool ideas

Don't waste time with trial and error schemes; life is too short to keep making the same or frequent mistakes.

If we believe that we are as smart as other people, then we can build a business or innovate in order to achieve success.

We all have cool ideas but the majority of us don't know how to start or what to do to achieve success in life.

In 1999, it was possible to create a business plan that could last for between 5 to 10 years. Today, that's not possible due in part to the evolution of advanced technology. Modern business tools such as the Internet, smart devices, killer app and games and even the quickly growing AI (Artificial Intelligence) segment have altered the business world. These cutting-edge technologies have been developed based on self-adaptation for success.

Twenty years later or nowadays, a business plan is projected for a year or less. Thanks to the said evolution, the world is developing and changing rapidly with people as the main propeller of changes in attitudes, values and beliefs held by society. Consequently, people need to adjust and adapt themselves all the time. So, if you think you have enough time for trial and error schemes like you did in the last decade, you might be able to do it. But if you want a shortcut and a direct path to the door of success in no time, you need to have an individual plan for success.

As people are different, success is an individual matter for each specific person from which we should learn from, but not make absolute imitations.

GeniusX Business Intelligence is, therefore, designed to help people to learn about themselves and others according to the Creative Thinking concept. Understanding the six types of people and the strategies they are likely to use can provide you with a unique understanding and lead you to success in business and your personal life.

BEING **A ROLE MODEL.**

ACT!

PENDING!

ACT!

MORE **PROBLEMS ENCOUNTERED!**

FIND **NEW IDEAS.**

HAVE **ADDITIONAL GOALS.**

IGNORE **OBSTACLES.**

LOSE!

SET GOALS

ACT IMMEDIATELY!

SOLVE **PROBLEMS AT HAND.**

PROBLEMS ENCOUNTERED!

Game Changer

Game Changer – a person who likes challenges, always finds new ideas before the next person. Such new ideas usually enable the **Game Changer** to quickly set clearer goals than his/her competitors and make them act immediately while ignoring obstacles. When this group encounters problems along the way they are always able to find solutions or solve the problem at hand in a timely manner. They don't surrender easily. A stumble here and there leads them to come up with more ideas in regards to problem solving and additional goals are put into action that often result in the achievement of their predetermined objectives, i.e. they simply won't give up.

Game Changers intentions are generally serious and they feel proud of their achievements each time they succeed. **Game Changers** are trustworthy and reliable people. If they fail or make a mistake, they can become frustrated and don't easily let go of such feelings. As a result, those around them will also begin to feel uncomfortable. However, after giving issues a lot of thought, **Game Changers** ultimately learn from their mistakes and put in place a process that can be applied down the line when they face new problems.

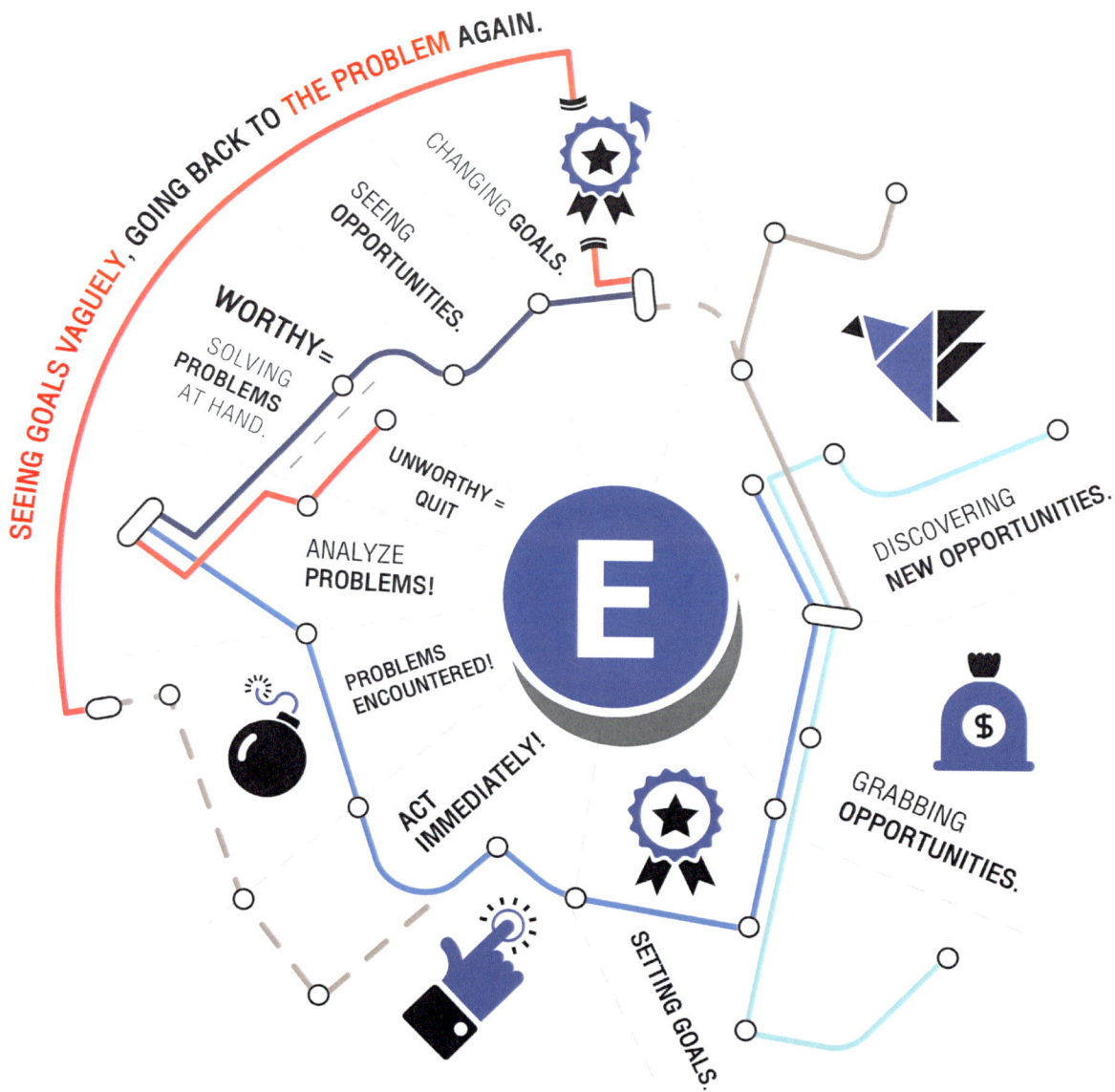

SEEING GOALS VAGUELY, GOING BACK TO THE PROBLEM AGAIN.

CHANGING GOALS.

SEEING OPPORTUNITIES.

WORTHY =
SOLVING PROBLEMS AT HAND.

UNWORTHY = QUIT

ANALYZE PROBLEMS!

PROBLEMS ENCOUNTERED!

ACT IMMEDIATELY!

E

DISCOVERING NEW OPPORTUNITIES.

GRABBING OPPORTUNITIES.

SETTING GOALS.

Entrepreneur

Entrepreneur – a person who starts doing things when they see an opportunity. **Entrepreneurs** seize such opportunities without hesitation. But if no opportunity arises, this type of person is willing to create their own. They will set goals and objectives of what they want to achieve and ask questions such as "Why I am doing this?" "What is it for?" and "Who will benefit from what I am doing?" **Entrepreneurs** are goal–oriented individuals who evaluate situations and look to see if the outcome is worth–while. If it is, they take immediate action and continue until they achieve success. Even with success in the bag, **Entrepreneurs** keep looking for new opportunities.

Nevertheless, in life there is no easy way to success. Obstructions and problems always hinder plans as a company grows. What **Entrepreneurs** are good at is pausing for a while to analyse situations, pinpoint problematic areas and find solutions to cure problems at the root. In case a problem is too hard for them to solve, or it is not worth solving, **Entrepreneurs** always go back to the start and review their plans and set new goals if necessary.

If they consider that a problem can be solved or it is worth solving, they will tackle it head on and resolve issues so that they can proceed with the next step until they finally reach their goals. **Entrepreneurs** are creatures of habit and will always look for new opportunities and openings.

USING **CONNECTIONS**
TO **SOLVE PROBLEMS**.

CONSULTING
OTHER **PEOPLE**.

SOLVING PROBLEMS
ON ONE'S OWN.

**PROBLEMS
ENCOUNTERED!**

CREATING
TEAMWORK.

CREATING
NETWORKS.

FINDING
OPPORTUNITIES.

CREATING
RELATIONSHIPS.

SETTING **GOALS**

Network

The personality trait of a **Network** type of person is typified by their ability to build lasting relationships with other people. Whether they know the people or not, **Network** people have a natural ability to get along with others. So, the Network type of person is likely to have a considerably wide **network** of assorted acquaintances. By forming large networks of like-minded people, the **Network** person is always presented with opportunities.

After being presented with an opportunity from their networks, the next step for this type of person is to find someone to join them rather than acting alone. The **Network** type of person will try to find competent team members who may be a known acquaintance or someone who they've just formed a new relationship with, **so that everybody can achieve their goals together.**

Absolutely no one can avoid **problems**. A common method used by people who have an enormous number of friends is to consult and seek advice from experienced persons they know. By harmoniously blending good advice with their own ideas, they are ready to face any problems in order to go forward to reach their desired goals.

Apart from the **Network** person achieving success, we can see that other people, both old and new faces, are always involved in every step of the way. This helps to expand their networks whereby new opportunities are likely to emerge.

GO BACK AND SEARCH FOR INFORMATION OR NEW POSSIBILITIES.

INSOLUBLE PROBLEMS;

REVIEWING

UNSUCCESSFUL =
SEARCH FOR
NEW POSSIBILITIES

UNSUCCESSFUL =
SEARCH FOR
NEW INFORMATION

PROBLEMS
ENCOUNTERED!

GO STEP BY STEP,
ONE THING AT A TIME.

MAKE A PLAN.

ANTICIPATE PROBLEMS.

POSSIBILITIES

SEARCH FOR
INFORMATION.

ANALYZE
INFORMATION.

COMPARE
INFORMATION.

GATHER
INFORMATION.

Information

People who search out **Information** are a group of people who like to collect all types of information. They like to study and learn new things, thus giving themselves the option of considering all possibilities before taking action. Even though they have a high possibility of success, they need to find information as a preventive measure rather than trying to solve problems at a later stage.

Hence, the **Information**-driven person mostly dedicates their time to gathering information from a wide variety of sources. Once the information has been thoroughly compared and analysed, a systematic plan is put in place to cope with any problems. The **Information** person takes great pride in foreseeing problems and will reuse or rehash a previous plan to achieve their goals.

However, if they encounter an unpredictable problem after following their known procedures, the **Information** person will try to figure out what mistakes have been made by recalling all the information they acquired before starting the project. Reviewing all data is the way in which this type of person is able to make successful plans. If they are unable to find a solution for their problems, there is a good chance they will abandon the project at hand and look for a new opportunity that's less risky.

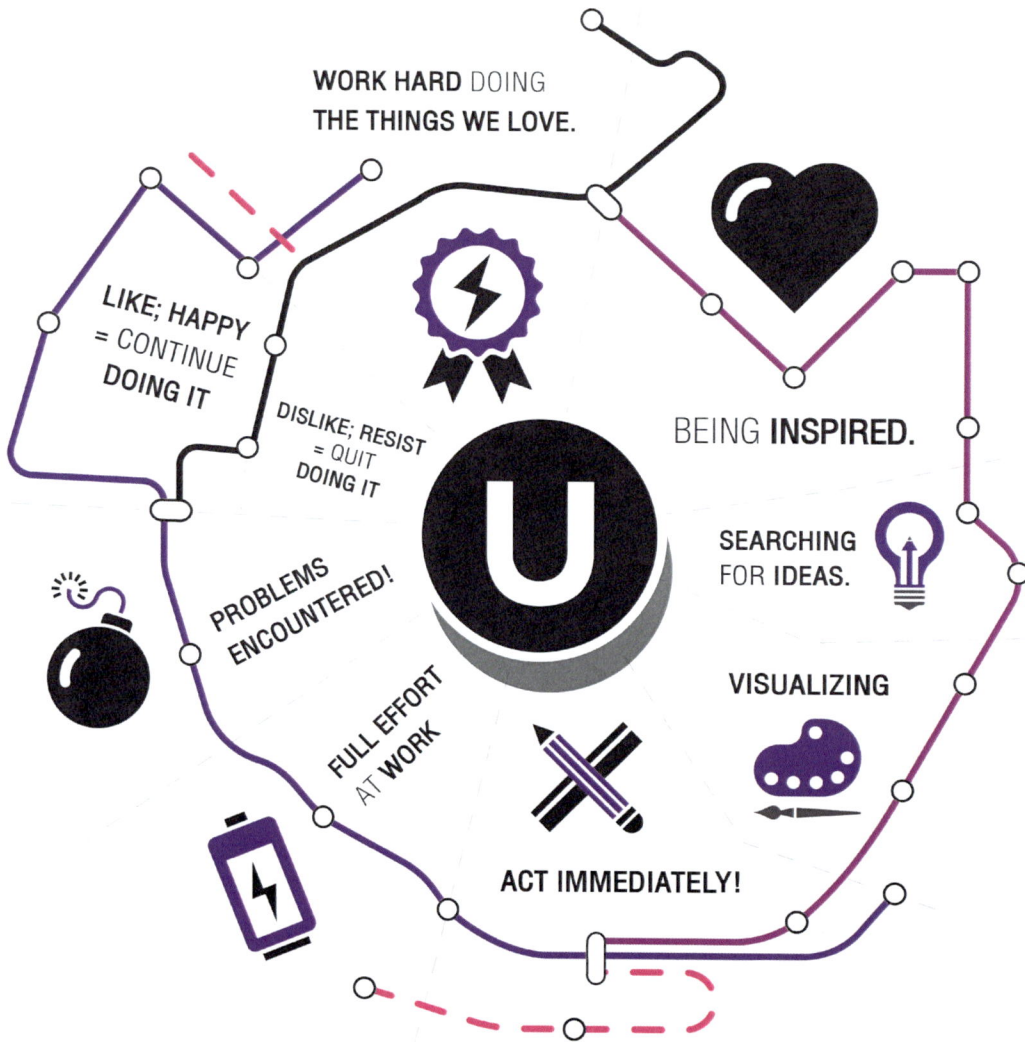

WORK HARD DOING THE THINGS WE LOVE.

LIKE; HAPPY = CONTINUE DOING IT

DISLIKE; RESIST = QUIT DOING IT

BEING INSPIRED.

SEARCHING FOR IDEAS.

PROBLEMS ENCOUNTERED!

VISUALIZING

FULL EFFORT AT WORK

ACT IMMEDIATELY!

U

Unique

An artist like the **Unique** species always starts doing everything by heart. They have inspiration to nourish their life and their projects. If they really adore or have a passion for a specific theme, they dedicate themselves to doing the best possible job and keeping on doing it without feeling tired.

If the **Unique** person develops more intense feelings of love and a bond for what they are doing, they do it wholeheartedly, ignoring whether other people understand or not. They won't listen to negative opinions and prefer to follow their heart. Even though they could possibly face a very serious problem, the **Unique** person is ready to fight in order to protect their pet project. The only reassurance they require is being able to do the things they love.

However, when working with heart and emotion as the main drivers, if the day comes when the **Unique** person becomes bored with what they are doing they will cease doing it immediately and without giving any specific reason. Although someone else may plead with them to continue doing it, they won't listen. They prefer to stay true to their heart, rather than compelling themselves to do a job they don't like and feel unhappy with.

LET GO;
OVERLOOK
PROBLEMS

FEELING **HAPPY**.

HAVE PROBLEMS
WITH **ASSOCIATES**.

HAVING **SYMPATHY**.

S

ADDICTED
TO **HAPPINESS**

WANTING TO
HELP OTHER PEOPLE.

FEELING HAPPY
AND **CONTENT**.

DEDICATED TO
OTHER PEOPLE

Sharing

The behavioural pattern of Sharing people is mainly dictated by sympathy and compassion. In fact, these feelings are not confined to the Sharing group of people. Whenever people in the sharing family are touched by sincere feelings they will crave more and offer more help than other groups of people. From providing support and talking about things they have seen or sensitive issues that happened, Sharing people like to help others overcome problems and be free of obstacles.

This group of people feels happy and content with their dedicated thoughts and labour. Many are even willing to share their money and often give to other people in need. They want to see smiling faces and hear people laughing. They are addicted to happiness through the virtue of giving and witnessing the outcome. But if the outcome is contrary to their expectation, the Sharing people will be more sensitive to mistakes than people of other groups. This is due to the fact that all events promote an impact and so it is their wish to help others. Sometimes, though, Sharing people can give too much care and offer to much sympathy, which can cause grievances to their other associates. This is the reason why Sharing people are required to reflect on their lives, take care of their families, let go and overlook problems and to abstain from always being preoccupied with things they wish to do for other people. This will, therefore, make those in the Sharing group settle for their own happiness first and foremost.

A baby will emerge from the womb
with more than 100,000 billion neurons
or brain cells, roughly ten times as many as
found in a fully grown adult human, although
the size of **a baby's brain** is perhaps half
the size of an adult's brain.

This overproduction of neurons is necessary
to ensure that babies have the best chance
of survival, although many brain cells will be
lost in utero. **In its first year of life** a baby
has so much to learn and with over 100 billion
brain cells, many more are lost as the brain
gets rid of unwanted synaptic connections.
Almost all development takes place
in the brain and by 90 days the brain
has more than doubled in size as it
forms larger and larger synaptic pathways.

Chapter 1

GeniusX Brain Intelligence

1

Pruning

At birth, a child's brain consists of billions of nerve cells or **neurons;** a little like the stars in the night sky. In total, it is thought babies have twice as many neurons as adults.

In the first three months, the child grows quickly, developing its sense of hearing as the auditory neurons start to connect to one another forming a pathway and remembering certain sounds. A child's eyesight also develops as visual nerve cells start to connect to one another from the eyes and the retina, through to billions of the brain's nerve cells and linking the occipital lobe, thus enabling sight.

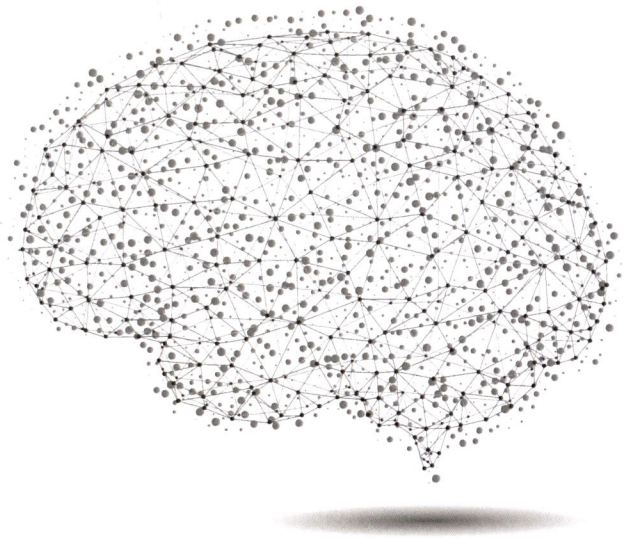

Neurons in other parts of the quickly developing brain also begin forming life-long neural pathways for speaking, reading, writing, thinking, analysis and calculation.

As specific parts of the brain are used more frequently, this creates stronger synaptic connections throughout the brain.

Weaker neurons are eliminated in a natural manner (similar to the elimination of skin cells). For example, if a baby rarely uses its auditory nerves, the neural connections will gradually fade and eventually be eliminated. According to Neuroscientists, the elimination of unused nerve cells is called Synaptic Pruning, after which only the strongest and most regularly used connections remain.

2

Neuron

When we exercise any part of the brain regularly, that part of the brain becomes stronger – like any muscle – and we establish long-lasting synaptic activity as a result. But if we stop utilising that part of the brain, we slowly lose the skill we acquired such as speaking another language. Another example is being proficient at mathematics as a child, but as we age we stop using that part of our brain and take up another activity such as a work skill.

As we focus more on a particular neural activity such as the brain cells used in language skills, the pathways become stronger, while the neural pathways once used for calculation become weaker. So, if your children struggle in any particular skill at a younger age, the chances are they will be able to improve in adolescence with continuous practice.

Babies are capable of learning any language and those who listen to multiple languages have been shown to form better executive function. Multilingual children are more focused and are thought to be quicker at learning new skills.

None of us are born stupid; our brains just need time to acquire the neural connections needed in life. Quite simply, we do not use many areas of our brain to allow sufficient neurons to become interconnected. Therefore, pathways take longer to form in later life. Many people may believe they are not good at calculation, but in fact their synaptic nerve cells relating to that particular skill are not sufficiently used.

3

Neuroplasticity

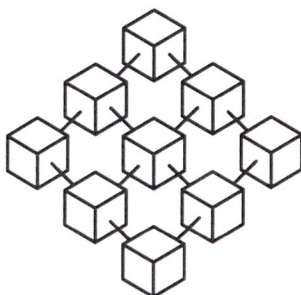

Since the late 20th century, scientists have made huge breakthroughs in the final medical frontier of the human body: our brain. We now understand how the brain creates neural pathways and how synapses strengthen and weaken over time. Neuroscientists call the brain's ability to adjust to changes "Neuroplasticity", meaning the brain is capable of adapting by remapping itself.

The nerve cells in our brains are constantly being rewired as we stop doing certain tasks and start learning new ones. For each new process, some synaptic pathways will fall dormant while others are formed. Canadian neuropsychologist Donald Hebb summed it up perfectly when he stated, "Neurons that fire together wire together, while neurons that fire out of sync fail to link."

Actors, musicians and sommeliers are constantly rewiring their neural pathways as they research new roles, create new music and grade new wines. In business, entrepreneurs also need to form new synapses as they tackle the ever-changing business climate. But perhaps the most revealing cortical remapping of the brain can be seen in people who suffer traumatic injuries and need to readjust their lifestyle.

As neuroplasticity allows the formation of new connections and pathways, neurogenesis relates to the brain's ability to grow new neurons, especially in people who have suffered brain injuries. Although the field of neurogenesis is in its infancy, it is an exciting development that could be lead to the treatment of degenerative diseases such as dementia.

In short, as humans we need to constantly adapt to our environment and by learning new tasks and skills we can ensure we have a healthy, fully functioning brain.

4

Cognitive Dissonance

At some point in our lives we will all experience a state of mind called **Cognitive Dissonance.** For example, we know that stealing is immoral and illegal, but those who commit this crime resolve their conflict over right and wrong by thinking that they need the money to take care of their family. This conflict of the mind is also played out in the lives of smokers, drinkers and to some extent political beliefs.

Gamblers for example often say they know when they have lost "enough". However, the following day they may buy a lottery ticket, scratch card or place a bet on a horse race or football match. They convince themselves that their next bet is going to win.

The three levels of perceived reality and cognitive dissonance include consonant relationship, dissonant relationship and irrelevant relationship, where ideas and thoughts are constantly at odds. However, as we are frequently aroused by stimulus and enticed by aspirations and passions, people are always faced with these mental challenges.

Cognitive Dissonance is a repetitive occurrence in almost everyone's life. We know that eating too much oily food is likely to cause high cholesterol levels in our blood and increase the risk of disease, but we continue eating. We also know that drinking alcohol is unhealthy and will damage the liver, but many people are happy to raise a glass on just about any occasion. When we feel happy, we drink and yet when we feel unhappy we also drink.

In business, we can work hard for years only to see our company fail, but we balance our failure with what neuroscientists called 'effort justification'. It allows us to convince ourselves that the effort expended was worthwhile.

It is clear that the cognitive side of our brain is filled with internal conflicts and we strive to figure out how to balance our discomfort.

We are all born with the innate sense of 'Ambition', whereby we want to progress and improve our life and the lives of those around us. Ambition is a positive term I've written about before and I firmly believe that people want to progress in life and reach their goals.

However, due to a myriad of circumstances not everyone achieves – or even attempts to achieve – their Life Goal. It may be down to negative beliefs or a lack of opportunity, so they idly spend their life not knowing what they live for. It's unfortunate that people lack the motivation to achieve their goals, because making the effort to do so would bring immeasurable benefits to their life.

People who regularly engage in idleness or are fearful of doing something that is outside their comfort zone only serve to encourage those closest to them that giving up on life is an acceptable outcome. There are huge differences between Western societies that provide a welfare safety net and Eastern societies that do not provide such luxuries. At the end of the day, those who fail to grasp opportunities presented to them will be a "failure" at life.

5

Priming

Priming can have both a positive and negative effect on the brain.

World-class athletes prime themselves by constantly saying they can do it, while regular people often say "I'm too old.... I can't run." Talking positively to your inner self can have fantastic outcomes, while being pessimistic and thinking negatively is likely to result in failure.

As a child, I was pretty bad at mathematics and I almost convinced myself that I was incapable of calculation. As I grew up I constantly practiced various fields of calculation, telling myself I could do this. When I was 26-years-old, I established my own business, Rester Massage Chair, in Thailand. In 1998, most businesses in Southeast Asia, including mine and other businesses in Thailand, were suffering from the financial crisis. From a small investment of US$10,000 and with only three employees, my positive thinking allowed me to grow my business. Within four years, my company's revenue had grown to more than $4,000,000 and I was still a few months short of my 30th birthday.

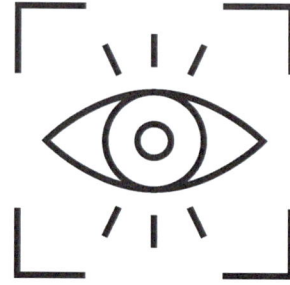

The reason I believe so many people fail in life is that they constantly underestimate their ability, and as a consequence, trick their brain into believing they cannot do a certain task. Can you imagine if Albert Einstein, Oprah Winfrey, Steve Jobs, Angela Merkel, Mark Zuckerberg and millions of other successful men and women told themselves they could not be successful?

Priming your brain is like exercising your body; it is an ongoing, life-long task.

6

Thorndike's Connectionism

S-R Bond

Edward Lee Thorndike (1874–1949) was an American psychologist who is recognised as the "Father of Educational Psychology".

Thorndike studied the theory of relations between Stimulus and Response.

This theory is called the S–R bond and is the connection between Stimulus and Response. *(Bond in this context means joint or connection.)*

Thorndike's theory of Connectionism is accepted by psychologists worldwide. It is an established theory that states learning is caused by the formation of relationships between stimulus and response.

In other words, when a situation or a problem occurs, our brain will try to do something to resolve such a problem by expressing various forms of behaviours in the Trial and Error manner until the best method or the right solution to the problem is discovered.

Three Major Laws of Learning

1) Law of Readiness

This law by Thorndike that states that...

Readiness in both physical and mental aspects plays an extremely significant role in creating learning behaviours.

When we are ready to learn and such learning renders satisfaction, this fosters a positive outcome. However, if we are not ready and are forced to learn, then we may experience a feeling of stress, dissatisfaction, dismay and discomfort.

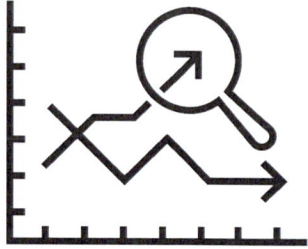

Reinforcement

Our ability to memorise previous behaviours through learning is revealed when we act on these behaviours in response when the same problem or stimulus occurs again. Another important aspect of learning that Thorndike was very interested in was Reinforcement, as it enhances the brain's memory in relation to the connection caused between stimulus and response.

2) Law of Exercise

This refers to the **Law of Use** and the **Law of Disuse**

2A) Law of Use

Learning behaviours frequently practiced are developed into expertise by the means of familiarity. The more these behaviours are exercised, the more accuracy is obtained. For example, athletes who practice their athletic discipline for years become familiar with every aspect of that discipline and gradually develop expertise in the sport.

2B) Law of Disuse

Learning behaviours that are rarely practiced will become decreasingly effective. Lack of practice for an excessively long period of time will cause an existing learning pattern to gradually fade.

3) Law of Effect

This law states that...
Whenever we encounter the same situation or problem, we are likely to repeat the same certain responses that yield satisfaction, pride, delight, dignity, happiness and comfort (any response producing a positive outcome).

As for some responses that yield dissatisfaction, disappointment, sorrow, regret, failure, misery and discomfort, we are likely to gradually reduce these until they finally become redundant and disappear.

Five Subordinate Laws

Five Subordinate Laws of Learning That Support Major Laws.

1) Law of Multiple Responses

When faced with a difficult or problematic situation, each person will express their response using a variety of methods they have learned and are thus comfortable with. They may try to figure out if there is an alternative method and once they find a solution to their problem, their brain will store that response in their long-term memory.

2) Law of Attitude

People are more open to learning new skills when they possess a positive attitude towards the task at hand. A positive approach enables an easy learning process and goes a long way in successfully mastering a new skill.

However, people who possess a negative attitude towards a new learning experience most often than not fail to master that task regardless of how easy or difficult it is perceived to be.

We can see examples of this wherever we look; people give up learning because they desire the reward rather than acquiring the skill; others care too much about what other people think; and many lack the required discipline to overcome the smallest of obstacles.

3) Law of Partial Activity

People use a diverse array of methods to solve a problem or overcome a difficult situation and will always choose the solution that suits their needs. We have all learned what is important and what we deem irrelevant to situations we face. Choosing the shortest, easiest and most convenient way out of a tricky situation is a key indicator of partial activity and determines our appropriate response.

The law of partial activity states that learning should be conducted in structured lessons. This is truer in the case of children, but it also applies to adults and how they deal with new experiences.

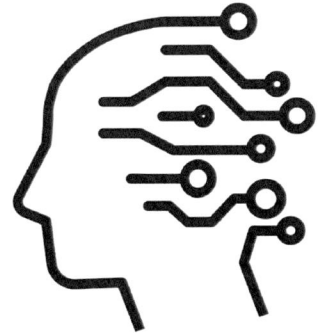

For example, if we want to travel from London to Paris we have the option of flying, driving, taking the train or taking a ferry. The easiest option would be the Eurostar via the Channel Tunnel but flying would be cheaper. So which is the easiest and most convenient option? We need to consult our previous memories for an answer.

Another example is when we use the World Wide Web to book a holiday, business trip or other online service. Although we know we can use various other websites to achieve the task at hand, the law of partial activity overtakes our reasoning and we succumb to the offer presented to us at one website that aggregates the price for us.

4) Law of Response by Analogy

People are adept at solving the problems they face regardless of the situation. If a new problem is similar to a problem previously encountered, people are likely to apply the same analogy that yielded a positive result.

We learn how to transfer the knowledge acquired earlier to resolve another situation, if and only if the situations are similar. Analytical thinking is crucial to human development and allows us to compare any situation we face to others we have stored in our long-term memory to work out a satisfactory outcome.

5) Law of Associative Shifting

When people associate a new stimulus or experience with any previous stimulus they have encountered, there is the possibility of faster learning.

The response or behaviour that's been embedded in our brain from a previous encounter can be transferred from one stimulus to another; like applying the skills learned to riding a bicycle to riding a motorbike.

Likewise, survivalists are skilled at finding food and water where most people would not think to look thanks to their ability in associative shifting.

Every second, more than 100,000 chemical reactions occur in the human brain. The speed at which these chemical reactions travel from one nerve to the next is in excess of 360 kilometres/hour, which is faster than **a Formula 1 car.**

Our body contains in the region of 100,000 miles or 160,000 kilometres of blood vessels from the four major carotid and vertebral arteries to the smallest capillaries. If placed end to end, the blood vessels in our body would stretch around the equator four times.

The brain is capable of producing new neurons throughout your life, so if you forget something, it's not necessarily associated with age-related memory loss. Constantly exercising the brain does lead to improved cognitive skills and helps prevent **memory loss.**

1

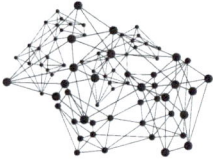

Pruning

+

2

Neuron

+

3

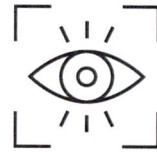

Priming

+

=

4

Law of Learning

+

5

Neuroplasticity

+

6

Cognitive Dissonance

Thinking System

At birth neural pathways in our brain are developing at lightening speed and the number of synapses per neuron is roughly 2,500. Within 36 months, more than 15,000 synapses are connected to each neuron. Every minute of the day (and night), a baby is exercising its brain by listening, looking, touching, tasting and moving. Some babies develop faster than others and in some cases even some of the baby's senses develop faster than others. As a baby stretches its arms and legs, different muscle groups are transmitting their information back to the brain. As babies start to use their fingers to explore their world, they begin to develop fine motor skills and when they begin to crawl, stand up and eventually walk, their gross motor skills begin to kick in.

As we continue to grow and mature, we learn more through trial and error and from a graded education. At this stage, we begin to form long-lasting synaptic connections that allow us to recall information of our previous actions that brought satisfaction, recognition and happiness. On the other hand, our memory serves to remind us to avoid actions that caused us loss, embarrassment, failure, disappointment, sorrow and despair.

In most people, there are between 86 and 100 billion brain cells or neurons that are constantly strengthening or weakening nearby connections depending on the frequency of usage.

Thinking System

When the brain is in full working order and concentration is at a peak, neurons are firing wildly, as seen in numerous MRI scans that reveal increased blood flow and neuronal activation. Thanks to neuroplasticity, we now know it is possible to reverse years of neural neglect and reactivate brain cells and synaptic connections that may have been disconnected.

With trillions upon trillions of permutations, the entire human race is completely different in the way each person's brain is wired. Each of us employs a specific part of the brain according to our skills. While some people are proficient at calculation, others excel at languages. Some people prefer to work with their hands while other are better at visualisation. It all depends on how we developed as we grew up and which parts of our brains formed the strongest synaptic connections. This is what makes understanding the different types of people you are likely to come across in life so important to building success.

All the experiences we encounter in life are thus individual and unique and help construct our personal **"Thinking System"**. Neuroscientists have identified six types of people by categorising them according to their specific **thinking methods** >>> **behaviours** >>> **actions** >>> **results** (which are totally different). Therefore, it is clear to see that each person has his or her own distinct method of dealing with situations.

GeniusX Thinking System

G	= Game Changer	A fighter who controls the game
E	= Entrepreneur	Brilliant business executive
N	= Network	Negotiator who loves making connections
I	= Information	Information Knowledgeable philosopher
U	= Unique	Artist who loves their freedom
S	= Sharing	Kind-hearted individuals

Categorising people based on their Thinking System enables us to understand that all people think differently and thus their actions differ. This information gives us insight into what business strategies they may also employ. It is important to realise that no two people are the same, each of us have our own unique Thinking System and to be successful we need to interpret how others think. Throughout our lives, our brain has been conditioned to react in certain ways to certain situations as everything stems from the thoughts in our brain.

Now we are beginning to paint a picture of what we are looking at, the next step is to learn about the different thinking processes and behaviour patterns. First though, we need to know..."Which type of person am I?" and "How does my Thinking System differ from other people?" As we begin to see the complete picture emerge, we are in a better position to ask questions such as "What type of people fit with my Thinking System and whom should I hire to work in my organisation?" and "Which strategy should I apply in order to build a successful business?"

Problem Solving **Process**

1. 1. Identify The Problem

What happened? We must be able to identify what the root cause of the problem was. What started the problem? What has led to our failure? Why did our business plan fail? What is the cause of quarrels in our organisation?

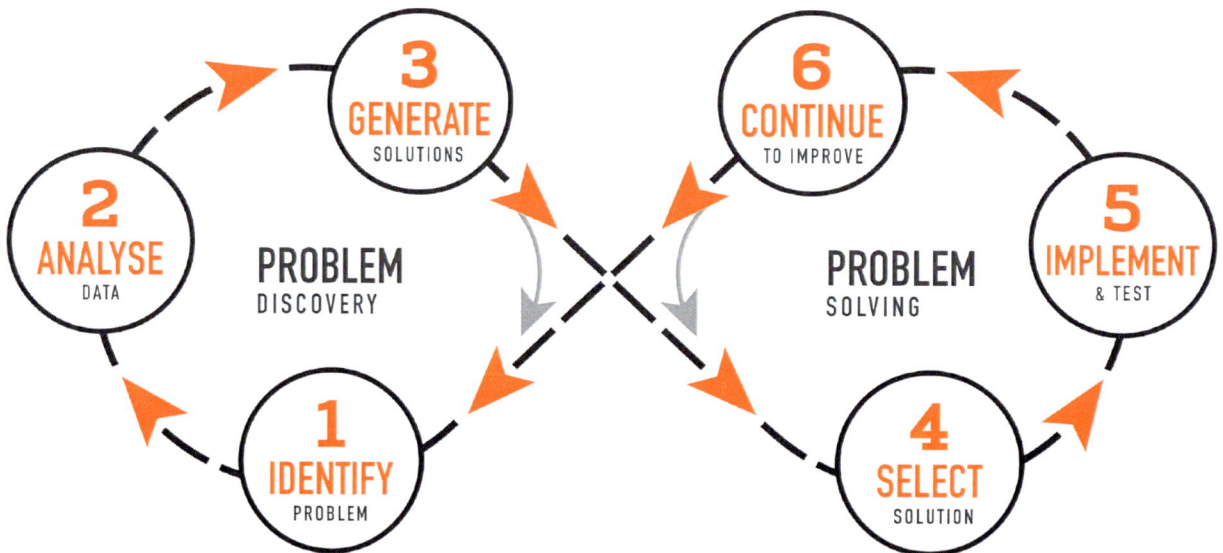

Problem Solving Process

2. Analyse Data

Identify specific pinch points and analyse problems at hand to find out whether they are caused by internal or external forces so a targeted plan can be implemented. Insufficient knowledge about such problems always leads to mistakes, therefore it is imperative to seek additional information before administering the problem.

3. Formulate Solutions

It is always best to have as many contingency plans as possible. A problem always has more than one solution, so have several solutions at hand regardless of whether they are difficult, easy, short, quick or slow to implement.

4. Select First Solution

Select the first solution you think it is the "best". Plan to resolve the problem using the best idea or one that brings the fastest result. It will always boil down to how urgent or significant the problem is.

5. Implement & Test

Put the solution into practice. Whether you get a clear vision of your chosen method depends on how effective you can solve the problem. It is necessary to gather and record figures so as to measure the outcome.

6. Next is Plan B

If your first plan does not provide the expected outcome, you need to have other plans ready. After performing a detailed assessment of the outcome and if your backup plan still yields poor results, start a third and a fourth plan; never be afraid of problem-solving as there is always a way.

"Smell"

Our sense of smell can evoke long lost memories because nerve impulses relating to the olfactory senses have been stimulated, interpreted and recorded in the "hippocampus," an important part of the human brain.

The hippocampus is a part of the Limbic System, which plays a significant role in creating short-term memories, long-term memories and emotion.

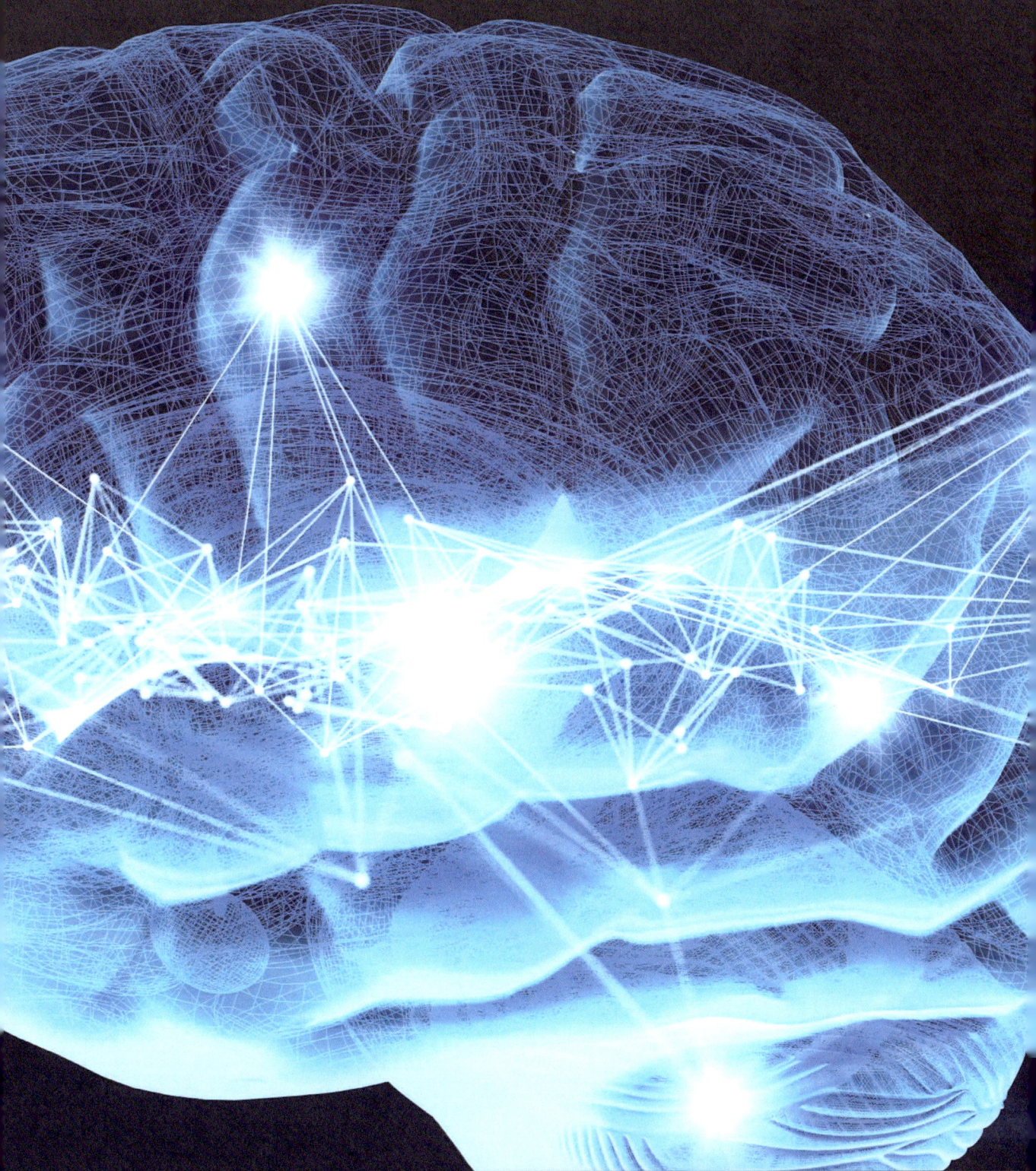

Chapter 2

GeniusX
Six Personalities

Creativity
is
our boundless ability to think.
Each man has this ability at different levels
and in various forms,
and the outcome of creativity
can be enormously unlimited.

E. Paul Torrance

Creativity
is
a personal ability to connect components
to create new things.
If two remote elements can be associated,
more creativity is yielded.

Sarnoff A. Mednick

Creativity
involves
breaking out of expected patterns
in order to look at things
in a different way.

Edward de Bono

Elements of Creativity

In 1999, Joan Dalton, a consultant and educator, defined two elements of creativity as follows:

The first element is the intellectual ability and comprises four traits, while the second element is the emotional and mental ability, which is composed of four traits, namely:

1) Originality
2) Fluency
3) Risk-taking
4) Flexibility
5) Complexity
6) Elaboration
7) Imagination
8) Curiosity

Creativity in Action

American psychologist J.P. Guilford studied and built on the research around creativity and then defined the following:

1) Originality
2) Fluency
3) Flexibility
4) Elaboration

Personality & Characteristic		Thinking & Behaviour
G	**Game Changer**	Creative, adaptable, self-improving, fond of progress and challenging jobs; gets bored very easily; impetuous; a fighter who does not surrender to obstacles
E	**Entrepreneur**	Focuses on work performance and profits; fond of calculated risks; always sees business opportunities first; likes trading; has fun with new projects
N	**Network**	Loves and beloved by friends; likes parties and socialising; good people relations; adaptable to most situations; gets along with other people
I	**Information**	A thinker who likes to find information before making decisions; organised and thoughtful; plans before taking action; never acts in haste; dislikes risk; observer of rules
U	**Unique**	Likes to imagine; visualises everything; has habits of an artist; loves freedom; dislikes hassles; makes decisions based on emotion rather than reason
S	**Sharing**	Good-hearted, generous, fond of sharing and making a good impression; a giver rather than a taker; benevolent; feels happy with other people's happiness

Eight Important Elements

by Haefele 1962

1) Originality

innovative and extraordinary ideas – able to create new things – applies existing knowledge to build on and create new products or services.

2) Flexibility

able to find multiple solutions – provides answers and directions in a variety of formats for different situations – flexible and capable of modifying and utilising their surroundings to their benefit.

3) Fluidity

able to think outside the box – seeks new ideas – avoids and solves problems quickly.

4) Dominance

ability to be a leader of a group – creative in leadership and provides inventive channels.

insightful ideas – clearly distinguishes points and sources of issues – rational approach to situations.

combination of diverse ideas – develops new ideas or concepts – offers alternatives from older ideas.

shows awareness and sensitivity to problems – ready to quickly resolve problematic situations.

ability to define specific characteristics – issues or objectives easily discernable – key points of situations highlighted.

Divergent Thinking

by Torrance 1974

1) Originality

innovative and extraordinary ideas – ability create anew –
apply existing knowledge to build on and create new things.

2) Flexibility

ability to find many solutions – provides answers and
directions for a variety of circumstances – flexible and capable
of modifying and utilising surroundings for benefit.

3) Fluency

ability to think of an abundance of answers quickly and
fluently – works in a limited amount of time.

4) Elaboration

ability to think thoroughly and carefully – considers all aspects
– realises both positive and negative results may occur.

Four Elements of Thought

by Guilford 1987

possesses innovative and extraordinary ideas – creates from new – applies existing knowledge to build on and create new ideas, products and services.

ability to find solutions – provides answers and directions in a variety of forms for different circumstances – flexible and capable of modifying and utilising surroundings for own benefit.

ability to create thoughts which are beneficial to any required area – ideas can be instantly realised.

ability to think thoroughly and carefully – considers all aspects – understands both positive and negative results may occur.

Creative Thinking

by Dalton 1999

1) Originality
innovative and extraordinary ideas – able to create anew – apply existing knowledge to build on and create new things.

2) Flexibility
able to find solutions; provides answers and diretions for a variety of different circumstances – flexible and capable of modifying and utilising surroundings for own benefit.

3) Risk Taking
ability to think outside the box – seeks new ideas – avoids and solves problems quickly.

4) Fluency
ability to think of an abundance of answers quickly and fluently – works in a limited amount of time.

5) Complexity

ability to figure out more than one solution or to solve problems at various stages, producing a chain effect that changes other things.

6) Elaboration

ability to think thoroughly and carefully – considers all aspects – understands both positive and negative results may occur.

7) Imagination

ability to visualise, i.e. both still and moving images, although such things may not exist or have not yet actually been invented.

8) Curiosity

interest in any issue – undertakes research to seek understanding – looks for inconsistencies to get useful data.

Having a lot of complexities in our brain
does not mean that we are smart.
Decades of research work has shown smart
is learned. Ultimately, it has been discovered
that the levels of complexity in our brains
are due to increases in active neurons as we
grow up. The brain increases its synaptic
mapping area to cope with this growth,
but the brain has its limitations and cannot
increase its volume. Therefore, instead
of adding more space, the brain simply
creates layers of complexities instead.
Smartness is more related to the brain's
density and the amount of synapses than
the brain's complexities. This is because
synapses are formed only when we learn
new things or do new activities, such as
learning a different language or a new recipe.
This learning stimulates the brain to develop
new neural pathways while at the same time
committing to memory (long-term
and short-term) what we are learning.

GENIUS**X**

Network

A great negotiator
Good people relations
Attentive to friends
Cares for other people
Has lots of supporters

Entrepreneur

Brilliant business skills
Likes trading
Good at investment
Sees opportunities
Has fun with investments

Game Changer

A fighter
Dares to think and act
Likes challenging jobs
Enjoys new things
Takes action
Does not surrender to
obstacles

I

Information

A knowledgeable
philosopher
Good at researching
Likes to collect information
Focuses on facts
Rational,
logical thought process

U

Unique

An artist who loves
freedom
Creative
New perspectives
Loves differences
Always creates
new things
Follows their heart

S

Sharing

A kind-hearted
person
Benevolent
Generous
Cares for other
people
Helps others while
holding on to positive
thoughts

G

ORIGINAL
THINKING

COMPETITIVE
THINKING

FUTURISTIC
THINKING

FLUENT
THINKING

RESOLVED
THINKING

E

STRATEGIC
THINKING

FLUIDIBLE
THINKING

SYNTHETIC
THINKING

BENEFICIAL
THINKING

EVALUATIVE
THINKING

N

COLLABORATIVE
THINKING

ADAPTIVE
THINKING

NEGOTIABLE
THINKING

INTEGRATIVE
THINKING

DIVERSE
THINKING

I

ANALYTICAL
THINKING

LOGICAL
THINKING

THOUGHTFUL
THINKING

COMPLICATED
THINKING

DETAILED
THINKING

U

CREATIVE
THINKING

IMAGINATIVE
THINKING

DISTINCTIVE
THINKING

PROFOUND
THINKING

THINK **OUTSIDE THE BOX**

S

FAITHFUL
THINKING

SENSITIVE
THINKING

ETHICAL
THINKING

POSITIVE
THINKING

PEACEFUL
THINKING

We all have different Thinking Methods

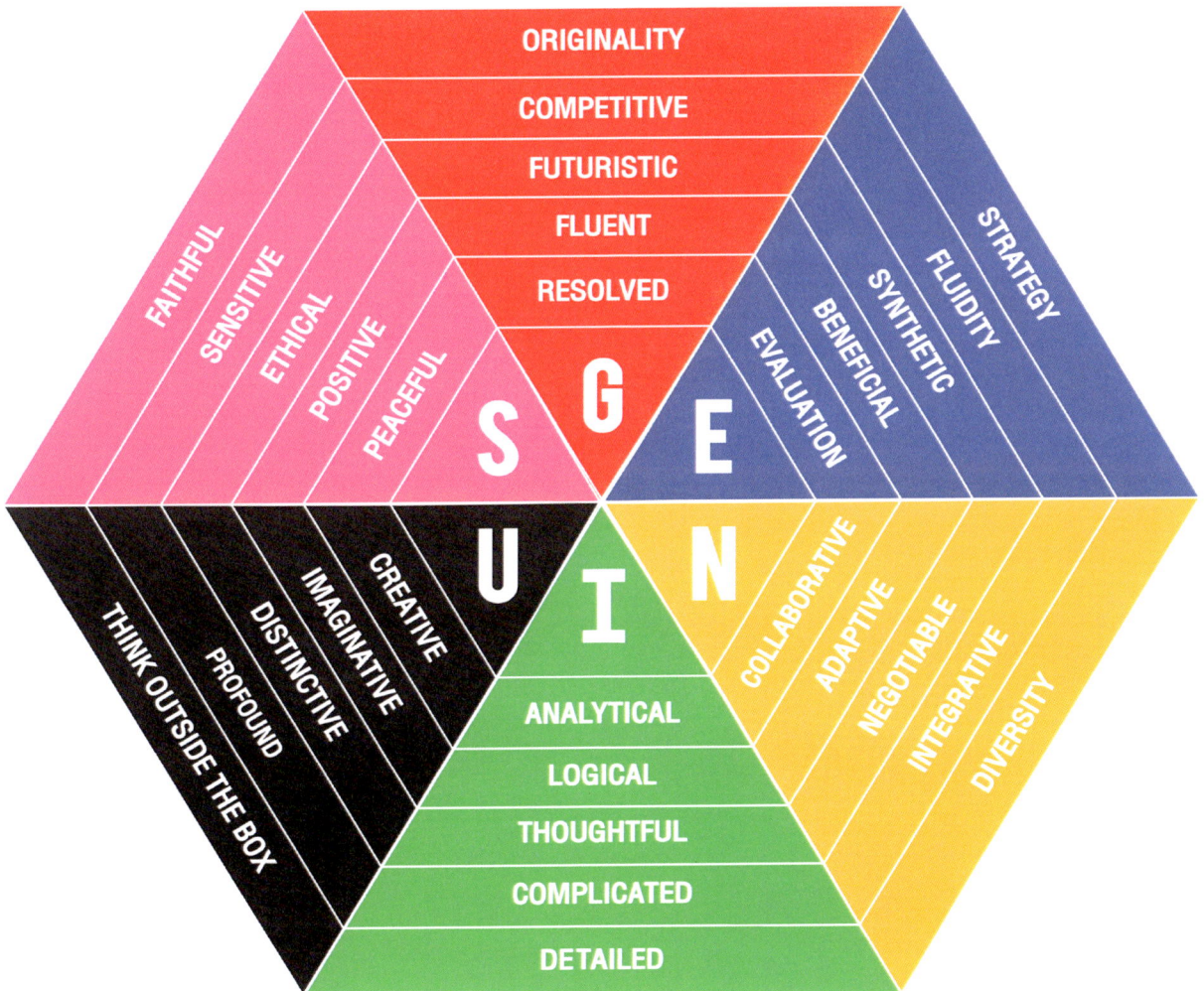

GeniusX Thinking System

G

Game Changer type of people

They have the highest Thinking System that focuses on their goal. The only thing they think about is how to achieve that goal without having to consider other factors.

E

Entrepreneur type of people

They have a Thinking System that's a winner. They won't let themselves get in a position of disadvantage. Their perspective always provides a channel whereby they can gain an advantage; no matter which situation they are in.

COST | REVENUE | LOSS | PROFIT

N

Network type of people

They have a Network Thinking system and will use existing connections to help reach their target goal quickly.

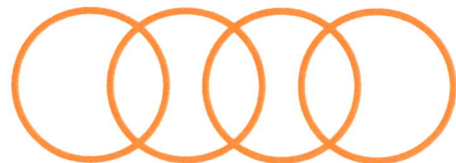

I

Information type of people

They have a Thinking System that follows procedures. To succeed in achieving their goal, they need to be careful, gather enough information and prepare a thorough plan. This will ensure an error-free procedural driven operation.

U

Unique type of people

They have an independent Thinking System with limitless boundaries and one-of-a-kind pattern. They usually use their free spirit and feelings to drive themselves forward. Using unique methods, they capture success.

S

Sharing type of people

They have a generous Thinking System. They can see goodness in every situation and every person. With this outlook these people are loved by others, which may cause discomfort to their family.

Game Changer

A Fighter

Thinking Process

G-type people: Game Changers

GAME CHANGER

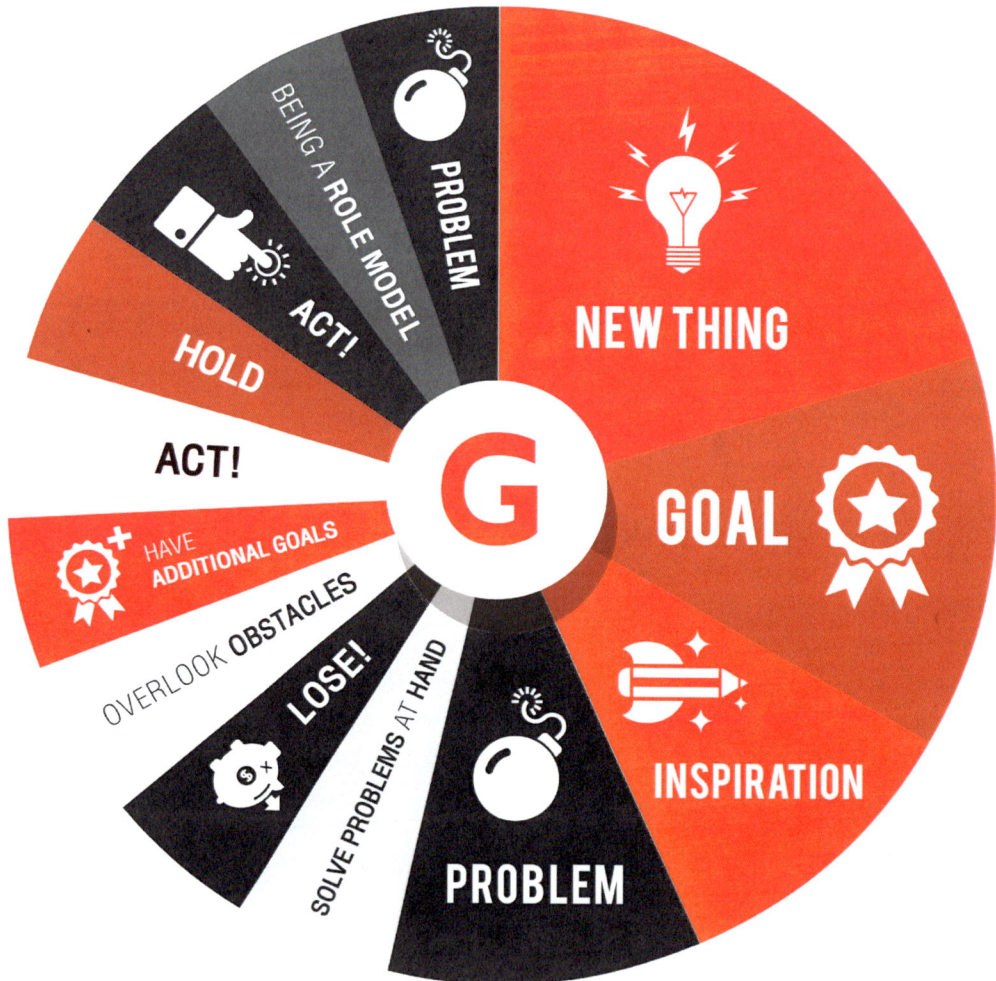

G

NEW THING

GOAL

INSPIRATION

PROBLEM

BEING A ROLE MODEL

PROBLEM

ACT!

HOLD

ACT!

HAVE ADDITIONAL GOALS

OVERLOOK OBSTACLES

LOSE!

SOLVE PROBLEMS AT HAND

General Characteristics

G-type People
Game Changers

The **G-type** person always does things by going to the extreme. They are determined and decisive, i.e. if they can not get as far as they can to the left then they must get as far as they can to the right; when they say they are going to do something, they do it. **Game Changers** will not sit on the fence and are prepared to give everything they have, even if it means losing now and again. Once the **Game Changer** has set their goal it is almost impossible to stop them.

Almost every person who falls into this category is comfortable with their thoughts, making the first move and creating something of value. They are a true **"starter"**. As impetuous souls they occasionally forget to think clearly before acting.

Moreover, the **Game Changer** always gives 100% effort and has a lot of self-confidence. This self-confidence does mean they are prone to ignore those around them. When faced with a problem or obstacle, **G-type** people are ready to confront the problem and will attack obstacles head on.

With the spirit of a fighter, **G-type** people strive to complete tasks they are assigned quickly and efficiently. If they are team leader, their subordinates must try to keep up with them. If they are a subordinate, their leaders must always seek for new challenges for them.

G

Game Changer

The thinking system of the **Game Changer** tells them to **"create new things that make the world a better place"**. **G-type** people are easily bored when working on old systems and are eager to create something new. As soon as they have an idea, they **"act immediately"** without wasting valuable time. Like modern 'disruptive' businesses, **Game Changers** are willing to shake up the market.

Among the six types of people, the **Game Changer** group is considered a **"pioneer" who dares to do new things** without paying heed to anyone. They are not even bothered by the shape of the economy; good or bad. All they need are new goals as that is the best thing to drive their life.

When faced with a problem, a **Game Changer** will fight to find a solution to solve their problem. They don't easily surrender although they may be trapped in a cul-de-sac.

Due to the fact that **G-type** people possess a brain that is capable of coming up with new ideas and they are deeply committed to their cause, their ability to communicate their intentions is not always clear. As long as things are moving along nicely on the surface, if there are underlying relationship problems, **Game Changers** are willing to let such issues slide for the sake of the bigger picture. It is not unusual for **G-type** people to speak bluntly and offend those around them, although they don't always mean what they say as they are totally focused on the task at hand.

A Game Changer's life is filled with Commitment

The **Game Changer's** win-at-all-cost attitude often brings problems, which can sometimes severely test their spirit. If they prove to be determined and decisive enough they will overcome that hurdle only to face another later on the road to success. People sometimes think **G-type** people are aloof, but in actual fact they are actually totally preoccupied with setting new goals. For the majority of people, constant thinking and tinkering is a major worry, but for **Game Changers** it is a way of life.

When a **Game Changer** decides to act, others better follow or they'll get left behind. Like a marathon runner who makes a break for the finish line with 10 kilometres left to run, those behind must keep in close proximity or they will be cast adrift. This makes **G-type** people natural **"leaders who are followed by others"** without them often being aware of this fact.

Not always a charming leader or humanitarian, **Game Changers** can – and often do – foresee **"the future world"** before someone else does. They challenge the invisible as if they are a "prophet" because they are prepared to do things no one has ever imagined before. They want to change the world with their superabundant competence.

Unlikely to entertain despair, obstructions are no barrier to **G-type** people and they want the world to spin on their thoughts.

"A leader who lacks relationships" is like a **"lonely wolf"**. While they are happy in the company of others, loneliness is their true life-long companion.

Strong points & *Weak points*

The **G-type** person should be careful of working too hard and neglecting those they love. After a full day's work, they need to turn off for a while and concentrate on their personal and family relationships. As world-beaters, **G-type** people like challenges and want to see new things. They are bored with routine jobs and are unsuitable for work that includes repetitive tasks. **Game Changers** would rather die than stay doing the same old job over and over again. Their brain constantly runs at 100 km/h and they are always looking for the next big idea.

A Game Changer is a person who loves progress in their life and career. They don't consider starting a business risky as they would rather work for themselves than someone else. Their ideas are usually more advanced than their competitors because they see the future in a way others can't. Although they may try to explain, very few people understand them. In the end, they are so wrapped up in their thoughts they have no true friends.

Strong points

1) They are fighters who never retreat.
2) They are good at getting the best out of others.
3) They dare to think and initiate new ideas.
4) They live for challenges.
5) They are confident in themselves.

Weak points

1) They don't plan before taking action.
2) They rarely listen to other people.
3) They are often over-stretched.
4) They get bored easily.
5) They have excessive self-confidence.

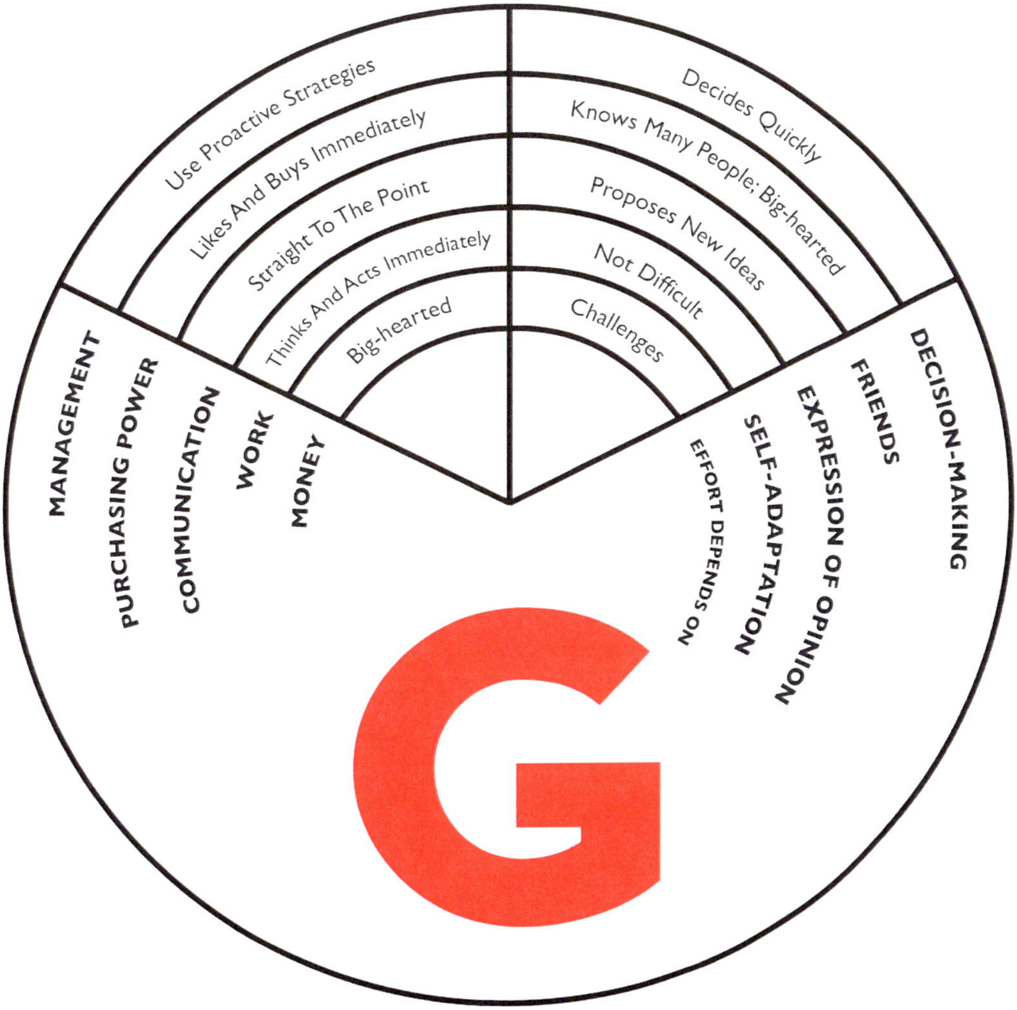
Use Proactive Strategies
Likes And Buys Immediately
Straight To The Point
Thinks And Acts Immediately
Big-hearted
Decides Quickly
Knows Many People; Big-hearted
Proposes New Ideas
Not Difficult
Challenges
MANAGEMENT
PURCHASING POWER
COMMUNICATION
WORK
MONEY
DECISION-MAKING
FRIENDS
EXPRESSION OF OPINION
SELF-ADAPTATION
EFFORT DEPENDS ON
G

GAME CHANGER

Famous Game Changers

Steve Jobs, Apple Inc.: Creator of the iPhone/iPod/iPad

Jack Ma, Alibaba: Father of Chinese E-commerce

Mark Zuckerberg, Facebook: Took Social Networking to the next level

Elon Musk, Tesla: Pioneer of electric cars, spaceships and tunneling

Six Characteristics of *Game Changer*

1) Future Thinking A seer of the future world – knowledgeable and competent, **Game Changers** are capable of seeing the future in such a manner that's difficult for others to grasp. All inventions that have had a profound impact on the world were created by **Game Changers.**

2) Fast Moving A person who can quickly adapt – the world around us continues to change because of this group. They move forward before anyone else, they are natural leaders and founders of trends, creations and innovations. They have the world in their hands.

3) Fearless Doers not dreamers – this type of person is not only prepared to think but also to act. They are afraid of nothing. In the blink of an eye they can come up with a new idea that might change the world. More importantly, they act fast without being worried whether they will be able to make their idea work. **Game Changers** don't think; they act immediately.

4) Do It Now

Immediately – highly impetuous, the **Game Changer**'s ideas must be implemented quickly. They don't like being idle and waiting for results. They are always on the go: thinking, acting, thinking, acting. If they set a new goal, they make a plan to get there without waiting for anybody.

5) Innovation

A true innovator – if we want something new, we must let **G-type** people think on their own, in their own world. **Game Changers** are not good at being dictated to and prefer to follow their own path. As an event organiser, the **Game Changer** might arrange an unconventional yet innovative and surprising event.

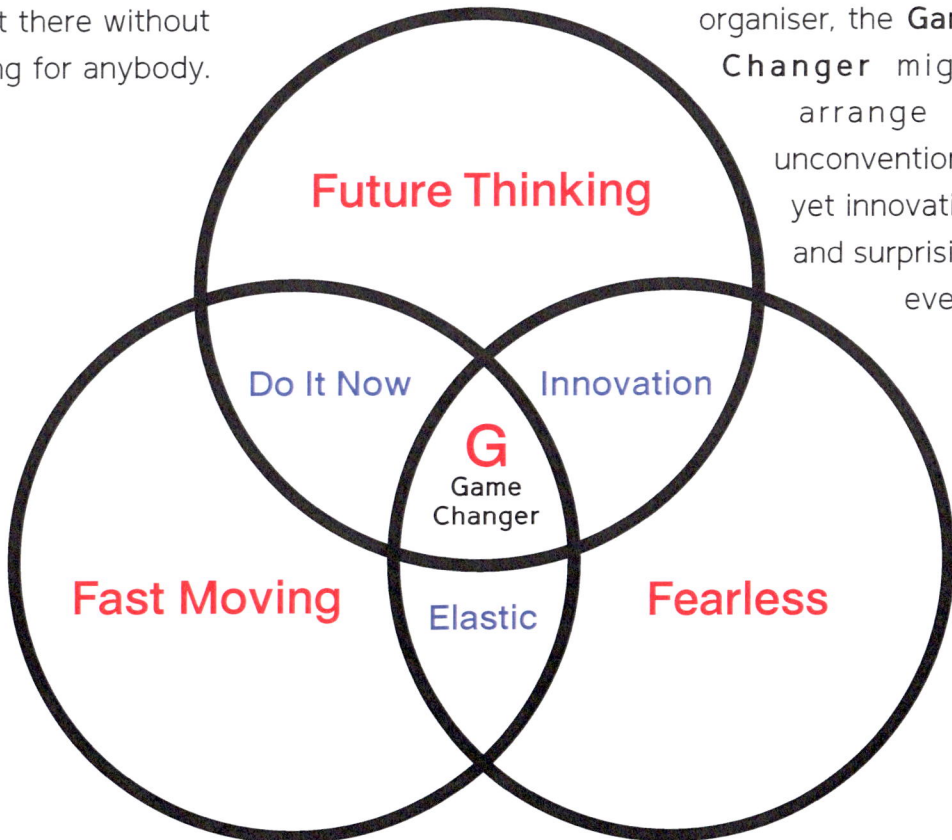

Future Thinking

Do It Now   Innovation

G
Game
Changer

Fast Moving   Elastic   Fearless

6) Modify Flexible and easy to adapt – clinging to nothing, if a **Game Changer** can make life better they will do it without waiting for the approaching apocalypse. The **Game Changer** adapts faster than anyone else does.

Entrepreneur

Brilliant Business Executives

Thinking Process

E–Type people: Entrepreneurs

SEE GOALS VAGUELY; GO BACK TO THE PROBLEM AGAIN.

CHANGING **GOAL**

WORTHY = SOLVING PROBLEMS AT HAND.

UNWORTHY = QUIT

SEEING OPPORTUNITIES.

ANALYSE PROBLEMS!

PROBLEM

ACT IMMEDIATELY!

E

OPPORTUNITY

GRAB **OPPORTUNITIES.**

GOAL

General Characteristics
E-type People
Entrepreneurs

The **E-type** person is business oriented such as a merchant who seeks profits or a person with a new idea. When an **Entrepreneur** finds something financially beneficial, they attempt to build on it by creating a business or making profits from such an enterprise.

Although opportunities do not come along every day, an **Entrepreneur** has the wherewithal to create one. This is a special talent most other people do not possess. Even during a crisis, an **E-type** person still sees opportunities where others do not. For example, when the economy sinks and investors pause to see what the markets are doing, **Entrepreneurs** are willing to take a calculated risk. They see "a chance to make money" by betting on business segments that are able to grow in a sluggish economy.

By calculating the advantages and disadvantages, **E-type** people make sure they're getting something in return.

Nevertheless, everything does not always smell of roses, for the path of the **Entrepreneur** is filled with pitfalls. Typified by their desire to gain financial benefits, **E-type** people sometimes forget to pay attention to the people around them and often face relationship problems at work and at home.

Some **Entrepreneurs** do not have many close friends, but those they allow into their inner circle have been selected due to their qualifications or track record. If by chance an unqualified person gains the trust of an **Entrepreneur,** they have either proven themselves a trusted supporter or a good adviser.

E

Entrepreneur

The **Entrepreneur** type of person is a seeker of profits first, success second and friendships third. When they spot an "opportunity" they will seize it.

Among the six types of people we've identified, the **Entrepreneurial** group is considered to have **"business blood that always sees business opportunities".** They are expert investors and everything they do involves money. They are more proficient at analysing business situations than all other types of people.

Brilliant **Entrepreneurs** are known for their ability to intelligently calculate the chances of profits and losses. Their calculations are often so far advanced that other people feel dazed and are unable to compete.

Their standpoint is obvious: they are **"pros"** in the field of trade and business. They scan every channel to see where they can earn a profit. Whether the Gods of fortune are smiling over them or not, **Entrepreneurs** will always follow their gut feeling and go after their prey.

The **Entrepreneur** fights tooth and nail to avoid losing money as profits are the most important driver in the world for them. Every minute is money and it's better to implement an idea than sit idly by waiting for something to come along.

In general, most people find it hard to make enough money to make ends meet. But the **E-type** person seeks to make money at every turn. They analyse every option and are usually ahead of the pack. They are adept at selling a wide array of products from toothpicks to automobiles and bottles of custom shampoo to smartphones.

Life is *Valuable* to the *Entrepreneur*

It is apparent that the successful **Entrepreneur** is associated with financial reports, banks, land, properties, investment, trading and speculations every day.

The **Entrepreneur's** skill in business tends to make them an **"eye-catching leader"** who others always look to. The new-generation **E-type** people are finding alternative investment channels where they can make money and in a matter of hours others are following suit. When a successful **Entrepreneur** starts to invest large sums of money in a project, other investors become interested and start investing in the same area as well.

By employing clever business tactics and strategies, **Entrepreneurs** can make other people feel distrustful and worried as investing their hard-earned money is a sensitive issue for everyone.

Not every leader possesses the techniques to transform everything into **"wealth"**. But the **E-type** person is a legend of **business investments**.

They **"see opportunities...in places that lack opportunities"**. This thinking power renders them more successful in business than most other people.

When a business begins to go bad, **Entrepreneurs** are usually the first to escape the incoming storm, taking their capital to new business markets.

Strong points & *Weak points*

One thing that **E-type** people should consider is that because of their dislike of being at a disadvantage, they regularly cause friction among their friends. There have been occasions when **Entrepreneurs** have foregone certain projects to protect their relationships with close friends as they place a higher value on friendship rather than the money they will earn. Still, **E-type** people have an eye for opportunities they believe can be transformed into tremendous "assets". Even in an adverse situation, they think they can still make it a success.

Strong points

1) They always see chances to make money.
2) They are good at trading.
3) They preserve their benefits.
4) They are careful about money.
5) They are competent at negotiating.

Examples of **Entrepreneurs** taking huge risks include Sarah Breedlove (aka Madam CJ Walker) who made millions selling beauty and hair products to black women, Bill Gates who sold the DOS operating system to IBM even though Microsoft had no such product at the time, Steve Jobs who dropped out of college because he could not afford the tuition fees only to start Apple with close friend Steve Wozniak and J.K. Rowling who lived on benefits and struggled financially before writing her first Harry Potter novel. All **Entrepreneurs** have the same courage to continue when others would have given up the chase. They are not tricky people at all, but they are staunch believers in their own unique talent.

Weak points

1) They overlook good relationships.
2) They mainly look for financial benefits.
3) They are hardly ever at a disadvantage.

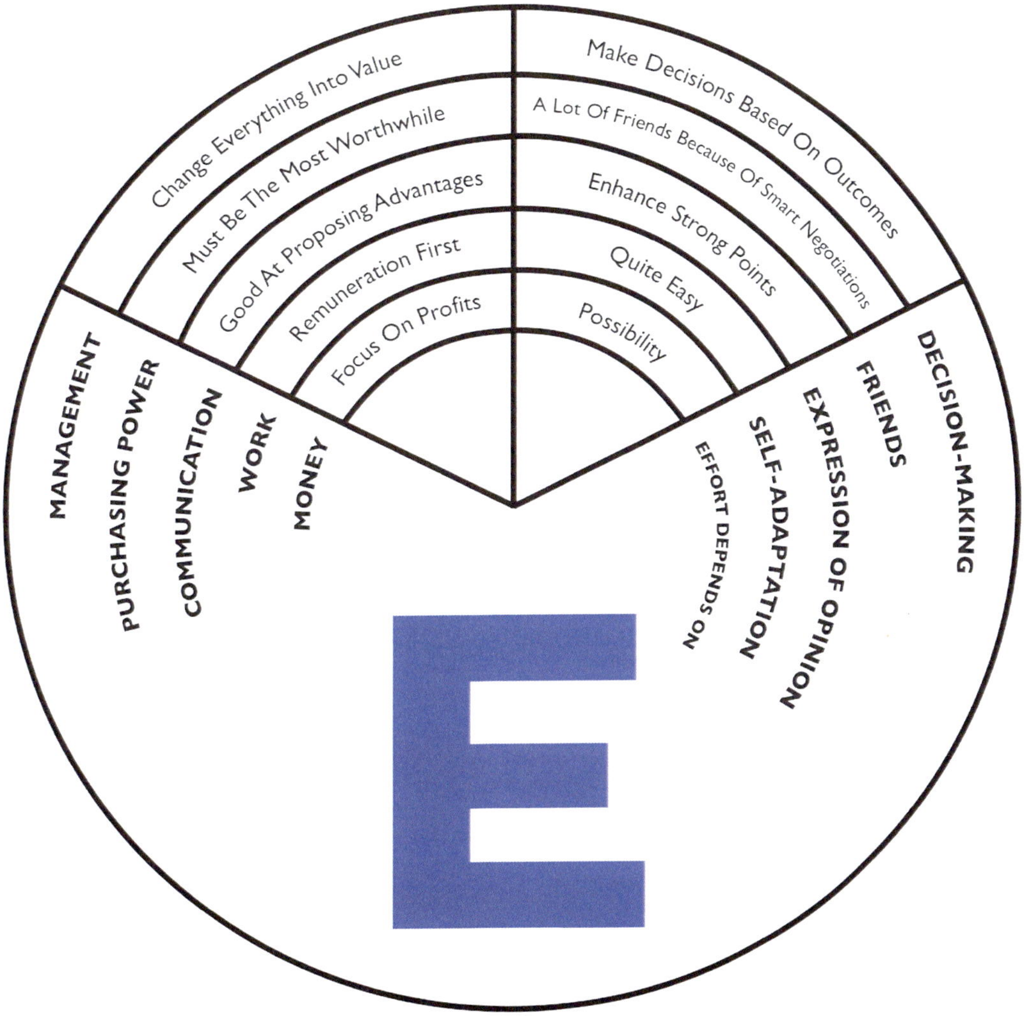
Change Everything Into Value
Must Be The Most Worthwhile
Good At Proposing Advantages
Remuneration First
Focus On Profits
Make Decisions Based On Outcomes
A Lot Of Friends Because Of Smart Negotiations
Enhance Strong Points
Quite Easy
Possibility
MANAGEMENT
PURCHASING POWER
COMMUNICATION
WORK
MONEY
DECISION-MAKING
FRIENDS
EXPRESSION OF OPINION
SELF-ADAPTATION
EFFORT DEPENDS ON
E

ENTREPRENEUR

Famous Entrepreneurs

Warren Buffett, an American investor (3rd richest man in the world, Oct 2019)
Jeff Bezos, founder of Amazon (and the world's richest man, Oct 2019)

Six Characteristics of an *Entrepreneur*

1) Opportunity An observer of opportunities; an optimist sees

"everything as an opportunity". No matter their circumstances or the economy in which they operate, the **Entrepreneur** can see what other people cannot, i.e. "how to make profits." They regularly start businesses that provide profits. Every decision they make is connected to making money.

2) Money Money is a big thing; nothing is more important than a

channel that earns money. The average **E-type** person could plant a tree that will later bear fruit in the shape of money. **Entrepreneurs** are not synonymous with lending money to other people or allowing their investments to become a loss. However, **Entrepreneurs** will borrow other people's money to further their own cause. Personal relationships take a back seat as far as earning a profit is concerned. If an opportunity presents itself, an **Entrepreneur** will invest if the scheme yields a good return on investment.

3) Carefully A careful thinker; investments are not a big problem

and the wise **Entrepreneur** can sniff out an opportunity like a trained dog can find truffles. **E-type** people are always doing mental arithmetic in their mind as to how they can grow their investment or make their money work for them. This principle is at the heart of all business executives and is a trait in the **Entrepreneurial** species. On the surface they may come across as being stingy, but for **Entrepreneurs** it's a case of penny wise and pound foolish.

4) Profit

A profit maker; whatever the situation, an **Entrepreneur** can always see a channel where profits can be made. They are, in a sense, natural born traders. Many of the most prominent **Entrepreneurs** of all time actually lacked a full education, giving up learning for the sake of making lots of money. The right knowledge and right connections are always in the **E-type** person's arsenal as they seek continual profits.

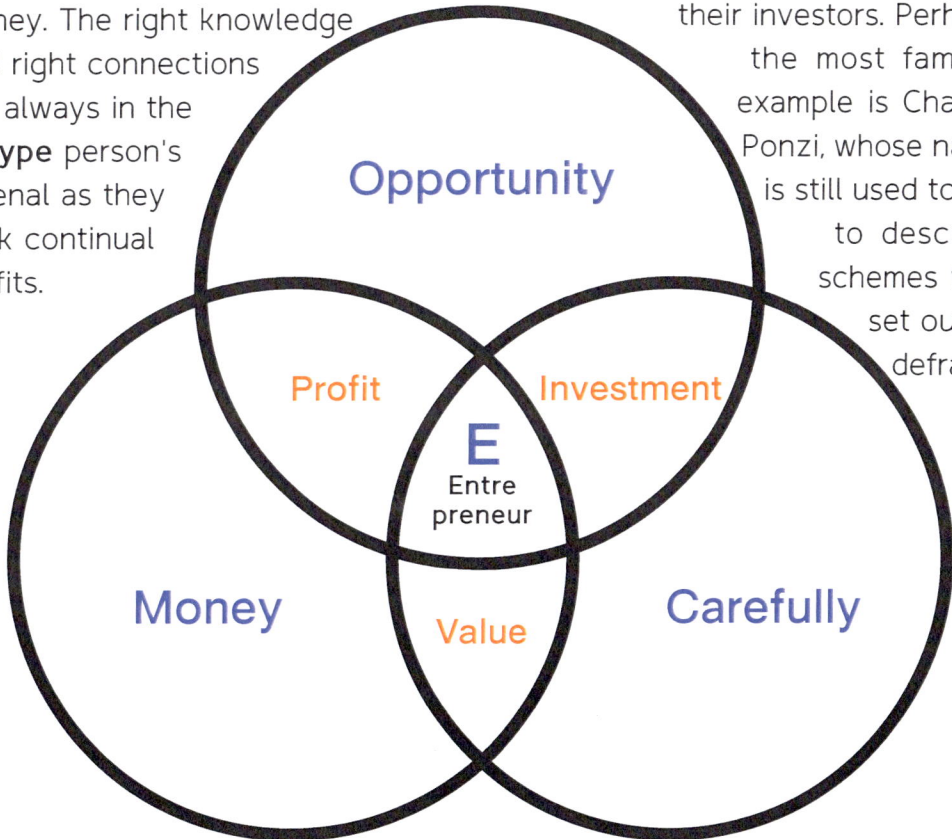

5) Investment

A true investor; undoubtedly, most leading businesspeople belong to the **E-type** group as they are extremely capable of spotting a channel for investment. However, some **Entrepreneurs** have fallen foul of the law as they've conned their investors. Perhaps the most famous example is Charles Ponzi, whose name is still used today to describe schemes that set out to defraud.

Opportunity

Profit   Investment

E
Entre
preneur

Money

Value

Carefully

6) Value Awareness of the value of money; **Entrepreneurs** are sharp investors and place their money in the most valuable positions. **E-type** people are great mathematicians and instead of banking their money to earn measly returns, they will look for other avenues with larger margins to invest in, such as bonds and debentures. For those who are risk-takers, stocks and multiple business lines are more favourable.

N

Network

A Negotiator Who Makes Connections

Thinking Process

N–type people: Networker

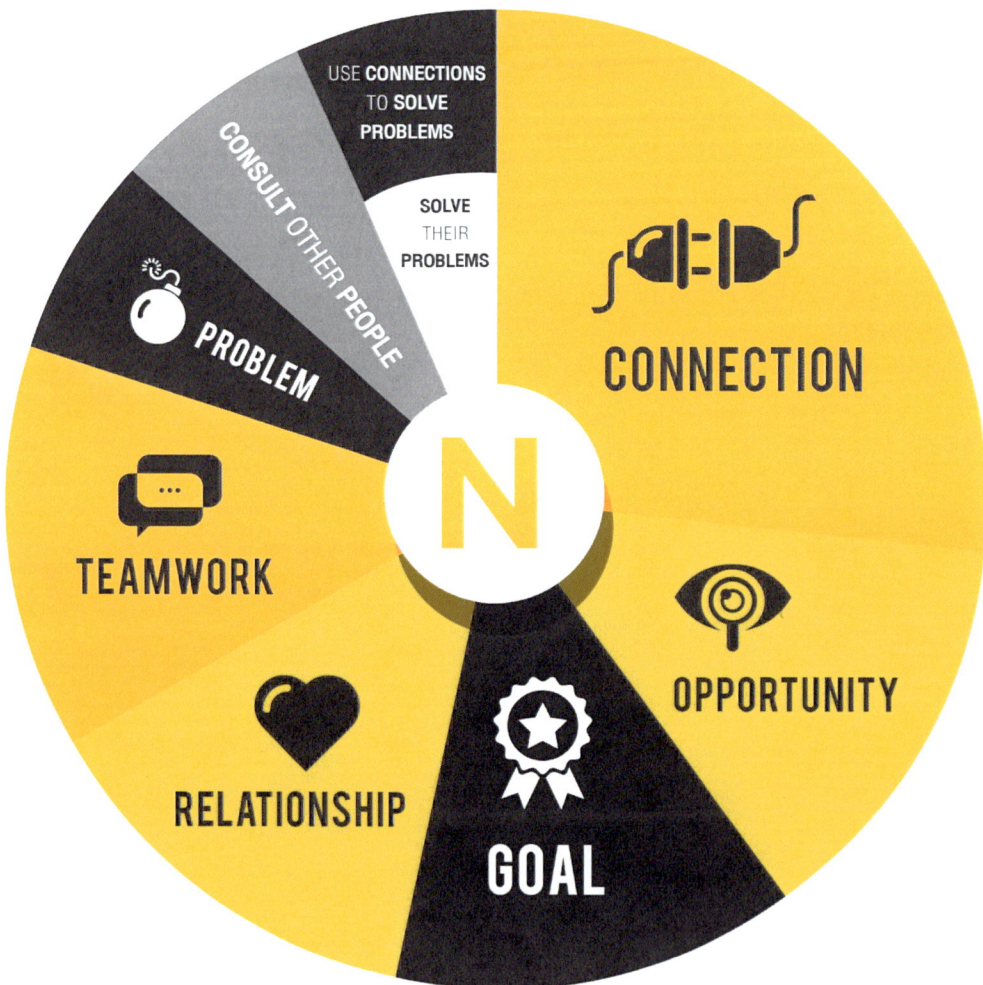

USE **CONNECTIONS** TO **SOLVE** **PROBLEMS**

SOLVE THEIR **PROBLEMS**

CONSULT OTHER PEOPLE

PROBLEM

CONNECTION

TEAMWORK

OPPORTUNITY

RELATIONSHIP

GOAL

N

General Characteristics
N-type people
Networker

The **N** or **Networker** type of person is an expert at creating and maintaining relationships and they surround themselves with close friends and business associates. No matter where they go, they often attract people's attention and become the centre of interest thanks to their sociable and cordial personality.

Their companions can always depend on them in times of need, while in a family scenario the **N-type** person is usually **"the focal point of the family"** who strengthens the family's relationship and unites its members. Among friends, a **Networker** will become **"the go to person in a group"** and when missing from an engagement everyone will enquire as to where they are.

As a result, the **Networker** knows a great deal of people. They know everyone by their first name and are aware of everything that happens to the people close to them. If anyone needs to know the status of someone else, the **Networker** is able to pass on details as if they have only just seen it with their own eyes, such is their attention to detail. When it comes to personal problems between friends or lovers, the **Networker** is the perfect mediator and generally achieves natural reconciliation thanks to their personal knowledge.

A **Networker** is the type of person who strives to establish and uphold good relations between everybody in their group. To live and do things for their friends is more important than to live and do things for money and reputation.

N

Network

Among the six types of personalities and characteristics as defined in this book, the **Networker** is considered **"a superb creator of relationships"**. They care for everyone around them, mediating when necessary and constantly reinforcing the group's close-knit relationship.

The **Networker** never makes other people feel uncomfortable, in fact they are much more likely to make a newcomer feel relaxed. They happily listen to others' tales of happiness and sadness and they are usually the one who people turn to when in need of confidential conversation.

Happiness to the N-type person is openly and sincerely sharing their experiences with old friends, new friends and close friends without concealing anything. When a **Networker** opens their heart, what they expect to get in return is sincerity.

The sharing of knowledge between friends is paramount to **Networkers.** As society has evolved so have they and today **N-type** people turn to social networks to share their happiness. Giving without expecting in return is part of their nature, because for them **generosity comes first.** New business clients are given a sample of products before anything is requested. When the time is right, their associates return the good deeds. Such deeds may not be in the shape of a windfall, but it is the idea of being a sincere giver that appeals to **Networkers.**

The Life of a Networker is all about Human Relations

As they go through life, **Networkers** acquire friends just as other people acquire personal belongings and as relationships mature, their friends develop a deeper trust in them. The **N-type** person does not have to pay people to gain their trust as their unique trait lays in the fact that when people open up their hearts to them, they receive a friendship like no other.

Networkers become **"leaders who have the most supporters"** and in time they become **"the alpha wolf"** with the most trusting followers.

Ask a **Networker** how they've become so popular and they wouldn't say it's their attractive charm, but their total **"sincerity"**. They do not deceive people nor do they exploit or take advantage of their friends.

Not all leaders possess the technique of creating lasting relationships among their peer groups or how to create **"intimacy"**. But **N-type** people **are genius at creating personal networks.**

They are known as **"the most trusted person"**. They dislike quarrels and fights and are willing to surrender personal benefits for the greater good. Now and again they may be a tad boastful, but this is to garner love from their friends.

Many people depend on them to help mediate and although they are not the **"wealthiest"** people, they are the **"richest"** as they have the most friends.

Strong points & *Weak points*

Most **N-type** people worry about their own image because they want to look good and cheerful all the time, but deep in their heart they feel quite lonely. So, they always want to meet new faces and do new stuff. They'll never refuse to hang out if someone requests their company. Moreover, they tend to adapt themselves well to all types of situations. **Networkers** despise fighting and anger and prefer to create a pleasant atmosphere wherever they go.

Most **N-type** people love having fun over everything else. They are content with what they have and don't feel the need to compete with others. **Networkers** dislike being in a situation that causes annoyance. The fact that they know how to adapt and get along well with others has fascinated those around them in such a way that it's hard for them to withdraw from such a friendship. From an early age, **N-type** people have shown sincerity that constantly draws others to them.

Strong points

1) They adapt well.
2) They get along easily with other people.
3) They have a lot of friends.
4) They are an excellent entertainer.
5) They have a good image.

Weak points

1) They don't like working alone or going out alone.
2) They tend to follow society's rules.
3) They are playful.
4) They hardly have time for private matters.
5) They rarely refuse a request.

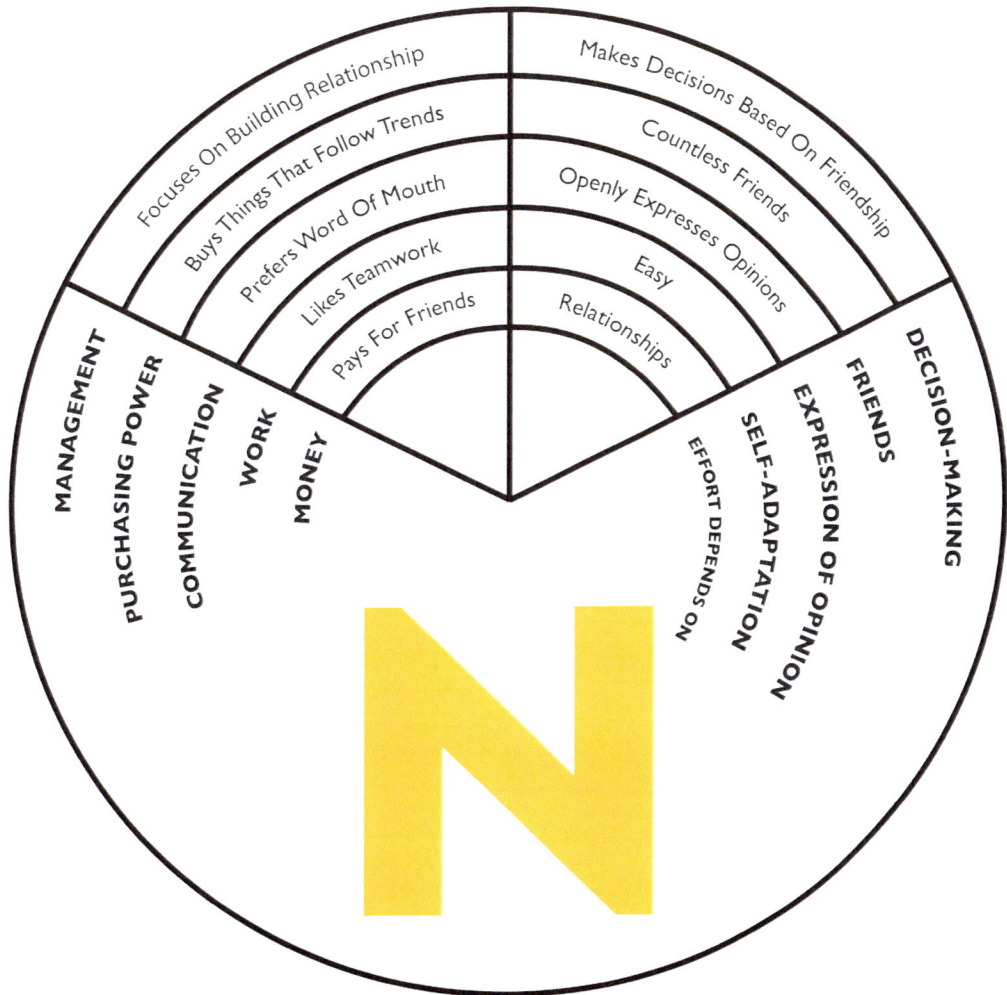

Famous Networkers

David Beckham – who went from being a good footballer to global icon.
Muhammad Yunus – founder of Grameen Bank providing loans to those in poverty.

6 Characteristics *of a* *Networker*

1) Openness An open-hearted person; being broad-minded gives **Networkers** an air of charm. As a **"senior"** member of the group, newcomers are quick to forge friendships. As their network of friends grows it attracts more people who are captivated by the genuine warmth of the group. The **N-type** person can easily persuade his or her followers to support projects close to their heart without people feeling exploited.

2) Honesty True moral compass; **Networkers** are totally reliable and never attempt to deceive or lead their friends astray. The **N-type** person possesses a pure heart and shows their friends the best way forward in most situations. For many, **Networkers** are the trustworthiest person they can turn to for advice. They don't want money or benefits from their friends and it is their true honesty that makes their associates admire them and feel comfortable in their company.

3) Leadership A reliable leader; **N-type** people are the light in a dark room giving warmth amidst the cold. Throughout history they have given people their freedom, been a pathfinder for those who have lost their way and have held out a helping hand to those in need. These traits are not created; they are present in **Networkers** from birth. People may sometimes be jealous of **N-type** people because of their ability to genuinely carry people along with them, but whether they operate in business, society, religion or in the family, **Networkers** are the people that we turn to for honest advice.

4) Friendship

A friend in need; in today's world, it is refreshing to meet people who genuinely open their hearts to others without expecting anything in return. Good friends, as typified by the **N-type** person, are great at getting people to lower their personal walls with honest, icebreaking conversation.

5) Trust

A dependable person; a **Networker** never pretends to be sincere; they ARE sincere. They build a trust with their friends who can then rely on them for their support in whatever they do.

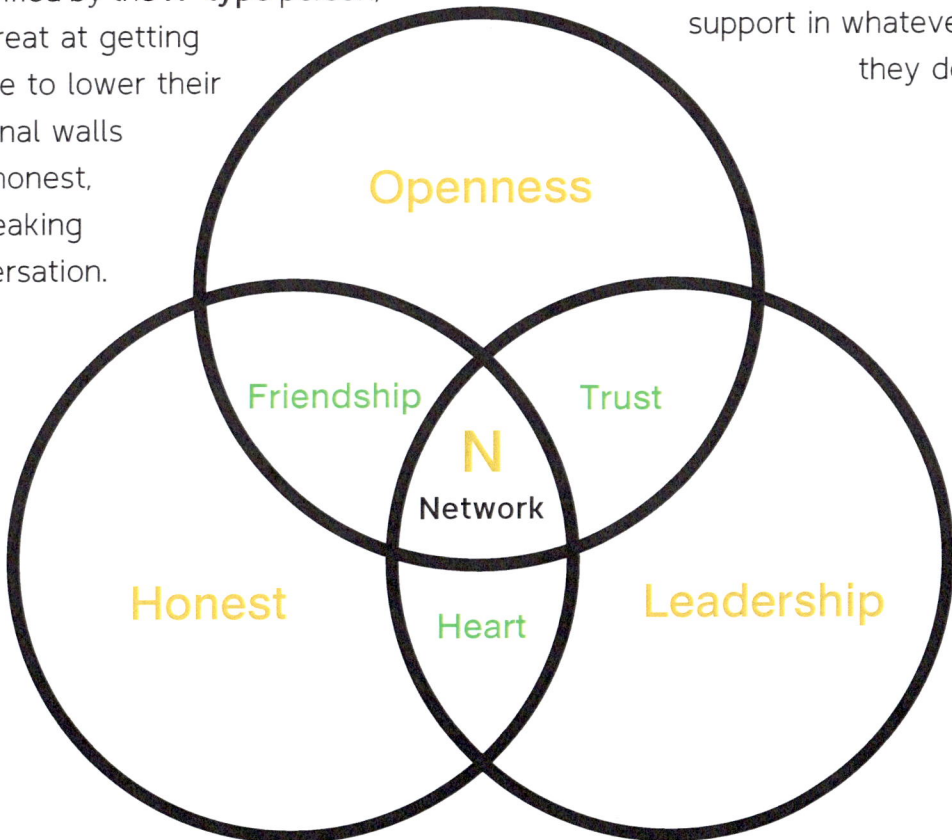

Openness

Friendship

Trust

N

Network

Honest

Heart

Leadership

6) Heart

Giving the heart; a compassionate heart is at the centre of everything a **Networker** stands for. People are happy to hang out with **N-type** people, pleased to be in their company, happy to work with them or for them and will do just about anything to stay close. When a **Networker** calls a meeting between members of their group, virtually everyone will attend. They are not seen as being the boss but more of a friend or more like a soul mate.

I

Information

A Knowledgeable Philosopher

Thinking Process

I–type of people: Informationists

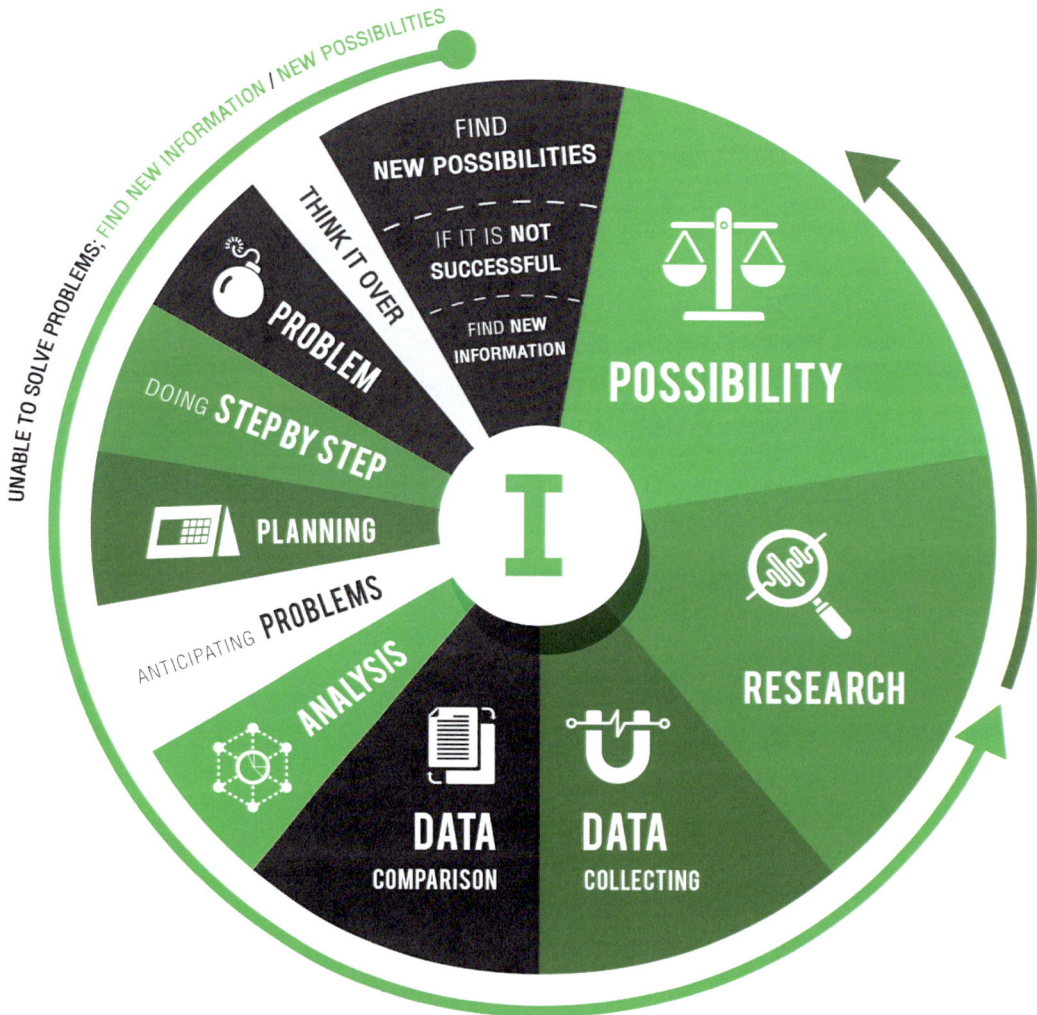

UNABLE TO SOLVE PROBLEMS; FIND NEW INFORMATION / NEW POSSIBILITIES

FIND
NEW POSSIBILITIES

IF IT IS **NOT**
SUCCESSFUL

FIND **NEW**
INFORMATION

THINK IT OVER

PROBLEM

DOING **STEP BY STEP**

PLANNING

ANTICIPATING **PROBLEMS**

ANALYSIS

DATA
COMPARISON

DATA
COLLECTING

POSSIBILITY

RESEARCH

I

General Characteristics

I-type people
Informationist

The **I-type** or **Information** person is a knowledgeable philosopher and a **"lifetime learner"** as reading and accumulating information comes easy to them.

They are useful in all circumstances for their credibility and knowledge as they possess a calm outer image like **"the all-knowing owl"** revered throughout history as a repository of wisdom and intellect. They are good at finding and gathering information from various sources, as well as being proficient analysts.

For **I-type** people, every action must be based on logic and reason, preferably an action that can be proved by scientific principles. Therefore, their mind is one of unwavering principles and clear procedures. They can be considered "a steady planner" as they prefer to live by the rules, playing it easy and safe.

Not one to believe what they hear, when the **Information** person has something to say, you can be assured it is very reliable. Nevertheless, **I-type** people's need to research and verify all types of information to make certain they will not make a mistake, can often result in them thinking and acting slowly. When you need a quick decision, the **Information** person is not always the right one to seek advice from.

The **I-type** person is an **"information"** specialist who needs to find an answer for every subject in order to understand its background and reasons before making a decision.

I

Information

Among the six types of people I've defined in this book, **Information** people are considered "theorists" who live according to rules and norms of society, the workplace and the family home. They don't like breaking the rules and will seldom innovate new and strange ideas. Their thoughts are based on principles.

The **I-type** person pays attention to and carries out research on one subject at a time. As we're now in the digital era, this is a time of "great opportunity" for this group of people. The information they wish to have access to is already online and they are able to access it via a smartphone. There is no need to spend hours in a library as used to be the case.

When an **Information** person wants to become an expert in their chosen academic field, they become "a wise researcher" who excels at finding and using the right information. They will not give up half way and are usually a savant amongst their peers. However, they are typically only knowledgeable about the subject they specialise in rather than the wider field of general knowledge.

An **Informationist** feels at home doing repetitive jobs. They dislike risk and frequent changes; changes cause them to think too much about the future or things that have yet to occur. Due to the fact that they are careful in leading their life and have well-rounded perspectives, an **Informationist** will plug every leak in an organisation as they abhor diversion and violation of the rules.

Data Means *the* World *to the* Informationist

"Knowledge is power and power is more precious than gold" is a truism that appears to ring true for the **I-type** person.

The more information they can attain, the more **"happiness"** they will gain. Their stand-out skill from birth has always been the **"leader with the most principles"**. Many of today's leading business people have never wavered from good ethics and have always put the customer first. People like Larry Page of Google, Brad Smith of Intuit and Tim Cook of Apple have all used the information available to them in positive ways.

"Omniscience" is a quality the **Informationist** gives special attention to. If they cannot find an answer they are looking for they will not stop searching until they find it. They must finish the job at hand before starting something new.

"Word of mouth can't be better than seeing with one's own eyes; seeing can't be better than touching". The **Informationist** only requires the truth. They don't entertain rumors or tampering and despise deceitful information.

Additionally, **I-type** people continue to seek perfection in every decision they take. Everything must have a plan. If they begin something, it must have a clearly defined path, i.e. a short-term, a medium-term and a long-term plan. The more they prepare for it, the more they feel confident in their work.

Strong points & *Weak points*

An **Informationist** must be careful about one thing: excessively clinging to the rulebook. This blinkered approach might make people feel uncomfortable and hesitant about proposing new ideas. The solution is for them to "have an open mind", listen to new ideas and try doing things outside the box. A "new experience" should be considered a fresh piece of information to be observed and studied.

Strong points

1) They are detail-oriented; prudent.
2) They are rational.
3) They are disciplined.
4) They are always eager to learn.
5) They are good at prioritisation.

Informationists mostly prefer working behind the scenes while feeding important information to their team and friends. When they are in full swing they hardly speak because their mind is so occupied. They employ a methodical approach when presenting their work, step-by-step with full details. They are known to practice their presentation so as to avoid mistakes, although this requires them to work hard prior to the big day. Sometimes, they might feel uncomfortable being around new people because they don't know what to say. As a result, they become a silent person who is a good listener and a clever thinker.

Weak points

1) They are slow at decision-making.
2) They cling to the rules.
3) They are cautious.
4) They are afraid to take risks.
5) They have low self-confidence.

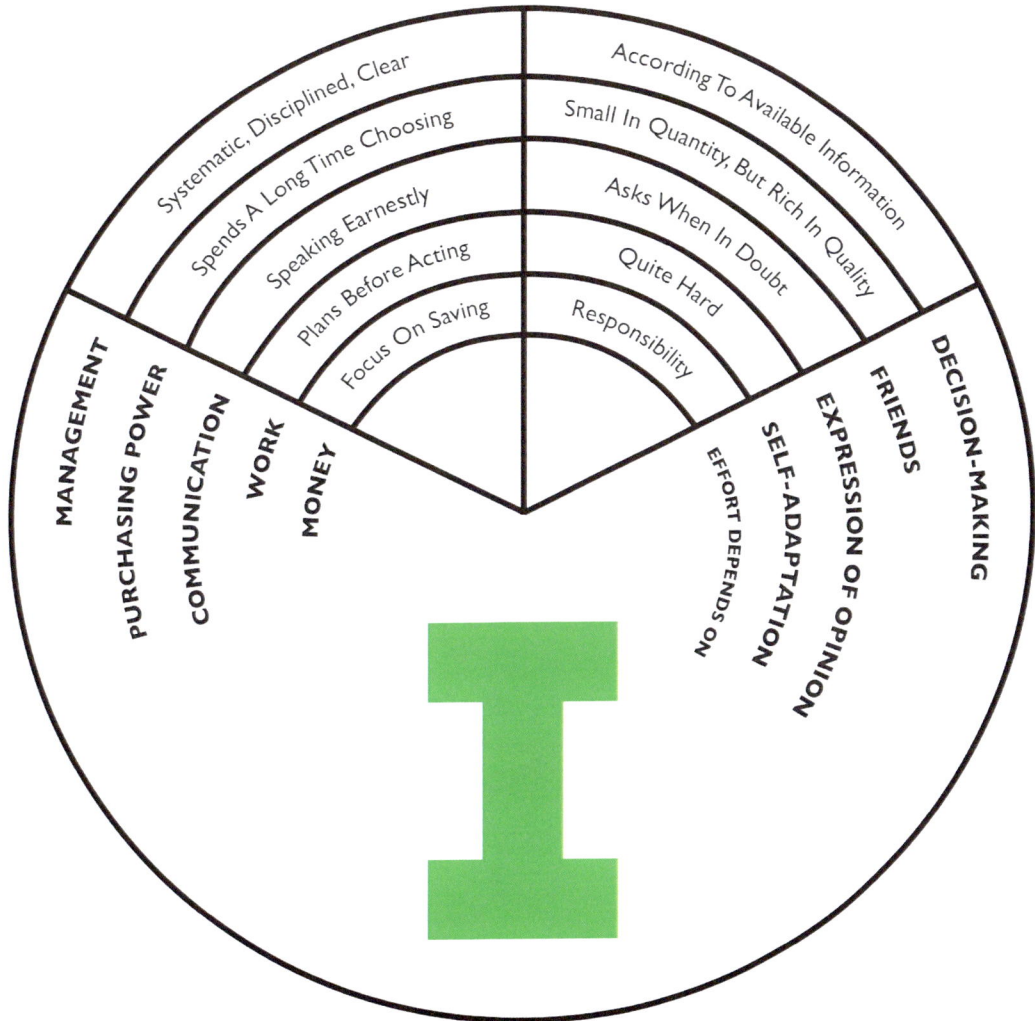

Systematic, Disciplined, Clear
Spends A Long Time Choosing
Speaking Earnestly
Plans Before Acting
Focus On Saving

According To Available Information
Small In Quantity, But Rich In Quality
Asks When In Doubt
Quite Hard
Responsibility

MANAGEMENT
PURCHASING POWER
COMMUNICATION
WORK
MONEY

EFFORT DEPENDS ON
SELF-ADAPTATION
EXPRESSION OF OPINION
FRIENDS
DECISION-MAKING

Famous Informationists

Sir Isaac Newton, theorist who spent eight years working on universal gravitation.

Albert Einstein, spent 10 years developing the theory of relativity.

Andrew Wiles, spent seven years solving Fermat's Last Theorem.

6 Characteristics *of an* Informationist

A———————→ B

1) Logical Thinking A logical thinker; the **Informationist** is a thinker whose ideas are based on reality. Their ideas can be linked and justified. Their thinking is based on discretion, consciousness, concentration and wisdom. They hold on to their principles and do not have irrational beliefs. The **Informationist** is like a scientist who must always find the proof.

2) Rule Observance of rules; An advantage of the **Informationist** is that they observe the rules. They do not like violations and do things step by step as they feel confident following established rules.

3) Learn A lifetime learner; The **Informationist** is always eager to learn and seek new knowledge. They find puzzles that create meaning to their life. An effective collector of information, **I-type** people like researching, reading and studying every subject they experience in life.

4) Principle

Life must be based on principles; The **Informationist's** life must include principles, such as the principle of justice, the principle of honesty and the principle of self. Their dependence on rules and order as well as logical thinking ensures they are good, honest people.

5) Reasonable

Being rational; An **Informationist** is a true believer in scientific fact as they accept as true that everything has a cause, action and outcome. They do not believe in things that are not supported by scientific reasoning.

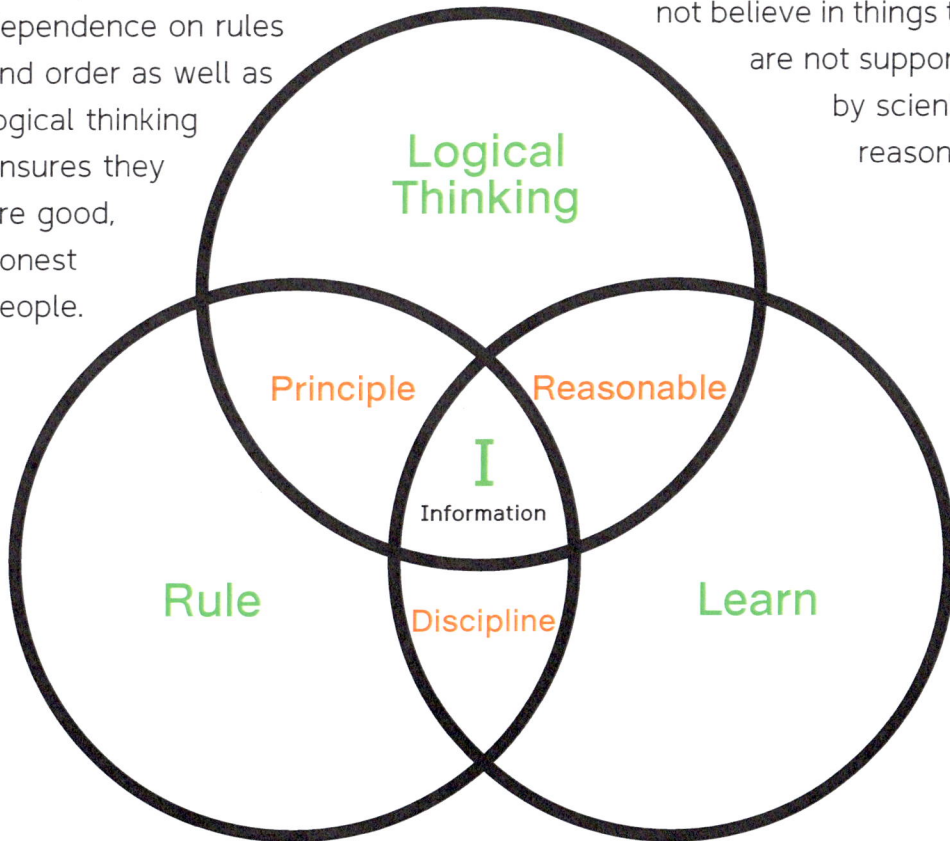

Logical Thinking

Principle

Reasonable

I

Information

Rule

Discipline

Learn

6) Discipline
Being disciplined; A business **Informationist** shows discipline and through their principles will not operate haphazardly. Before undertaking any new venture, they make sure they have all the facts. Being prepared for any eventuality is at the core of the successful business **I-type** person as they are disciplined in their business approach.

U

Unique

An Artist who Loves Freedom

Thinking Process

U-type people: Unique

U
N
I
Q
U
E

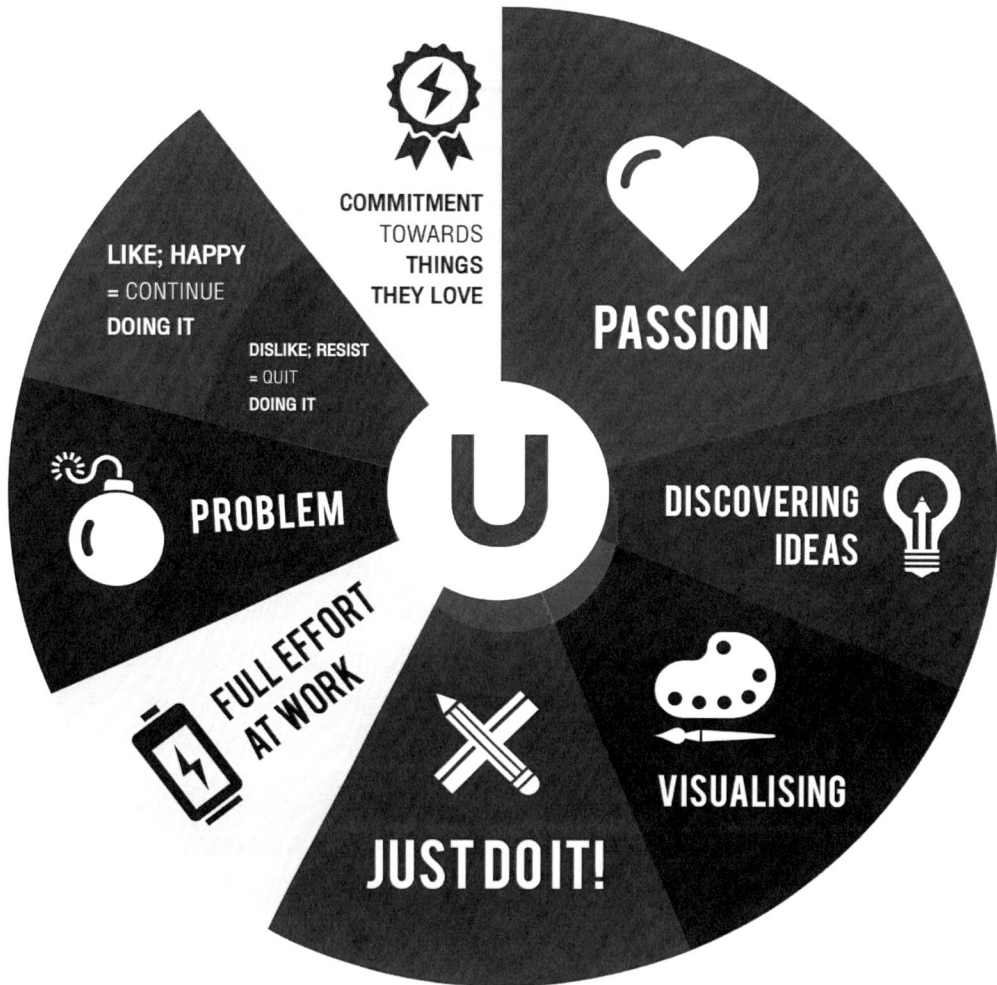

COMMITMENT TOWARDS THINGS THEY LOVE

PASSION

LIKE; HAPPY = CONTINUE DOING IT

DISLIKE; RESIST = QUIT DOING IT

PROBLEM

DISCOVERING IDEAS

FULL EFFORT AT WORK

VISUALISING

JUST DO IT!

General Characteristics
U-type people
Unique

The **U** or **Unique** type of person is **"a freedom-loving artist"** who likes the differences and aesthetic beauty of all fields of arts.

They are attracted to beautiful designs and do not care what other people think. **Unique** people always love what they do and choose to do what they love so it never feels like work. Peace of mind is their top priority, while financial reward is of secondary importance. In addition, they don't like being forced to do things in order such as following the rules and regulations because they believe and have faith in their creativity. Working in a disciplined system is stressful and **U-type** people easily become frustrated.

Some **Unique people** can be unsociable at times and feel uncomfortable being in a large crowd. Others enjoy their own company and will happily work alone on projects or go about their business with little social interaction.

However, at times they would like to be heard and understood by those close to them. The **U-type person** likes being distinctive and will shun the spotlight, preferring to silently retreat to their private world. Intruders beware because **Unique** people fiercely guard their privacy.

The outstanding traits of the **Unique** person is **"creativity"** and innovative viewpoints. Every piece of work created by a **U-type person** is fostered by their intention and spirit. The main reason **U-type people** are not good at social interaction is that they typically create visions in their mind and can find it hard to truly communicate their thoughts.

The **Unique** person is **"an artist"** who enjoys the comfort of their private world. It is not unusual for **U-type** people to appreciate things that others may find a little strange. Depending on their

U

N

I

Q

U

E

U

Unique

artistic nature, **Unique** people have a dedicated set of values and will usually have a specialised routine, which allows them to shine and reveal their remarkable attributes.

Among the six types of people I've defined in this book, the **Unique** group is considered **"the one whose lives are dominated by emotion".** They don't like being controlled and told what they have to do; their free spirit pushes back against restrictions. Most **Unique** people do not crave money; they are more interested in doing what they love.

Unique people have a distinctive lifestyle and at times they may feel confused about their place in the world. Passion and boredom are close bedfellows and **U-type** people will either throw themselves into a project or back off completely. Also, they are happy to hang out with like-minded people but feel just as comfortable being alone. This is a paradox that **Unique** people find hard to understand themselves.

When a **Unique** person puts their mind to undertaking a project, they do it with all their heart. But if they cajoled into doing something they'll resist, even if they are offered a huge sum of money.

Their sensitivity makes them aesthetically enjoy all types of surroundings. A small quirky cafe, a beautifully decorated restaurant or even a studio can make them feel inexplicably exhilarated. It's as if they are turned on by surroundings that other people don't understand or can't appreciate.

A Life of Differences with Unique People

"Emotion determines quality of life" is one of the unique habits that **U-type** people live by.

A person who has their own unique way of life will consequently create work blended with artistic features that clearly expresses their own identity.

"Innovative thinking" renders every step of their life different from others. When they have a feeling to do something, they do it. When they are pressured to do something, the chances are they'll refuse. They don't really care what other people think, as this is the way they are.

"Unique, an artist who exercises the right hemisphere of their brain". **Unique** people focus more on emotional details than other people do. They can find happiness without being richer, smarter, or better than anyone else. But they are happy in their own style.

When assigned to do a task, they will think it over a few times and can spend a considerable amount of time making a decision. But once they've decided, it's hard to change their mind. They might come across as being **"stubborn"** to other people, but this is just their personality trait.

One of their gifts is to see what other people can't see, i.e. something exotic and innovative that will grow their business. They artistically discover a balance in matters other people can't find.

U N I Q U E

Strong points & *Weak points*

When dealing with **Unique** people, you should be mindful of their emotional sensitivity. As they are different, they crave for other people to understand them. However, understanding their personality is difficult for other people to grasp. When a **Unique** person feels that no one understands them or that they have become less important to a mission, they withdraw. **Unique** people believe that everything in the world has its own integral value. So, they want to be in a workplace where people recognise their value, ability and importance.

An admirable quality of the **U-type** people is the expression of their unique identity. They dislike quarrels and if they have a problem with somebody, they will avoid confrontation and retreat to be alone. They tend to mull problems over and over again and although they won't admit to being angry, their close associates will see a difference as **Unique** people don't know how hide their emotions. Their true emotions are seldom shown as they believe their personal issues need to be guarded.

Strong points

1) They are confident in who they are.
2) They appreciate beauty and adore art.
3) They think outside the box.
4) They do not care what people think about them.
5) They are full of creativity.

Weak points

1) They are not good at approaching other people.
2) They do not like obeying rules.
3) It is hard for other people to approach them.
4) They act on their emotions (No Plan + No Reason).

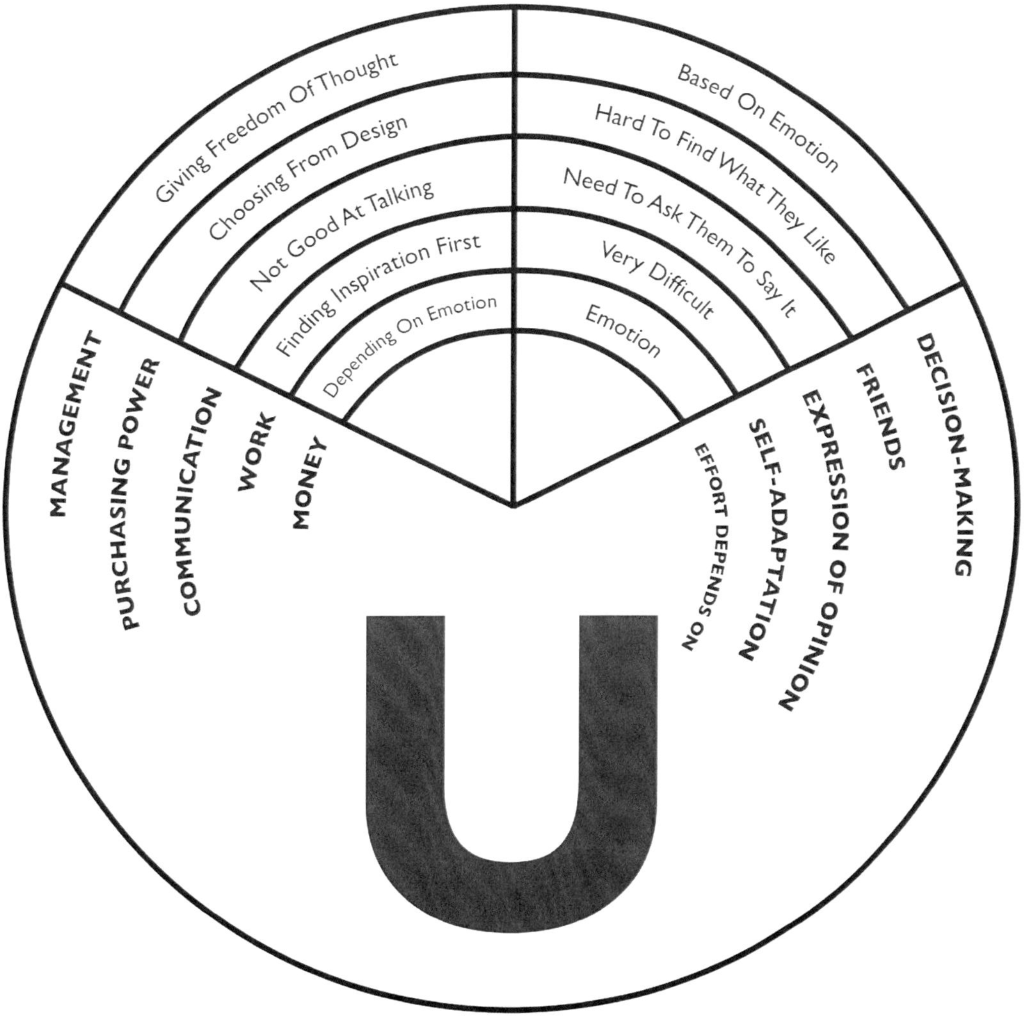
Giving Freedom Of Thought
Choosing From Design
Not Good At Talking
Finding Inspiration First
Depending On Emotion
Based On Emotion
Hard To Find What They Like
Need To Ask Them To Say It
Very Difficult
Emotion
MANAGEMENT
PURCHASING POWER
COMMUNICATION
WORK
MONEY
DECISION-MAKING
FRIENDS
EXPRESSION OF OPINION
SELF-ADAPTATION
EFFORT DEPENDS ON
U

U
N
I
Q
U
E

Famous Unique People

William Shakespeare, famous Elizabethan playwright and poet.
Vincent van Gogh, 19th century Post-Impressionist painter.
Johnny Depp, Hollywood actor who dislikes being in the public eye.

6 Characteristics of a *Unique Person*

1) Art

An artistic thinker; Thoughts and emotion have an extreme affect on their life as possessing artistic blood makes their lifestyle unique. They will fall in love with designs, paintings, photographs and vintage products at the drop of a hat.

2) Heart

Let's the heart rule the head; Unique people find it hard to discuss their reasons for living. Sometimes they are unable to justify the reasons why they do certain things. It's hard for them to find a rational explanation as their passion is rarely based on reasoning. Therefore, a **Unique** person's approach to life is hard to explain because they prefer to let their heart lead the way.

3) Smart

Hidden sophistication; U-type people are reserved and don't like to talk in meetings. They seldom volunteer to undertake group activities, but if they're forced to do a task they will show their superabundant abilities. The fact that they don't talk much doesn't mean they can't do what's asked of them, it may simply be they are not good at communicating. However, when it comes to showing their work ethics, they can stand out in the crowd.

4) Freedom

A life with freedom; Their thoughts, life and actions must not be "forced." The more **Unique** people are forced, the more they will **"resist + refuse to comply + be headstrong."** They shouldn't be seen as obstinate, but rather they don't like being forced to act against their will.

5) Different

Fondness of differences; Unique people love to be different. There might be many good ideas already on the table, but they tend to put all their effort into creating an innovative, outstanding and unique piece of work.

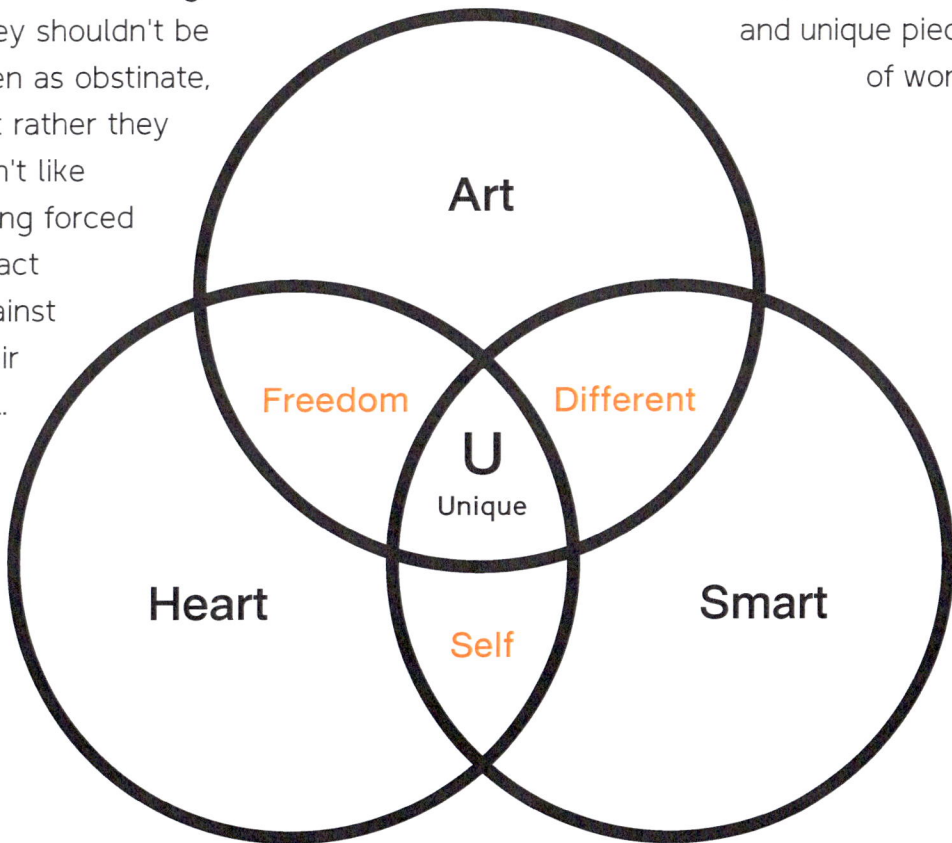

Art

Freedom   Different

U
Unique

Heart   Smart

Self

6) Self

Being oneself; A Unique person's identity can only be released if there is a stage for them on which to act. If they are assigned to create a new brand, they will be the one who shows how their brand differs from everyone else's and align it to the customer.

S

Sharing

A Kind-hearted Individual

Thinking Process

S-type people: Sharing

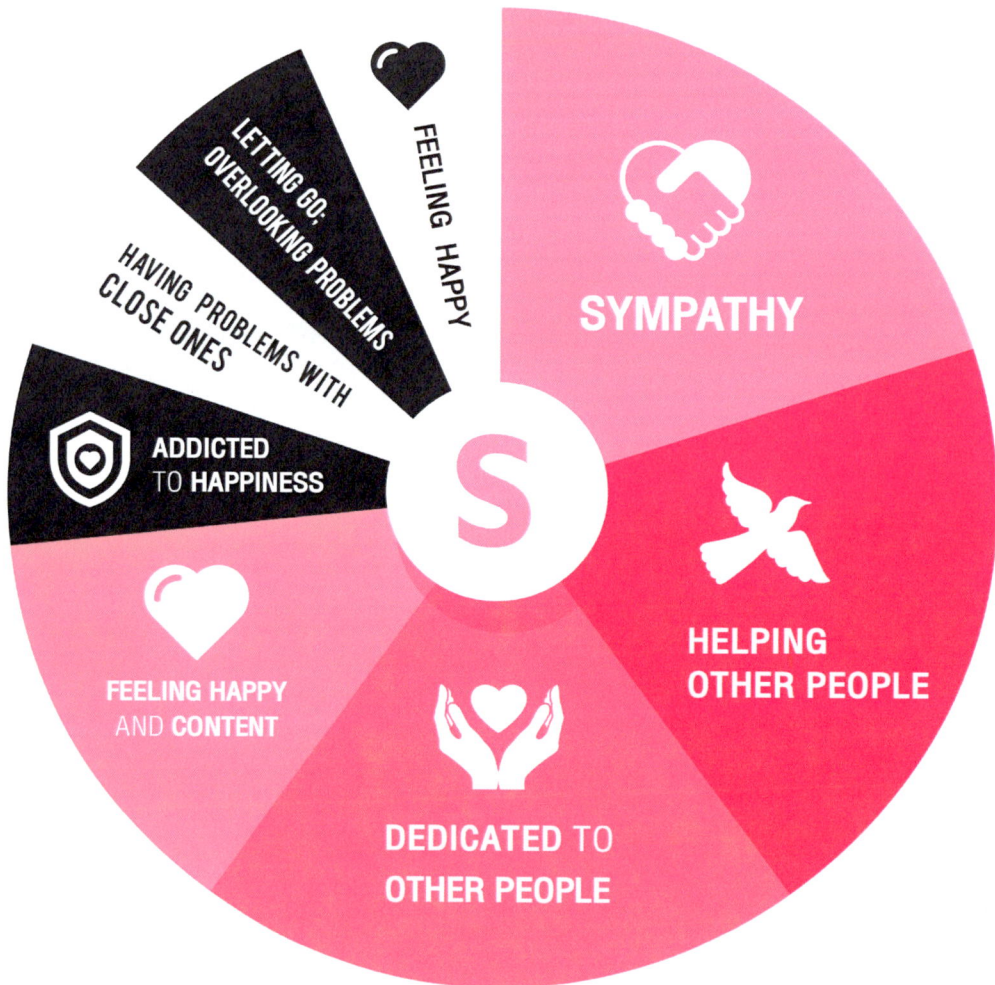

FEELING HAPPY

LETTING GO, OVERLOOKING PROBLEMS

HAVING PROBLEMS WITH CLOSE ONES

ADDICTED TO **HAPPINESS**

SYMPATHY

HELPING OTHER PEOPLE

DEDICATED TO OTHER PEOPLE

FEELING HAPPY AND **CONTENT**

S

General Characteristics

S-type people
Sharing

The **Sharing** type of person is like a **"kind-hearted aunty"** who is extremely generous and full of compassion. They are ready to help everyone, whether they know each other or not. **"Giving"** is at the heart of **S-type** people.

They constantly worry about other people and are always willing to offer their assistance if they think it will be beneficial. Moreover, **S-type** people are quick to share what they have with others without being asked.

In addition, **Sharing** people are eternal optimists and tend to see good traits in people that no one else can see. Consequently, **S-type** people are liked by everyone they come into contact with. No matter where they go, their aura of goodness and humbleness surrounds them in such a way that people can't help feeling a connection with them.

If **S-type** people are given a position of authority, they are sure to care for their subordinates. They will not hesitate to help any member of staff who faces a problem. They are compassionate business people, dedicated instructors and vital to successful organisations. If they are wealthy, they will not only make charitable donations, but their philanthropic mind also means they are likely to establish a foundation to support the less fortunate in society.

S

S-type people can be categorised as being kind and generous and by their very nature they are more of a giver than a taker.

Among the six types of people we've highlighted thus far, **Sharing** people are considered **good-hearted altruists who are willing to dedicate their hard work to help society without expecting benefits in return.**

Sharing people gain happiness from distributing their wealth, knowledge and kindness. It is not unknown for others to question why these people give so much. But **S-type** people do not need to provide a reason why they are happy to give generously. It is simply "pure generosity" stemming from their true sincerity to others. There is no deceit and pretension; what they do and how they give comes from their genuine feelings.

Sharing

A Life of Giving for Sharing With People

"Sublime kindness gives hope to humanity" is a great motto that brings immense pride to a **Sharing** person's life.

Sharing people are born to undertake beneficial deeds for the unfortunate in this world. Even with their last breath, they would say: **"The world still remembers my good deeds."** Ordinary people memorise these values and those who are prepared to share will be praised by future generations.

When **Sharing** people see someone in distress, they will be the first to assist with their physical, mindful or financial capabilities.

"Your happiness is more precious than mine": **Sharing** people want to see other people happy, although they gain nothing of monetary value in return.

Sharing people are sensitive and feel sad for the misery other people have to suffer on a daily basis. If they work for a charitable organisation where there are numerous sad stories, this undoubtedly has a negative impact on their feelings. **S-type** people tend to manage and address their emotions and sensitivities before offering their help.

Sharing people are considered a hero to the people around them. They are **"the one who changes the world with their good deeds."** Many **Sharing** people are the ones whose stories are recorded and retold throughout history.

Strong points & *Weak points*

"Self-sacrifice cannot be measured in terms of money" because it is more precious than that. **Sharing** people are good administrators since their management style does not cause trouble for anyone. All they have for their colleagues is kindness, generosity and encouragement. Therefore, they become a very important person to people who have problems at work or at home. **Sharing** people can be likened to a "large tree" where birds, insects, butterflies and other living organisms can depend on.

Strong points
1) They have a good heart.
2) They are willing to sacrifice themselves for the benefit of others.
3) They are optimistic.
4) They always think about other people's feelings.
5) They always see the good in others.

One area where **S-type** people should be cautious is their perceived weakness to grant anyone's wishes. With their pure hearts and forgiving nature, desperate people always seek their help. It is not unusual for **Sharing** people to feel a tinge of guilt if they are unable to help those in need. It is best to consider whether their help is truly useful or whether it will indirectly produce adverse effects to the ones who ask for help. The old adage that it is better to 'teach a person to fish rather than giving them a fish to eat' is always at the forefront of a **Sharing** person's mind and they take every request on its merits.

Weak points
1) They are seen as being weak-willed.
2) They may believe in people too easily.
3) They are afraid to refuse most requests.

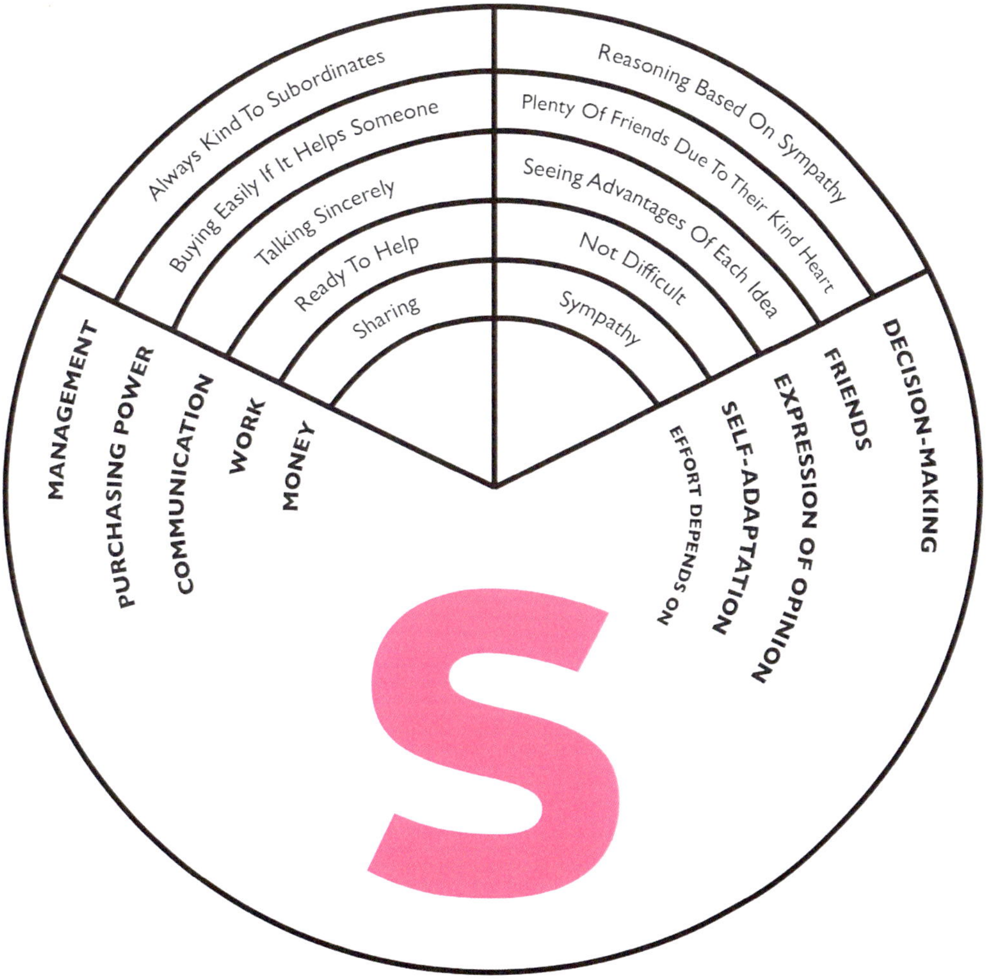
Always Kind To Subordinates
Buying Easily If It Helps Someone
Talking Sincerely
Ready To Help
Sharing
Reasoning Based On Sympathy
Plenty Of Friends Due To Their Kind Heart
Seeing Advantages Of Each Idea
Not Difficult
Sympathy
MANAGEMENT
PURCHASING POWER
COMMUNICATION
WORK
MONEY
DECISION-MAKING
FRIENDS
EXPRESSION OF OPINION
SELF-ADAPTATION
EFFORT DEPENDS ON
S

Famous Sharing People

Mahatma Gandhi, activist who fought for India's independence.

Mother Teresa, a nun who dedicated her life to help the poorest.

Bill and Melinda Gates, philanthropists who are committed to helping others.

6 Characteristics of Sharing

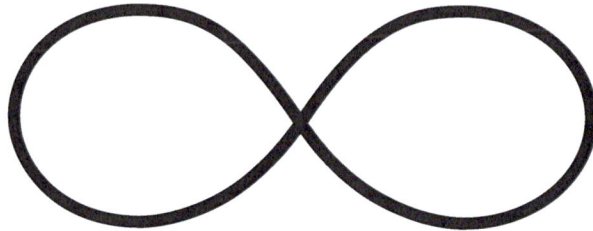

1) Give
A giver's spirit enables them to give without a hidden agenda; **S-type** people are ready to help people from all walks of life. They do it willingly, whether it is giving loose change to a beggar on the streets or a big thing like giving their physical and financial help to victims of disasters or volunteering for charity projects.

2) Kindliness
A kind-hearted and merciful person; To give without expecting something in return comes from a pure and humane heart towards fellow human beings. This is why **S-type** people always understand and feel empathy with those around them. They are keen to give their kindness although they are not always asked for it.

3) Public
Self-dedication for the good of the public; Whenever they feel the need to offer a helping hand to other people, **Sharing** people have the moral strength to take action and act on their feelings without thinking about how tired or stressful they might become. On the contrary, they are happy to do good deeds for the public and they have earned the title of being willing to sacrifice their happiness for the greater good of society.

4) Gentle

Tenderness; **S-type** people usually have gentle and soft expressions towards other people. They treat every person the same way due to their tender, sensitive and optimistic nature. They are sincere and honest and do not possess a wicked bone in their body.

5) Together

Go together, go further; Besides their faith in goodness, **Sharing** people also believe in harmony. If everyone unites to do the right and ethical thing and helps one another – like ants building a nest – then everyone will be happier and the world will be a better place to live.

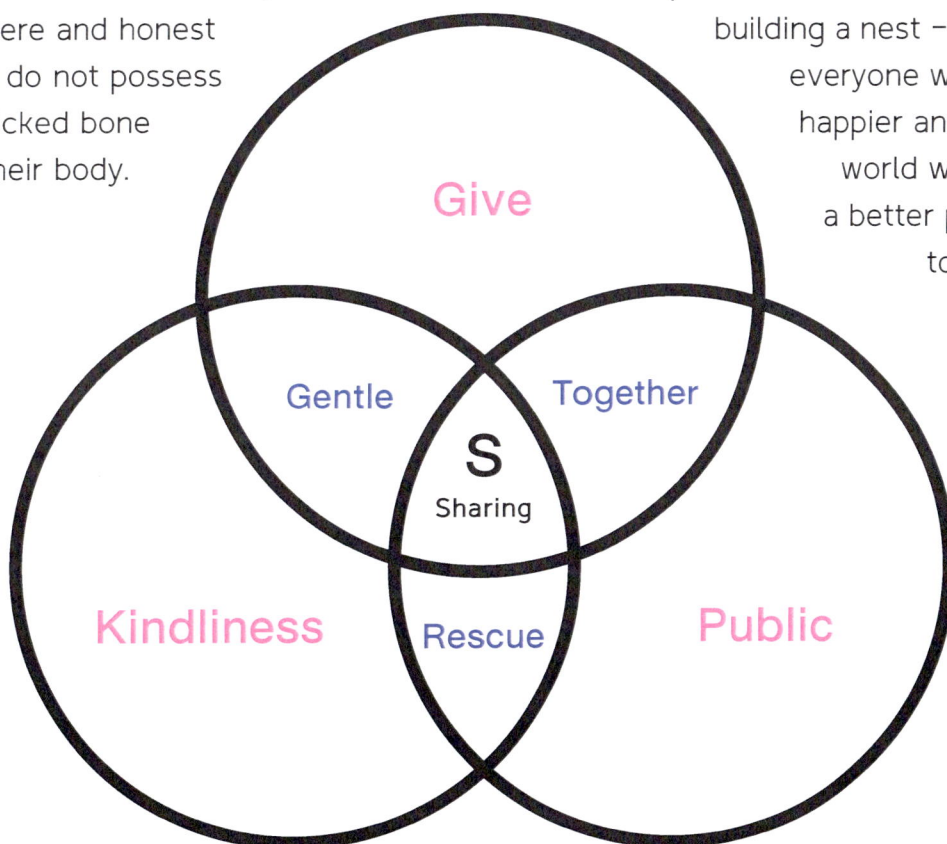

Give

Gentle Together

S
Sharing

Kindliness Rescue Public

6) Rescue Willfulness to help all people; **A Sharing** person is born to help and work for others without expecting anything in return, whether it is reputation, money or praise; this becomes the greatest happiness for **Sharing** people.

• The human brain produces around 23 watts of energy while we are awake. This is enough to power an LED light.

• Our brain can survive without oxygen for only 5 – 6 minutes. This means that our brain still functions even if we have been unconscious for that time and it is possible to recover.

• The human brain consists of 86,000 million neurons.

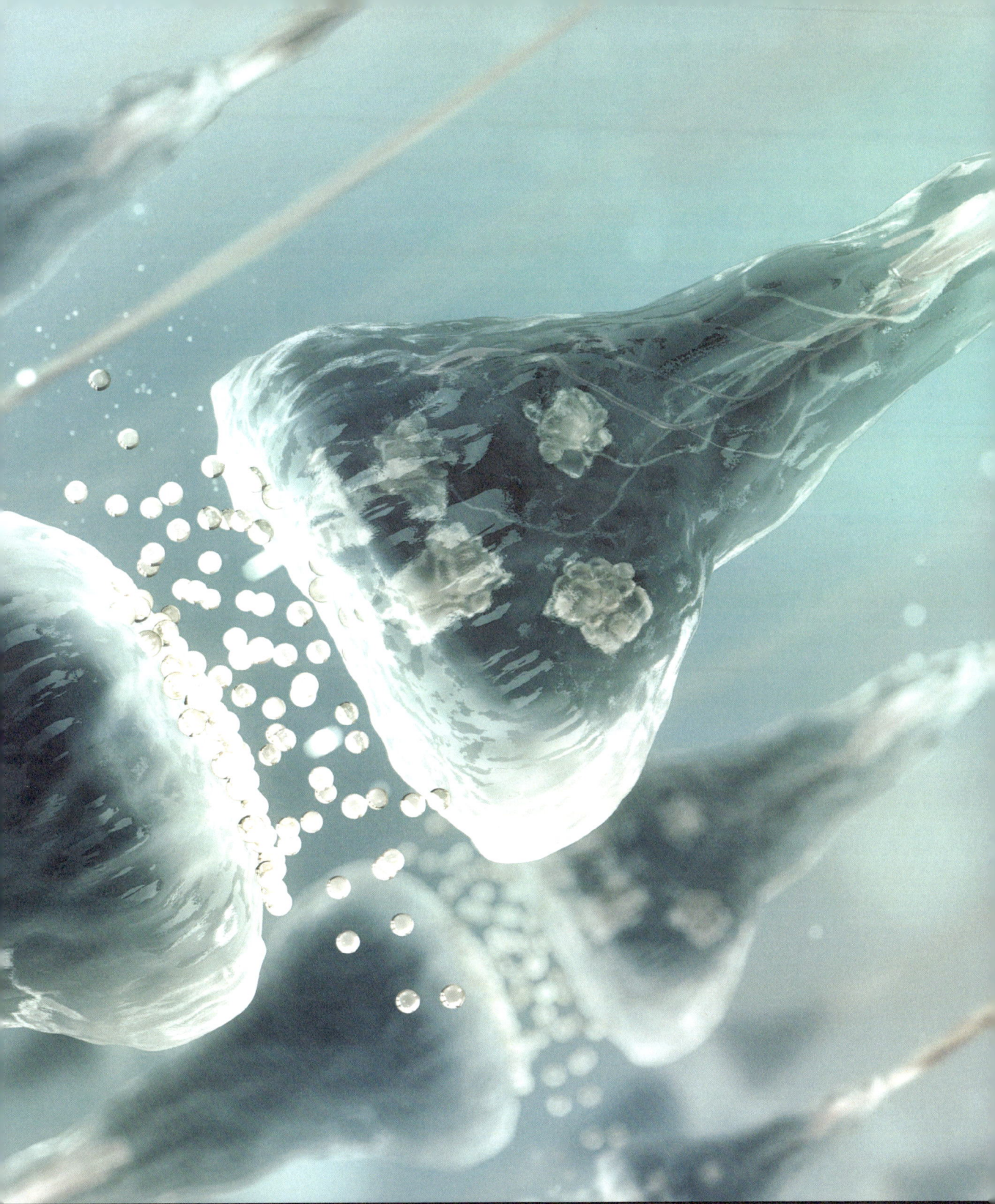

Chapter 3

GeniusX
Thinking System

In 1908, a French psychologist named Alfred Binet and his colleague Theodore Simon devised a method for testing the intelligence of children so they could be properly placed at school. The Binet-Simon Intelligent Test has now become the prototype model for other intelligent tests that are used around the world.

Alfred Binet introduced the term "Mental Age" or M.A. and when combined with a person's "Chronological Age" or C.A. an IQ score of a person can be judged. An IQ score is calculated by dividing the person's mental age by their chronological age and then multiplying the number by 100. For example, a child with a mental age of 12 and a chronological age of 10 would have an IQ of 120 (12/10x100)

In 1939, David Wechsler, an American psychiatrist, agreed with Alfred Binet that intelligence involved many different mental abilities and so designed a new test for adults namely the Wechsler Adult Intelligence Scale or WAIS in order to test people of 16 years of age and above.

The Intelligence Test has since been developed further by L.M. Terman of Stanford University, who developed the Stanford-Binet Intelligence Test along the lines of Binet's original test.

Guilford's Structure of Intellect Theory

According to American psychologist Joy Paul Guilford's structure of intellect theory, human intelligence is organised along three dimensions: operations, content and products.

1) Operations dimension knowledge and understanding of thinking and the general intellectual processes used by people are sub-divided into the following:

1.1) Cognition a person's ability to understand, comprehend, discover and become aware of information. Some people have visual understandings while other people may have alphabetic understandings.

1.2) Memory recording a person's ability to encode information and store such information as knowledge, which can be retrieved and applied at a later time.

1.3) Memory retention a person's ability to recall stored information.

1.4) Divergent production a person's ability to think and build on such thoughts so as to create solutions to a problem, give answers, perspectives and ideas.

1.5) Convergent production a person's ability to select the best answer and to summarise issues into one main point by standard problem solving.

1.6) Evaluation the ability to evaluate values, stories and opinions to determine if such things are accurate, consistent or valid.

2) Content dimension four areas of information to which the human intellect applies the six operations.

2.1) Figural real world stories, tangible objects and things in the environment that are processed via a person's sight, hearing and self-action.

2.2) Symbolic information observed as numbers, letters, symbols, traffic signs, musical notes, clocks and maps.

2.3) Semantic concerned with verbal meanings and ideas.

2.4) Behavioural information perceived as acts of other people.

3) Product dimension that shows results of thinking.

3.1) Units the brain's ability to distinguish between centimetres and feet, or between A, B, C and 1, 2, 3.

3.2) Classes the brain's ability to distinguish between Europeans and Asians, the status of water and oil, hazards and non-hazards, good and bad.

3.3) Relations the brain's ability to distinguish relationships among a group from the relationship among another group, such as human food from fish food and dog food; kitchen utensils from cleaning equipment; good friends from bad friends.

3.4) Systems the brain's ability to distinguish the working system's structure of one thing from other things, to carry out systematic works and to know the functionality of what they've learned.

3.5) Transformations the brain's ability to relate one thing to another thing, a question to an answer, a problem to a solution, an incident to another incident.

3.6) Implications the brain's ability to apply existing knowledge to various circumstances; for example, to apply theories about people in a workplace or to apply car production system to production of factory machinery.

G

Futuristic Thinking

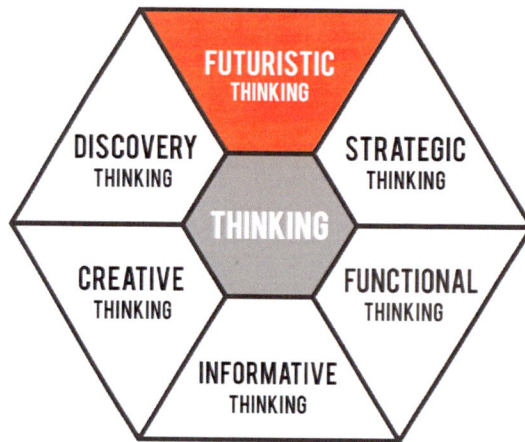

Futuristic thinkers like **Game Changers** only pay attention to their intended goals. Unlike other people, they are not akin to doing things step-by-step, although they sometimes want to be methodical in their approach. But being **G-type** people, as they come face-to-face with actual situations, they become impetuous and venturesome and are not afraid of overcoming obstacles. They might skip several steps from 1 to 10 without taking a break as they seek to complete their goals. **Game Changers** do not worry about being tired; they prefer to wait for no one. What **G-type** people like are new situations that bring excitement and make their lives more interesting.

Futuristic Thinking of *The Game Changer*

New Target

A new target is what **Game Changers** like the most as it makes their life more exciting. They will always look for new challenges, and more importantly, these encounters must be harder than anything they have achieved beforehand. Everything must be incrementally more difficult for them, despite the fact that most people would welcome an easier life as they age. But an easy life is not what **G-type** people want because they rise to a challenge. Their life must be full of extreme excitement. They like to play difficult games and apply complicated strategies. They are wired to enjoy living on the edge and love nothing better than a task that gets their adrenalin flowing.

New Things

Futuristic thinkers never feel excited by what they face in daily life; their excitement comes from new goals, new issues, new jobs, new products and new projects. They don't like tedious and repetitive jobs as they quickly become bored. To keep **Game Changers** functioning at the best of their ability, provisions should be made that nurture their natural talents.

Never Give up

Futuristic thinkers never give up; they are fighters who battle through obstacles and difficulties. Although they may have to work long hours, they never complain, stop or feel desperate. They have fighter's blood flowing through their veins. If they are physically strong, they will carry on regardless of what faces them.

Futuristic Thinking

This thinking method is based on considering what certain outcomes might be in the future. Suitable for people looking for new products and new ideas, this way of thinking helps create opportunities in the future. Futuristic thinking suits **Game Changers** as they are typically the people who determine the future and this draws upon 100% of their potential ability.

1. Need More Knowledge

To be a successful **G-type** futuristic thinker, you need to have boundless knowledge. If you lack sufficient knowledge, then you'll simply be a "dreamer". Knowledge is all around us and it's never been so easy to access thanks to the World Wide Web.

2. Study World Trends

By studying global trends it is possible to predict what will be popular in the future. For centuries, trends such as fashion and eating habits have flowed from one country to another. Today, we need to think digital.

3. Synthetic Thinking

If you can take the knowledge you've learned and combine it with changing global trends, you can create a new product or service in your country. These are the types of challenges that **G-type** people excel at. They build on other ideas to create new innovations. Think Uber and Lyft, LINE and WhatsApp or Muji and Uniqlo.

4. Set New Goals

A "new goal" or "new task" is very important to drive **G-type** people forward. If it is something they feel excited about taking on, it will drive them for many years or as long as it takes to complete the project.

5. Do it Now

Gamer Changers "out-of-the-box" strategies are unbelievable and many people may not truly understand them. Impetuous by nature, they tend to act without planning although this can sometimes lead to them taking the wrong path. Their "do-it-now" attitude is born from their fighter's spirit and they seldom surrender without a fight.

FUTURISTIC THINKING

01 NEED MORE KNOWLEDGE

02 STUDY WORLD TREND

03 SYNTHETIC THINKING

04 SET NEW GOAL

05 DO IT NOW

GAME CHANGER

A good tip for any Game Changer is to look for a partner or a team that includes at least one Informationist who is able to prepare a detailed business plan. Without this backup, G-type people are likely to make investments in new projects without proper thought.

The Futuristic Thinking technique is the most suitable method for Game Changers as they are always looking for a new future product, technique or idea in order to change their world.

E Strategic Thinking

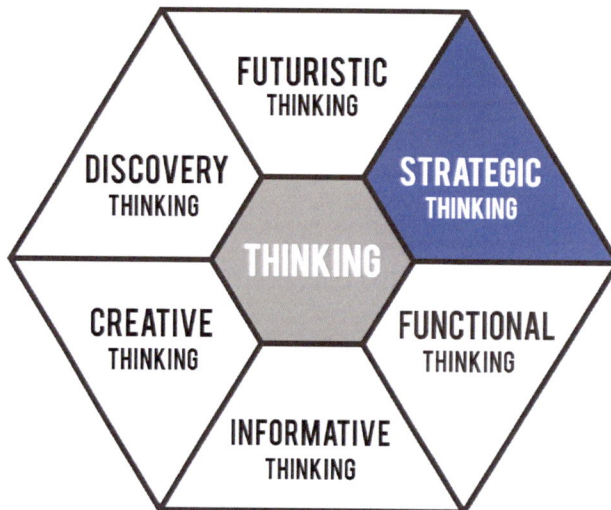

Strategic thinkers like **Entrepreneurs** possess personalised ideas about money, as they have a trader's instinct at heart. If someone asks: "What do you need to do to sell this product and get rich?" an **E-type** person might not be able to give a favourable answer. It's not that they don't want to or can't give the right answer; all an **E-type** person knows is that it comes easy to them to "trade" and to "make a profit". Look around you and you'll see **Entrepreneurs** doing business regardless of the economy and how hard up for money people might be. **E-type** people create a need for their product that other people believe they must have. Therefore, **E-type** people always attract money; whether it stays with them for long or not is another matter.

Strategic Thinking of *The Entrepreneur*

Winner's Thinking

Think like a winner: A simple idea often used by **Entrepreneurs** is "If I'm not able to win at this game, I won't play." Therefore, **E-type** people are very good at grabbing winning opportunities without hesitation. When an opportune moment presents itself, they will take it. If they face an obstruction, there is no need to tell them what to do as **E-type** people will try to eliminate problems by almost any means. In some parts of the world, this may include paying 'under the table' or offering a bribe in order to continue. The **Entrepreneur's** reasoning is that if no one knows about it and it's not hurting anyone, then why not do it.

Money Game

For the **Entrepreneur,** money really does "talk". They are born to create businesses, to grab opportunities, to seek money and to maximise their profits. They can make financial calculations so quickly it is amazing to witness. The more they gain, the more they'll invest. While most people have any number of other interests, **E-type** people are only interested in one thing: money.

New Project

The boss of projects: Business people at the top of the industry are exceptional because they are trading geniuses. If you have a friend who fits this description be careful when asking their financial advice. When you ask if your planned project will earn a profit, they won't be interested if they think it is likely to be a loss-making venture. On the contrary, if they think your project will make a profit, they may wish to become your partner. If your idea is really good, they might even start a new company to compete with you! **E-type** people are not afraid of losing friends; they fear losing money.

STRATEGIC THINKING

01 MISSION

03 STRATEGY

02 FINANCIAL PROJECTION: PROFIT OR LOSS

04 ACTION PLAN

ENTREPRENEUR

The Strategic Thinking technique is most suitable for those with an Entrepreneurial streak as they will always seek ways to beat or outsmart their competitors without hesitating. In most cases, E-type people hold the upper hand in every game they play.

Strategic Thinking

The strategic thinking method is a viable working style for **Entrepreneurs** who tend to calculate their expenses and profits. These types of people are always running through new ideas or strategies in their minds, many of which still need to be transformed in to clear operation plans.

1. Mission

Establish a definition for a task: What is the purpose of the task? What do we want from this task? For example: money, profits or reputation. Do we want to open 300 retail stores within 3 years or expand to 150 coffee stores within 2 years, etc.

2. Financial Projection

Create a financial plan that has various dimensions: normal sales, great sales and poor sales. Business people need a thorough understanding of what they are getting in to before they implement any investments.

3. Strategy

Determine a strategic direction that's appropriate for your task: set the direction and how far you are prepared to go forward or backward. Plan what to do in-between to achieve success.

4. Action Plan

Create a procedural operation plan: make an itemised operation plan in order to reach your goals within the set timeframe.

Successful business owners figure out a project and have their accounting team create financial projections in order to anticipate profits. If they speculate that a project will suffer a loss, they will cease investment and close down any such business line. Sentiment plays no part in their decision.

Functional Thinking

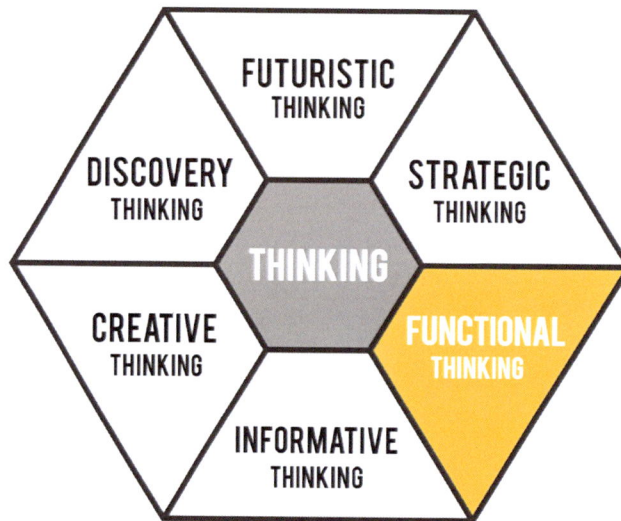

Functional thinkers like **Networkers** are able to recognise other people's abilities. Although they are not always considered the smartest people, if **Networkers** have clever friends to call on, they will quickly figure out what they need to do and their friends will probably help them. If they are successful, **N-type** people will share the profits with their friends. It could be said they appreciate the love of their friends more than money. **Networkers** are known for their skill in people deployment, of putting the right man in the right job. The founders of Apple, Steve Jobs and Steve Wozniak, had this skill down to a fine art and it was, and still is, the backbone of Apple today. So, it is not surprising that **N-type** people are functional thinkers who are expert in human resources management.

Friendly

Good human relations: thinking about friendships. It is hard for other people to imitate how **N-type** people express their sincerity towards their friends. The **Networker** is trusted and loved by their friends and are the cornerstone of their family; the one who unites the household. Without a **Networker** in the house, it would probably be dull and lifeless. **N-type** people can express their sincerity without having to speak and people close to them can easily perceive their sincerity.

Influencer

An influencer among friends: An advantage of a **Networker** is that they are a non-compelling negotiator and not a compelling seller. Instead, they are friends who ask for help from friends. Mostly, **N-type** people will give first and take afterwards. As they are always ready to give, they are hardly ever denied when asking for help from others. Therefore, they become an influencer among their friends. A get-together organised by a **N-type** person is rarely cancelled as people look forward to seeing each other.

Leader

A leader of grandeur: Typically, when we select a classroom leader, we do it voluntarily based on our preferences, admiration and friendships. The **Networker** is a natural leader who gets along easily with people from all walks of life. Their friends feel comfortable asking for and taking advice. If we open our hearts to this leader, we are sure to feel as if we've been friends for a very long time.

N E T W O R K

Functional Thinking

N
E
T
W
O
R
K

The functional thinking method is suitable for people who have a lot of friends. It's a very easy route because you never have do it alone. Please be reminded though that this method is for **Networkers** who have plenty of friends and not for those with only a handful of friends. This thinking method is appropriate for those who can call upon others like only **N-type** people can. If the method works well and is constantly fine tuned, it will be a fantastic tool to move forward.

1. Set Goal

Find a target and create a clear goal that's realistically achievable.

2. Function Analysis

Specify areas where help is needed; determine duties in terms of human resources.

3. Find the Right Person

Recruit people and create a team; seek friends who can help or outsource work that the team cannot accomplish.

4. Delegation

Delegate work to the most competent and smartest people in the team; always choose the best thinker in each field.

5. Assembly

Gather work results and combine them; collect all ideas to form one united concept.

6. Start

Collect and unite ideas into one concept and take action immediately. Do not wait or hesitate.

FUNCTIONAL THINKING

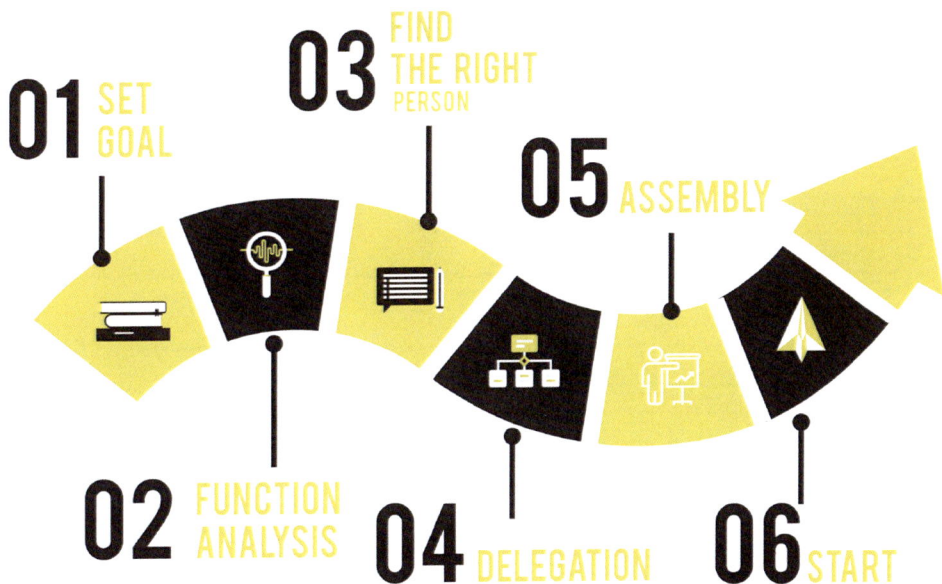

01 SET GOAL

02 FUNCTION ANALYSIS

03 FIND THE RIGHT PERSON

04 DELEGATION

05 ASSEMBLY

06 START

NETWORK

The Functional Thinking technique is the most suitable for Networkers because they usually have a "helper" to assist them all the time. Networkers I've spoken to always tell me they have "many solutions...given to them" and great "ideas have come from their friends."

Informative Thinking

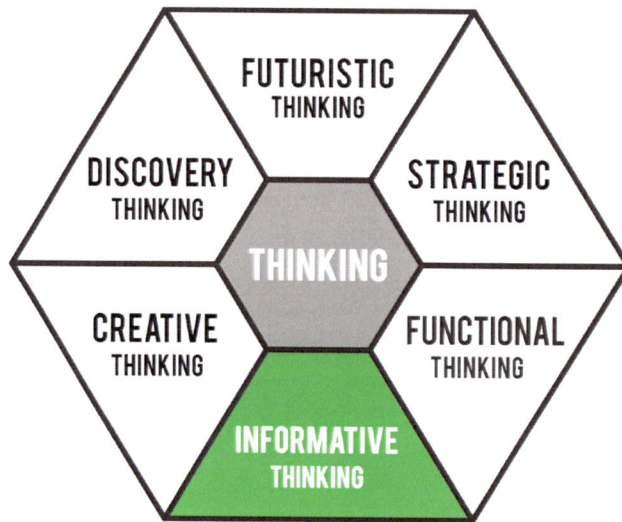

Informative thinkers love researching all types of things. They are adept at finding the information they want and seek knowledge accordingly. The world is now in their hands thanks to the proliferation of the World Wide Web and the hundreds of billions of web pages. **Informationists** can easily dig up information on just about anything from a friend's secret via social media to innovative ideas via TED Talks. What was once the domain of librarians and book-keepers has now become a global library of information where **I-type** people are free to research to their heart's content.

Informative Thinking *of* The Informationist

Research

A knowledgeable philosopher who holds the title of **"lifetime learner"**. They are passionate readers and studious gathers of information they believe is useful to their career or company. The **Informationist** is not easily fooled and everything must be backed up by ironclad evidence. Hence, you can be certain that any information from an **I-type** person is totally reliable.

Reasonable

In the world of logic and reasoning, **I-type people are skilled at finding answers to specific problems** – but their skills do not stop there. Now that the world is awash with information, some of which is misleading and more still that is downright lies, the intellectual knowledge and reasoning put forth by an **Informationist** brings untold value to an organisation. Their life is based on principles and they have clear processes to research each piece of information they are tasked with.

Knowledge

The Informationist does not seek information for no apparent reason. When an opportunity presents itself **I-type** people realise they have been given a chance to prove their knowledge beyond doubt. Keeping an **Informationist** close to hand in your organisation is one part of the jigsaw to finding success. Every business leader, politician and famous personality always has an **Informationist** next to them so they are never caught off guard.

Informative Thinking

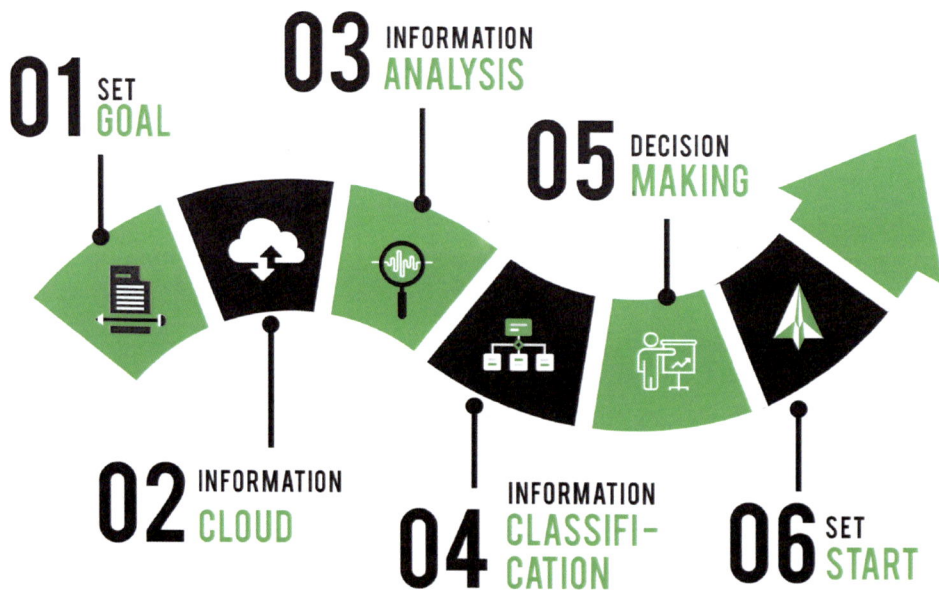

This thinking method is suitable for those who are used to dealing with vast amounts of data across multiple categories. By utilising this method, you will be able to extract the equivalent of pure gold from your **I-type** specialist who is the king of information. However, before being totally happy with any new information, the **Informationist** will screen, filter and double-check data until they believe it is accurate. From a confusing overall snapshot of a subject, **I-type** people are able to condense information into bite-sized information snippets, which can then be used appropriately.

INFORMATION

INFORMATIVE THINKING

01 SET GOAL

02 INFORMATION CLOUD

03 INFORMATION ANALYSIS

04 INFORMATION CLASSIFI-CATION

05 DECISION MAKING

06 SET START

The **Informative Thinking technique is most suited to Informationists since what they require to do their job is "information + information + information".**

Informative Thinking

1. Set Goal

Set achievable goals such as: What do we want to do? Where? When? What is the commencement date? When can we expect to wrap up the project?

2. Information Cloud

Find and store information in the cloud. Every piece of the puzzle is right there in the cloud waiting to be put together. Give your **Informationist** start and end points and let them gather, screen and distill the data to your liking.

3. Information Analysis

Analyse every piece of data; retain the most valuable pieces while discarding all unhelpful or unreliable information.

4. Information Classification

Classify all reliable information into categories; this is a task suitable for an **I-type** person as they thrive in such situations.

5. Decision-Making

Decide and choose accordingly with the requirements at hand now you have sufficient information. Typically, **Informationists** can slip up at this stage so take important decision-making seriously. Do not hesitate and make your selection based on good judgment gained from the data acquired.

6. Set Start

Start taking action as planned and make your project a success.

Normally, an Informationist is happy doing steps 1-4, but cannot be relied on to see through steps 5 and 6. This is partly because they have too much information and are afraid of making a mistake and thus they fail to commence.

U

Creative Thinking

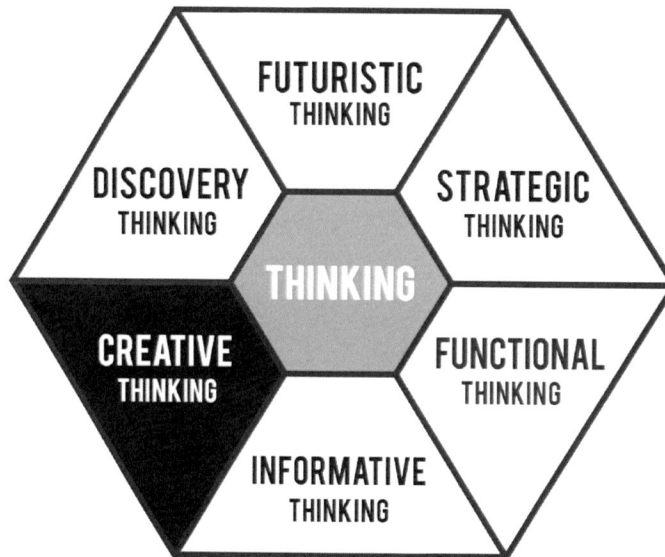

Creative thinkers prefer new and unique things that have beautiful designs. **Unique** people hardly ever pay attention to things that look unattractive. Most **U-type** people like to present themselves by wearing clothes that many others could not possibly wear; bright colors, bizarre designs, retro clothes. However, in most cases it does not matter what the person wears as long as they can fulfill the mission you give them. All **Unique** people can adapt to situations if they are given enough time to realise the end result. As, we've discussed before, many **U-type** people need to be convinced and feel at ease with what they are doing otherwise they simply turn off.

Creative Thinking of *The Unique*

Creative Thinking

A creative thinker versus an unimaginative thinker: If you are looking for a unique piece of work that's fresh in appearance, you have to depend on a **U-type** person to design it for you – be prepared to see something different because it has come from a unique source. **U-type** people who own a business, say a coffee shop or bric-a-brac store, have exceptional and remarkable displays that suit their style and preferences. They don't care what other people think or say, they are happy in their own beliefs.

Artist

An artist who embraces the sky: Loving your creative freedom is as vast as the sky above us. **Unique** people find it difficult to do repetitive jobs for too long; most will simply look for an escape to do something more interesting. They may not know where they are heading just as long as they get away from boring work. Keeping **Unique** talent happy is the key to getting the most from their boundless creativity.

Emotion

Emotion leads their life. The thinking principle of **Unique** people is based wholly on "pure emotion". Therefore, we cannot expect to find reasons or explanations about what they present as what they do comes from a pure heart. People from other groups we've discussed find it hard to understand **U-type** people. Sometimes, **Unique** people do not understand themselves as well. So, please, if you are looking for creativity choose wisely as everything they do is based on emotion.

Creative Thinking

U N I Q U E

Every positive outcome starts from having fun and being creative. This thinking method relies on a **U-type** person's imagination as the main tool; once implemented, creativity will be wonderfully displayed. This method is suitable for **U-type** people because they are creative and have "visualised thinking" that makes it easier for them to create almost any project from scratch.

1. Ask Yourself

Are we sure that we want this? How much do we really like it?
Does it represent who we are? How many years we will need this?

2. Imagination

Imagine a prosperous future that you will have with a newly-created, forward-thinking organisation, product or innovation.

3. Create Strength Point

Create a series of distinct features for your product; create a strong point for the organisation, which people can unite around.

4. Finish Product

Create a product or service that excites the customer.

5. Sell it

Sell the product or service created and if the product is a success then you might have a competitor want to buy your product or business.

Unique people love their freedom and cherish their creativity. They do not like being tied to something. But if it's a job they love, they will happily spend hours working on it. Let U-type people have complete creative freedom and you'll be rewarded with excellent work.

CREATIVE THINKING

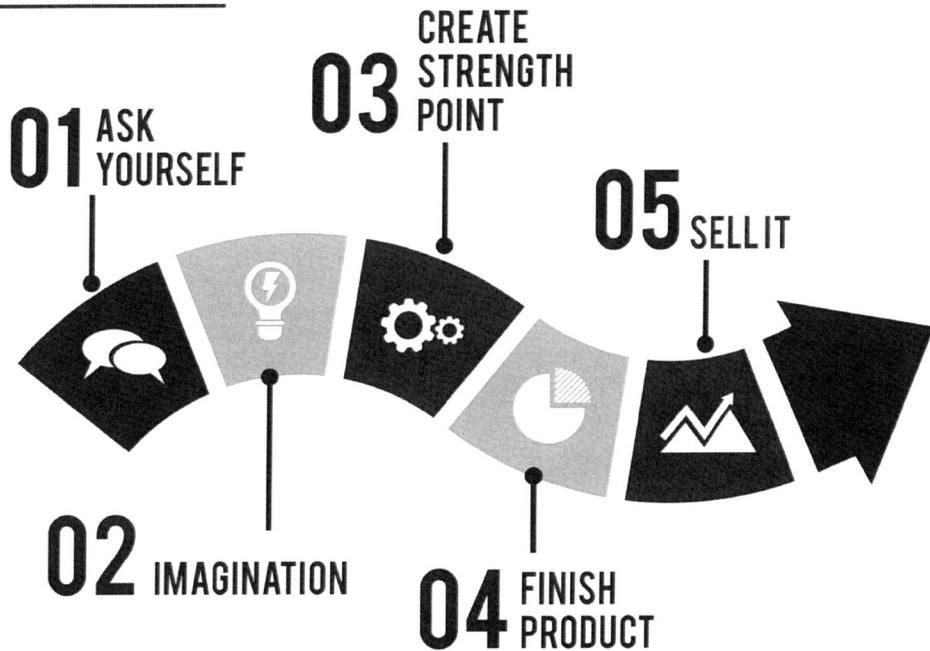

01 ASK YOURSELF

02 IMAGINATION

03 CREATE STRENGTH POINT

04 FINISH PRODUCT

05 SELL IT

UNIQUE

The Creative Thinking technique is best applied to Unique people because their inner talent gives birth to "magnificent ideas" that other people are incapable of achieving. Unique artists have a special talent that needs to be nurtured to bring out the best of their ability. Don't stifle their creative spirit because it is easier to put out the flame of imagination than reignite it.

Discovery Thinking

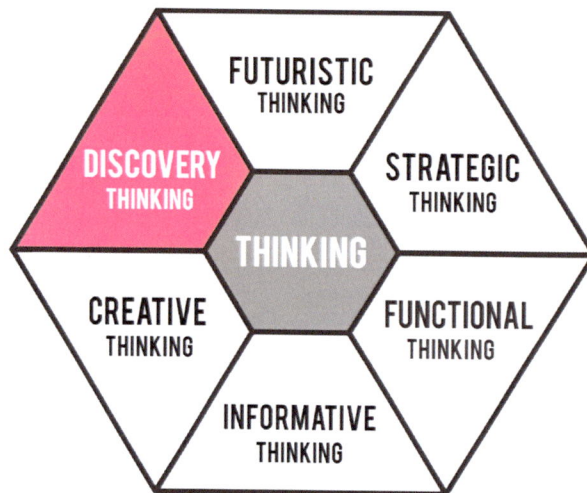

FUTURISTIC THINKING

STRATEGIC THINKING

DISCOVERY THINKING

THINKING

CREATIVE THINKING

FUNCTIONAL THINKING

INFORMATIVE THINKING

Discovery thinkers like **Sharers** seek happiness within their hearts. People who share are born to make the world a better place. Without this group of people, the world would probably lack much needed generosity and a great deal of good hearts. **Sharers** are ready to devote their strength and spirit to other people unwaveringly. They don't have a selfish bone in their body and always give priority to the public's interest. However, good people also have a weak point as their sensitivity and sympathy towards other people sometimes causes people with ill-intentions to take advantage and deceive them.

Discovery Thinking of *The Sharing*

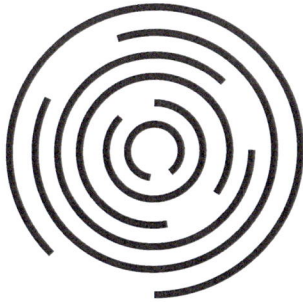

Spiritual Thinking

A spiritual thinker or a thinker who seeks only heaven's blessings: As the belief in goodness is in their blood, **Sharers** offer their help wherever possible. Due to their good nature, they help everyone regardless of gender, age or social standing. However, by applying spiritual thinking to their work, they might encounter problems. Because of their very nature, their heart often rules their head and although they would not harm with intent, they think they will always receive good things in return. This is fine in normal circumstances, but in a work environment, people need to employ their ability to move ahead and this sometimes means having to step over people to climb the corporate ladder.

Heart

Let the heart lead the way: An advantage **Sharing** people possess in abundance is they believe "happiness" can occur all the time. Due to the fact that they love and sympathise with their fellow workers, they are known to avoid all types of conflict with people. Sometimes, **S-type** people are let down by their excessively soft and sensitive heart, which tends to cause them more mental anguish than other people.

Devote

Sharers are known to devote themselves to volunteering: **S-type** people are willing to sacrifice their own happiness for the benefit of others. They will donate their money and offer their physical strength to help people in need. They are willing to devote their life to society, their family and their jobs. It is not about making money, earning praise or being famous, they simply have other people's interest at heart.

DISCOVERY THINKING

S H A R I N G

01 SELF STUDY

03 FIGHT FOR THE IDEAL LIFE

02 DISCOVERY YOURSELF

04 JUST DO IT

The Discovery Thinking technique is best utilised with Sharing people because deep down they wish to discover their own self, foster new ideas and help others in society, at home and at work in order to make the world a better place.

Discovery Thinking

This thinking method is most suitable for people who are good at **Sharing.** The application of this method will fill the divide caused by their exceptional kindness and extreme optimism. **S-type** people are able to finish tasks on time and apply creativity where needed by employing their outstanding characteristics as follows:

1. Self-Study

Perform self-study to achieve thorough understanding by asking a lot of questions while analysing every aspect of life.
Why are we born? What do we actually want to achieve in life?

2. Discovery Yourself

Discover yourself to find your true identity and gain a new lease of life through good ideas that help others.

3. Fight for the Ideal Life

Fight for your life and do things you love. To make the world a better place to live, turn your ideal world into reality.

4. Just Do It

Start doing things meaningfully and create the world you want.

Sharing people have a sensitive heart and love their friends, colleagues and family. What they do is for society and they are prepared to sacrifice their personal happiness to achieve their goals. They dislike taking advantage of other people, but more often than not S-type people end up being the victim in today's "me first" society.

Bad experiences are hard to forget.
We constantly remind ourselves that certain
things are dangerous
and that we shouldn't get involved
with other people's problems,
otherwise we might get hurt again.

Imagine the time when you were a child.
You played with a carefree mind
and never thought about hurting others.

If our memory didn't keep reminding us
about our past, as we get older we may forget such simple thoughts.
It is easy to repeat actions that might cause
us harm, so always keep thinking
of the dangers in life
and live your life to the fullest.

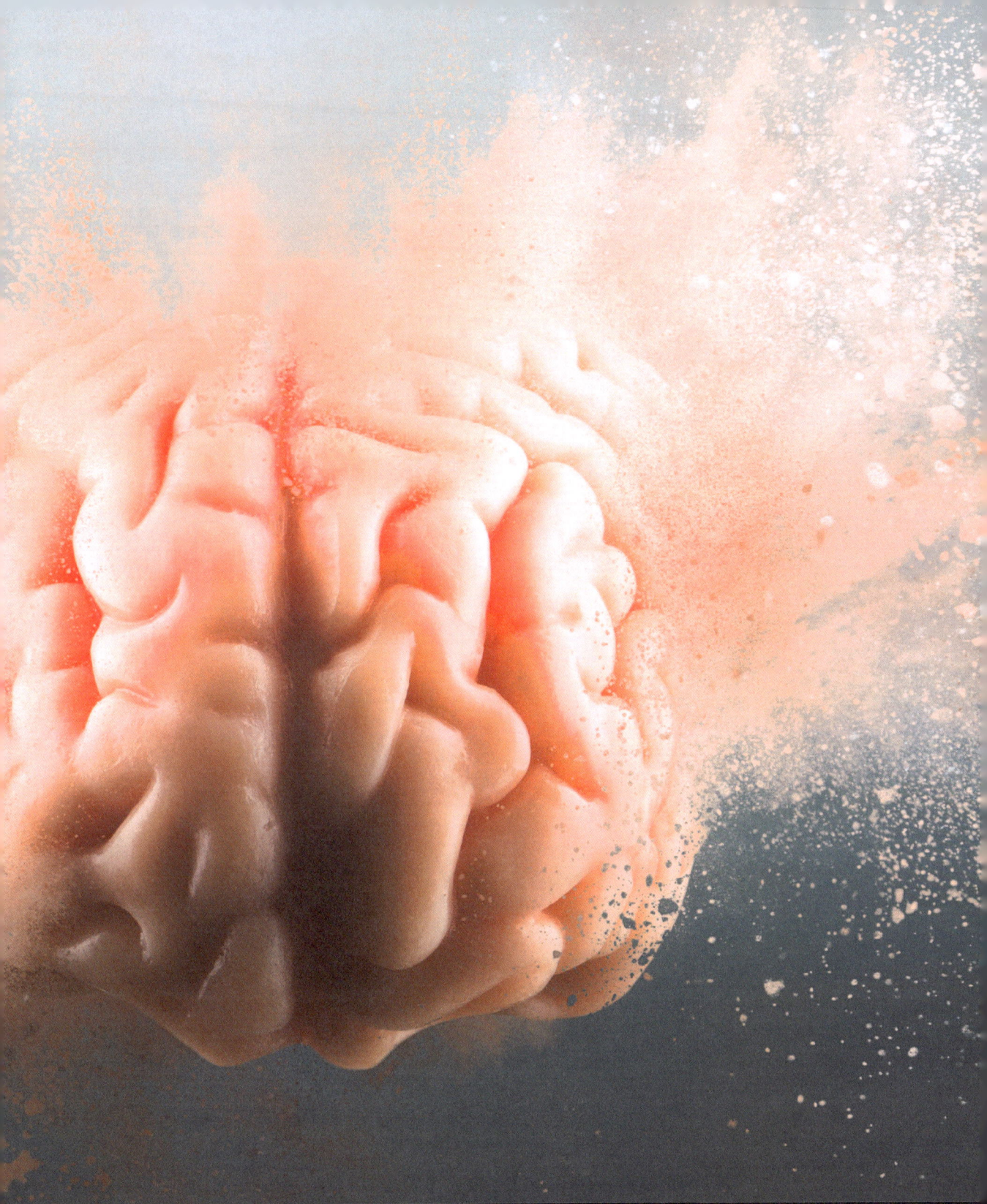

Chapter 4

GeniusX Inspiration

Over past 150 years, psychologists have attempted to explain and categorise people's motivation based on numerous theories. Carl Gustav Jung (1875 – 1961), a Swiss psychologist, divided humans into the following two groups:

A) Extraverts obtaining satisfaction from outside one's self. Extraverts enjoy interaction with other people and thrive in social gatherings.

B) Introverts being mainly concerned about one's own mental self. Introverts like solitary activities such as reading, writing and painting.

Jung divided the human mind into four categories:

1) Thoughts understand the world and nature; learn about our own world.

2) Feelings express emotion – happiness, suffering, anger, hatred, fear, love, sorrow.

3) Perception perceive stories and truth.

4) Intuition and premonition discovery of the path of the subconscious – facts, truth, feelings or thoughts.

Rule of Balance

People strive to create balance and harmony in order to have a strong body and a happy mind.

1) Sublimation Primitive desires are diverted into, and replaced by, culturally higher or morally acceptable activities.

2) Repression If instinctual desires are not sublimated in a proper manner, such powerful desires will be repressed within the subconscious. Over a long period of time, these desires will be discharged with stronger power than the function of conscious (ego). At this point, people will demonstrate unreasonable behaviour due to such pressure.

Inspiration is Competition

Inspired by Competition

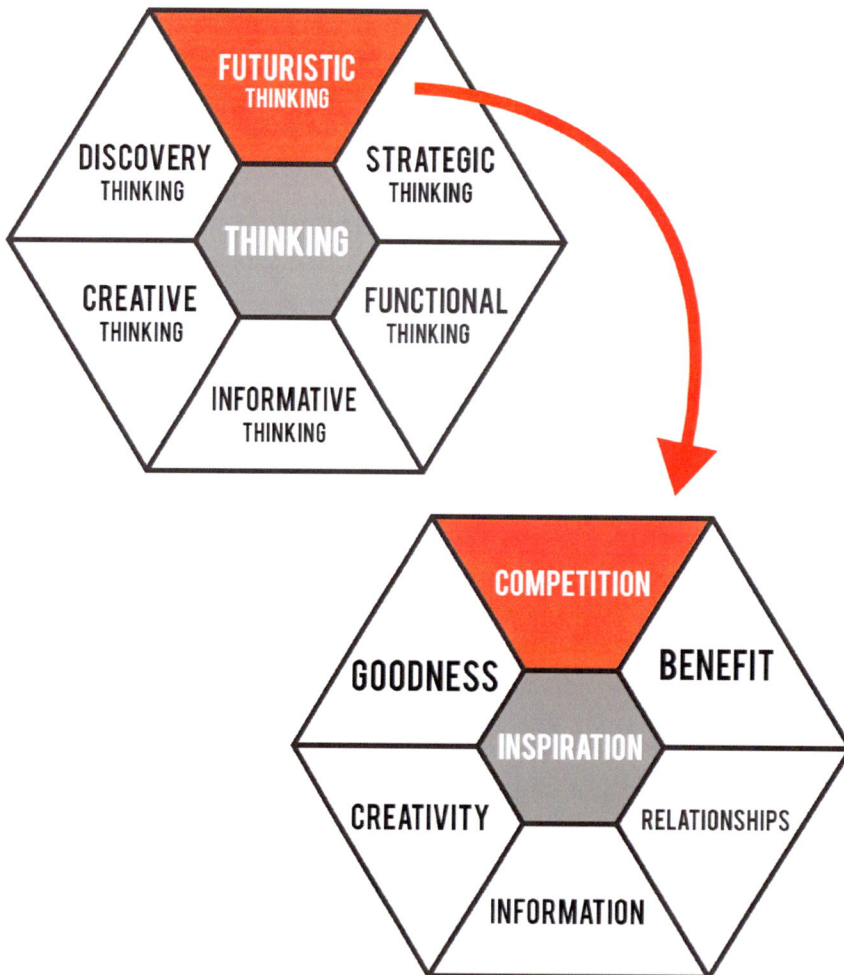

Inspiration is *Competition*

Competition

Game Changers like nothing better than taking part in a competitive challenge. The harder the challenge, the more fun they have. From a business perspective, if they can find a new product or open a new market, they will gain immense personal enjoyment. However, if they produce similar products that are already in the market and face competition, this becomes fun to them. They derive joy from going head-to-head with their competitors, employing fresh marketing ideas and trying new strategies to gain the upper hand. This trait is normal to **Game Changers** as they thrive on competition.

Determined Like a Game Changer

G-type people are eager to get involved in exciting and challenging projects. Therefore, whenever they are inspired by competition, they will feel a natural urge to start taking action immediately. Nothing can stand in their way until they ultimately gain victory. Inspiration by competition is one driving force you can tap into with **Game Changers.**

Inspiration is Benefit

Inspired by Benefit

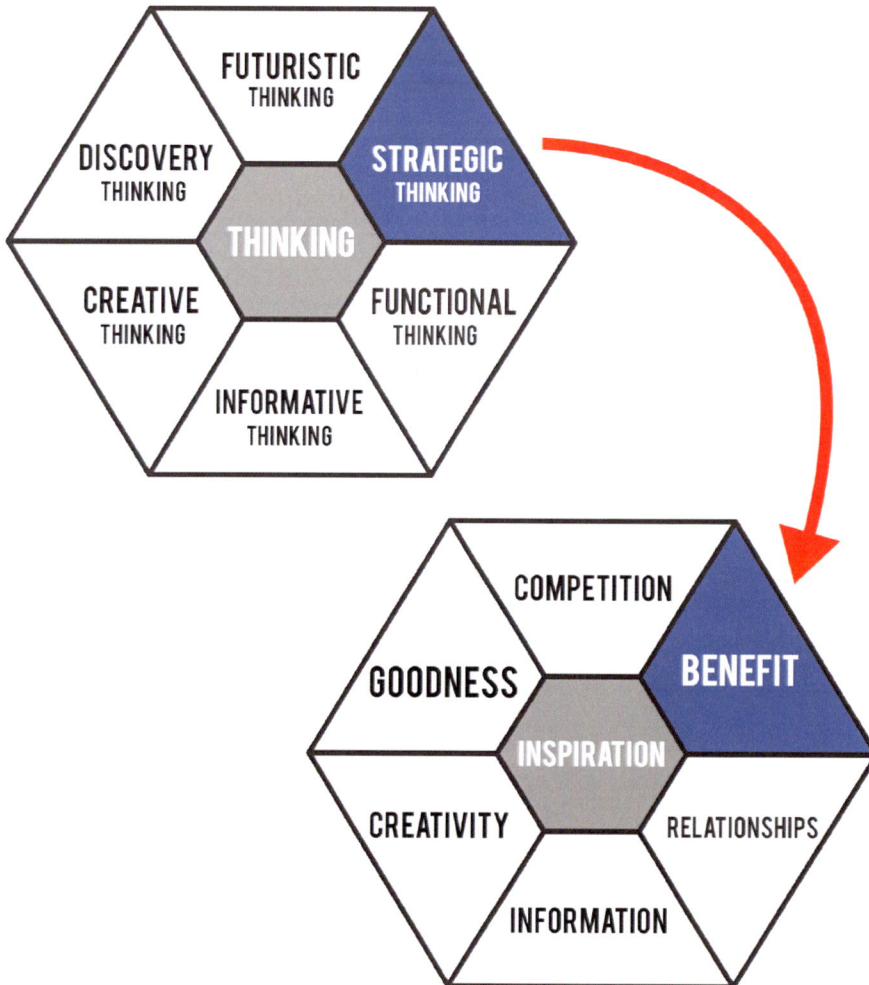

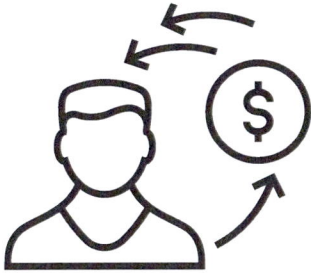

Inspiration *is* **Benefit**

Benefit

Entrepreneurs are driven by all types of benefits, be they in the form of money, profits, dividends, stocks, special income, commissions, bonuses and even air miles. If an **Entrepreneur** thinks they will accrue more benefits, their motivation will be stirred and they will continue creating business. More often than not, **E-type** people are prepared to work harder than most other people.

Smart Entrepreneur

Smarter than other people: Brilliant business people and skilled traders are your archetypal **Entrepreneur.** Constantly talking about superb ideas for investments, most **E-type** people are natural wheeler-dealers with little formal training. Many successful business people have written books about how they achieved success and now as popular authors, they are even richer. As talented business people who are always on the lookout for something new where they can make money, it could be said that **Entrepreneurs** are true "geniuses" when it comes to business and have a 'never say never' attitude.

Inspiration Leads to Good Relationships

Inspired by Relationships

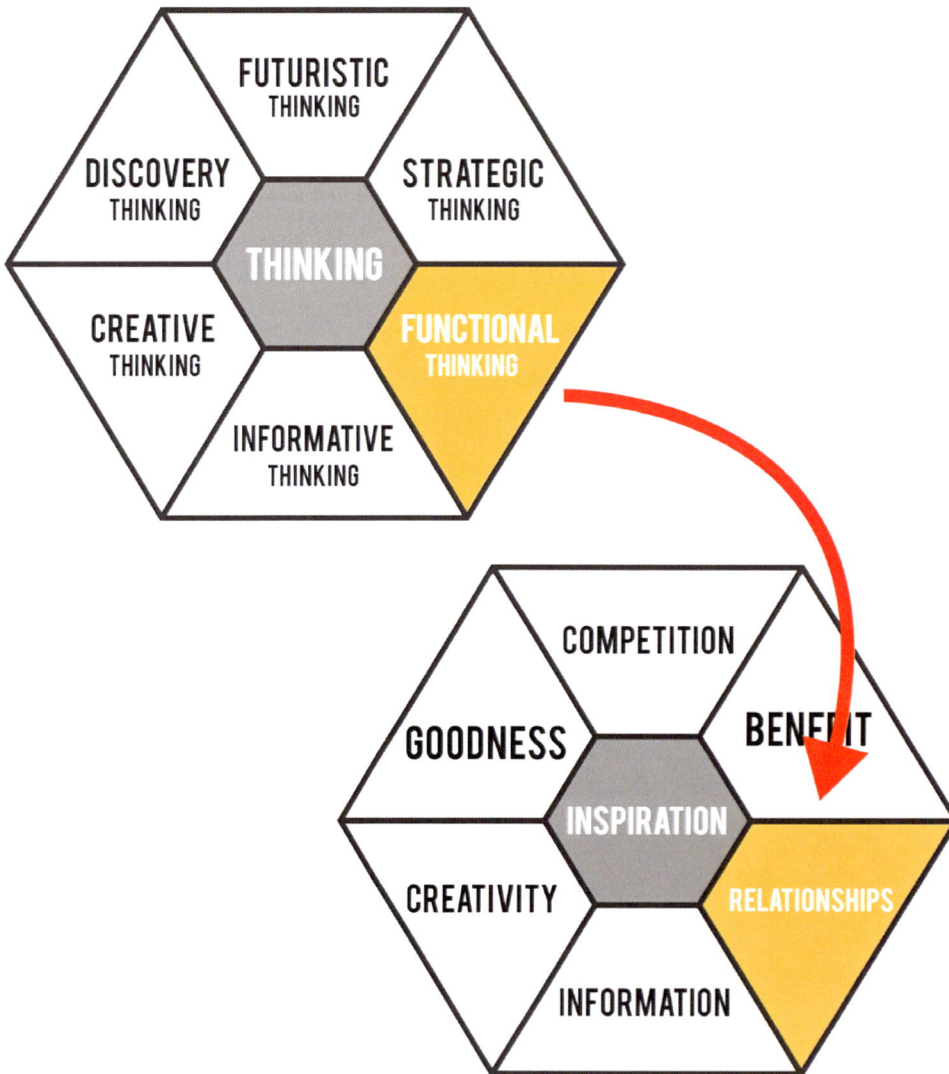

Inspiration Leads to *Relationships*

Relationships

N-type people are driven by relationships. Unlike other people, **Networkers** are very enthusiastic about meeting new people. They will not hesitate to greet a new face in their group or a friend's friend and are far from being shy. They enjoy social activities such as parties and get-togethers where there are likely to be a lot of people. **N-type** people get along well with most people thanks to their talkative and outgoing nature. They protect the relationships they have, which can lead to other people being a little jealous of their popularity.

Friendly Network

Networkers are prepared to go that extra mile for their friends. Their understanding of a good relationship is based on "sincerity," a simple trait that can rule the heart of other people. While the other five types of personality we've looked at are not always very attentive to their friends and relatives, the **Networker** remembers small details such as what colour their friends like, their friend's birthday, their friend's favourite food and even the types of food their friends are allergic to. This personal understanding of their buddies endears them to all their friends.

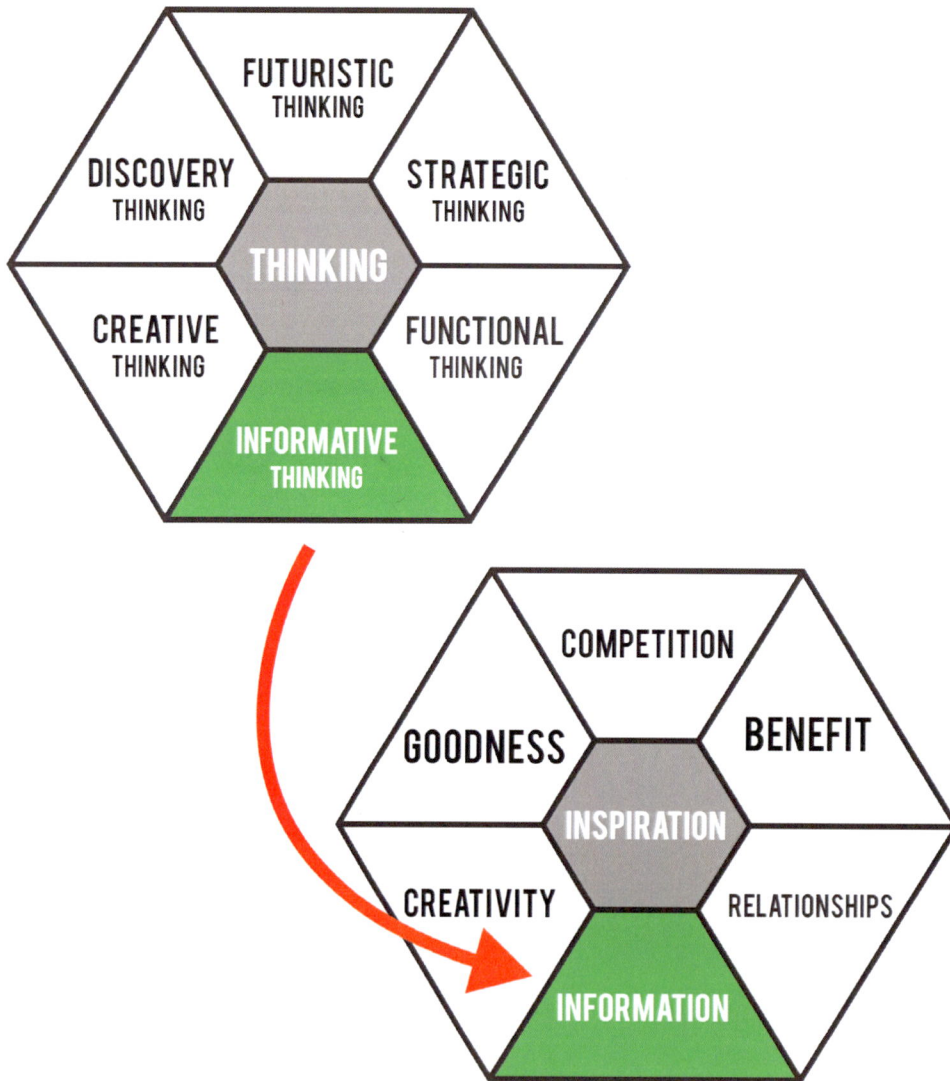

Inspiration is Information
Inspired by Information

Inspiration is Information

The Informative Researcher

What makes Informationists smart people is their ability to get to the bare facts; theirs is a smart life. As they are given more tasks to find information, they gain more mental superiority. Their confidence is born from their vast knowledge and while some people refer to them as geeks or nerds who are obsessed with information, in fact they are really smart people who are good at what they do. **I-type** people are deep thinkers who always look at both sides of every story to get the real low down. Therefore, their main task is to track down every piece of information to complete the puzzle. In an organisation their skills can never be underestimated.

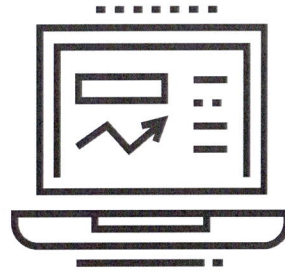

The Analytic Analyst

A competent researcher and analyst: The **Informationist** is born to study detailed information of every thing and any thing that comes into their sphere of interest. They are interested in issues that other people may consider insignificant and pay little attention to. But this is not what **I-type people** think, since they must know the most-minute details; even on a par with the world's leading news agencies. Let's say an **Informationist** was planning on buying a new product, they would study all other similar models, read all the specifications, look for the best offers and only then would they make an informed decision. Usually, they spend a very long time before they part with their money or their company's money.

Inspiration is Creativity

Inspired by Creativity

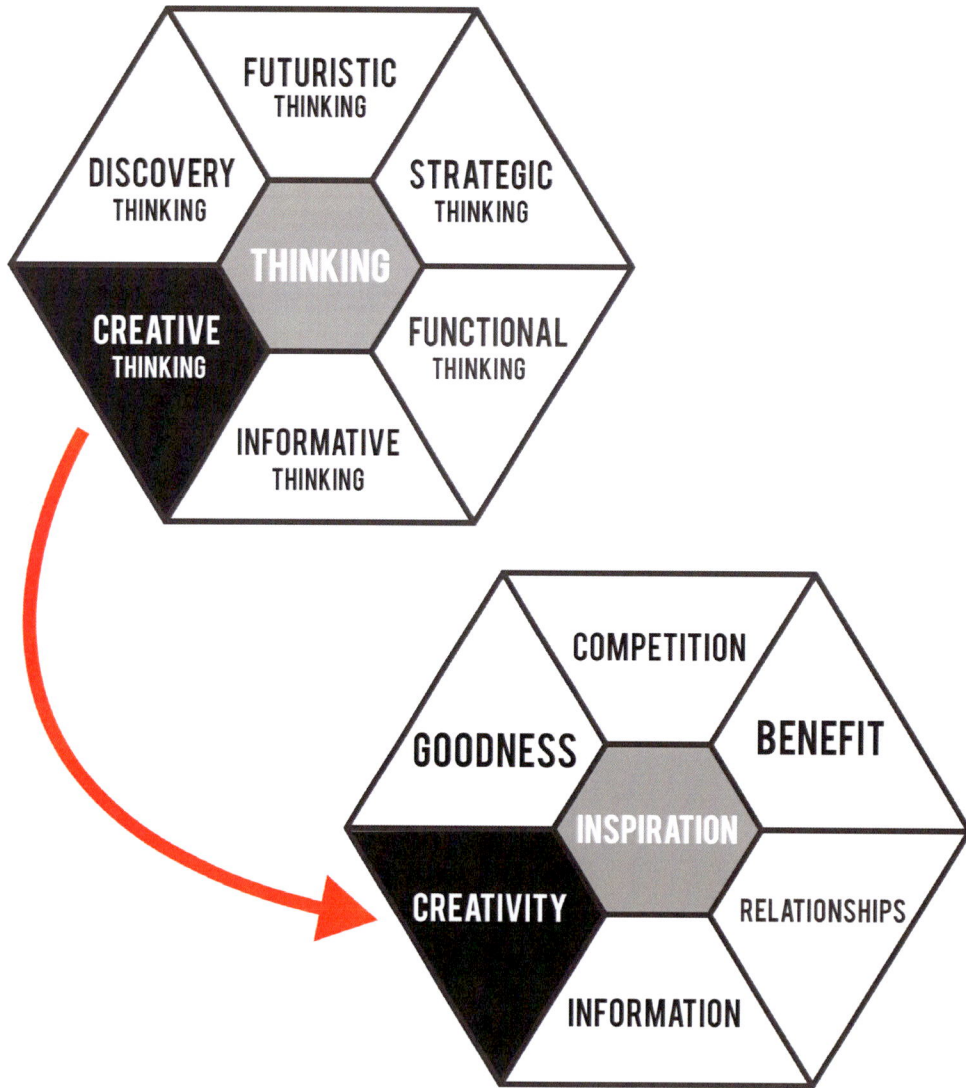

FUTURISTIC THINKING

DISCOVERY THINKING

STRATEGIC THINKING

THINKING

CREATIVE THINKING

FUNCTIONAL THINKING

INFORMATIVE THINKING

COMPETITION

GOODNESS

BENEFIT

INSPIRATION

CREATIVITY

RELATIONSHIPS

INFORMATION

Inspiration is *Creativity*

Creativity

There are only a few people whose creativity can stun the world. Only Unique people can create distinct and marvelous **innovations that are utterly brilliant.** When a company or country needs to hold a world-class exhibition, launch a roadshow, play, movie, product or organise a charity concert, they will undoubtedly turn to the talents of **U-type** people. Their unique characteristics are so outstanding that they leave their audiences amazed at what they've just seen.

Innovation is All Around

They like to dream of and create **innovative products. U-type people hardly ever imitate what other people have already achieved. Unique** people are born to create beauty and bring that beauty to a global audience. Designers such as Gianni Versace, Calvin Klein and Coco Chanel all took their inspiration and made it not only outstanding, but also a global brand. Singer-songwriters such as Bruce Springsteen, Adele and Ed Sheeran have put their words to music and inspired hundreds of millions of people to buy their records. While chefs like Jamie Oliver, Joël Robuchon and Anne-Sophie Pic have not only earned multiple awards for their mouthwatering cuisine, but have also opened numerous restaurants around the world so more people can be amazed by their culinary creations.

UNIQUE

Inspiration is Goodness

Inspired by Goodness

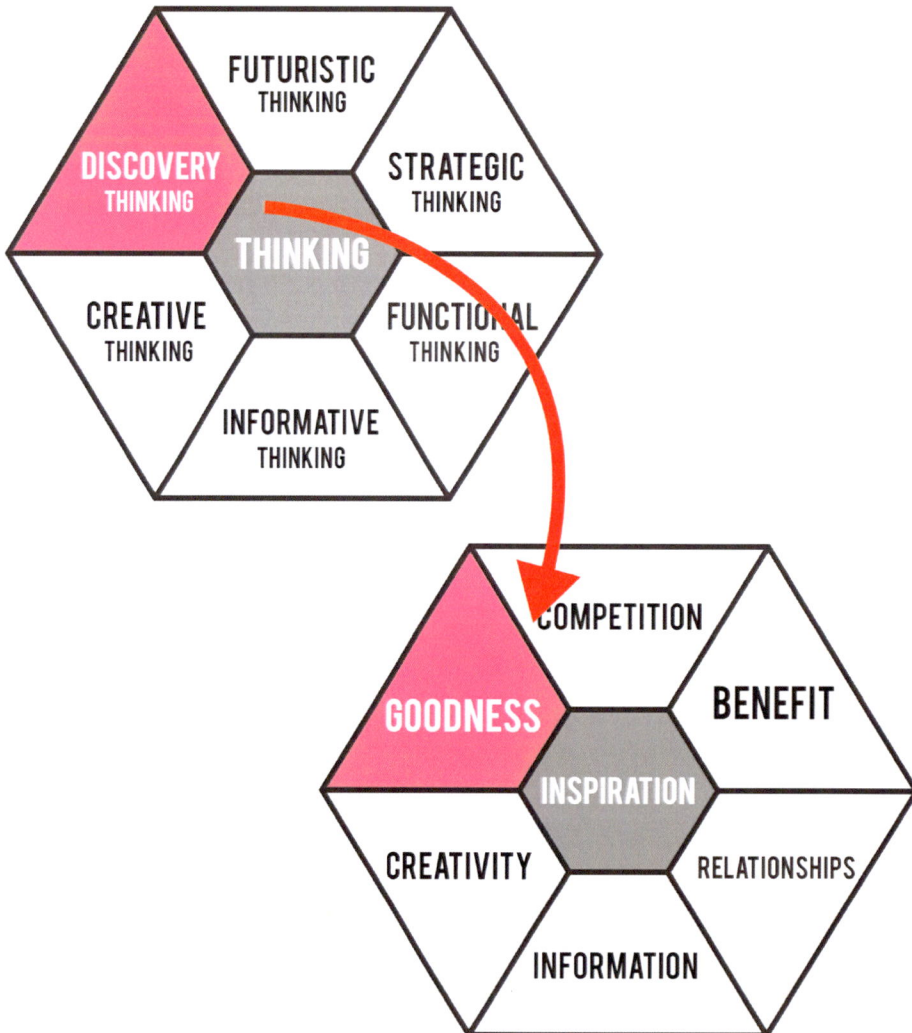

Inspiration is Goodness

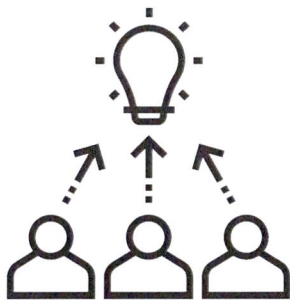

Creation of Goodness

Not everyone is capable of doing good deeds, but that does not make them bad people. When people do good deeds it means they are paying respect to their ancestors, but many people are now using this as a reason to share photographs on social media. But this is not what **Sharing people** do. They do not do good deeds once in a blue moon; they have been doing it all their lives. While some of their salary is used for personal spending, they also like to donate money to charity or buy items for people who really need help. When natural disasters strike, **Sharers** are usually the first to respond with offers of help. If they have spare time, **S-type** people will look at where in their community their time can be best used such as in an old people's home or community centre.

Happiness Leads to a Happy Life

Spiritual value is far more precious than money. There is no need to use money to ask **Sharers** to do things for you. If money is involved they will probably not waste their time. All of their actions come from a pure heart. The most valuable thing in their life is the happiness they gain after helping other people. It is a feeling that is hard to find. Giving without expecting something in return is the key that drives **S-type** people to continue doing good deeds. Sometimes they may feel tired, but as we all know there are millions of people in the world who need help. This is what **Sharing people** keep on fighting to alleviate.

SHARING

Researchers at Baylor University in Waco,
Texas, USA, discovered that
the brains of children
who are forced to limit
their ability to touch, play games
and express their responses will be
20–30% smaller than
the brains of children the same age
who are free to touch, play games and
give their natural responses.

Chapter 5

GeniusX Decision-Making

Decision-Making

Decision-making is a managerial process of taking into account all the information at hand to make an informed decision that will yield the best and most effective outcome. Decision-making is an experience that happens to each and every one of us on a daily basis in our personal lives, at work and in all businesses.

People have different and diverse thinking systems that allow us to make informed decisions. Therefore, each type of personality trait as defined in Genius X's classification is required to seek the most consistent method of decision-making that is appropriate for their own thinking system, behaviour and personality.

Decision-making consists of six forms:
1. Decision by Instinct
2. Decision by Result
3. Decision by Assembly
4. Decision by Logic
5. Decision by Inspiration
6. Decision by Desire

Decision by Instinct

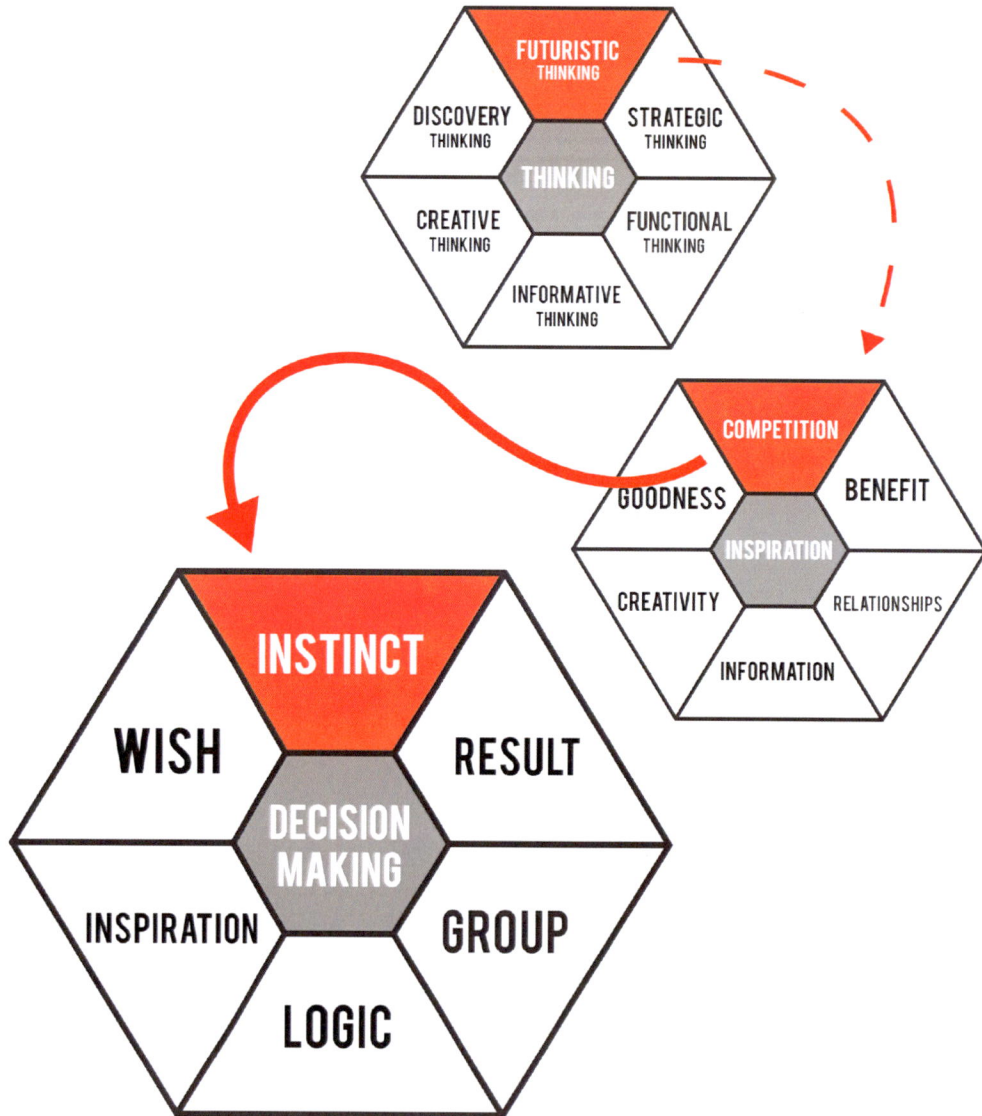

Decision by *Instinct*

1. Instinctive Decision (Relies on confidence, experience and intuition)

Game Changers make decisions based on their own instinct and the confidence they have built up over many years. They may also make decisions based on previous experience and occasionally by word of mouth recommendation. The overriding concept of Decision by Instinct is that it's based on quick decision-making because it is based on common sense and self-confidence.

For example, Mr. E inherits $10,000 from his father's will and wants to invest the money rather than putting it in the bank. His financial adviser recommends investing in Blue Chips stocks, but his close friend encourages him to invest in cryptocurrency. After looking at both options, Mr. E understands how stock markets work, but believes cryptocurrencies can provide a larger return and so he follows his instinct and buys into the Bitcoin phenomenon.

Application

Making decisions based on instinct, **G-type** always give priority to swift action. Once they've figured out something, they will do it immediately without listening to other people. Although their haste makes **Game Changers** the pacesetters who do things before the crowd, they often lack discretion and due prudence. Consequently, they are required to work while solving other problems.

Advice: Reduce speed; increase discretion
Taking a little longer to arrive at a decision can help **G-type** people's ideas become more concrete and reduce the chances of problems occurring, resulting in a smoother workflow and a quicker time to success.

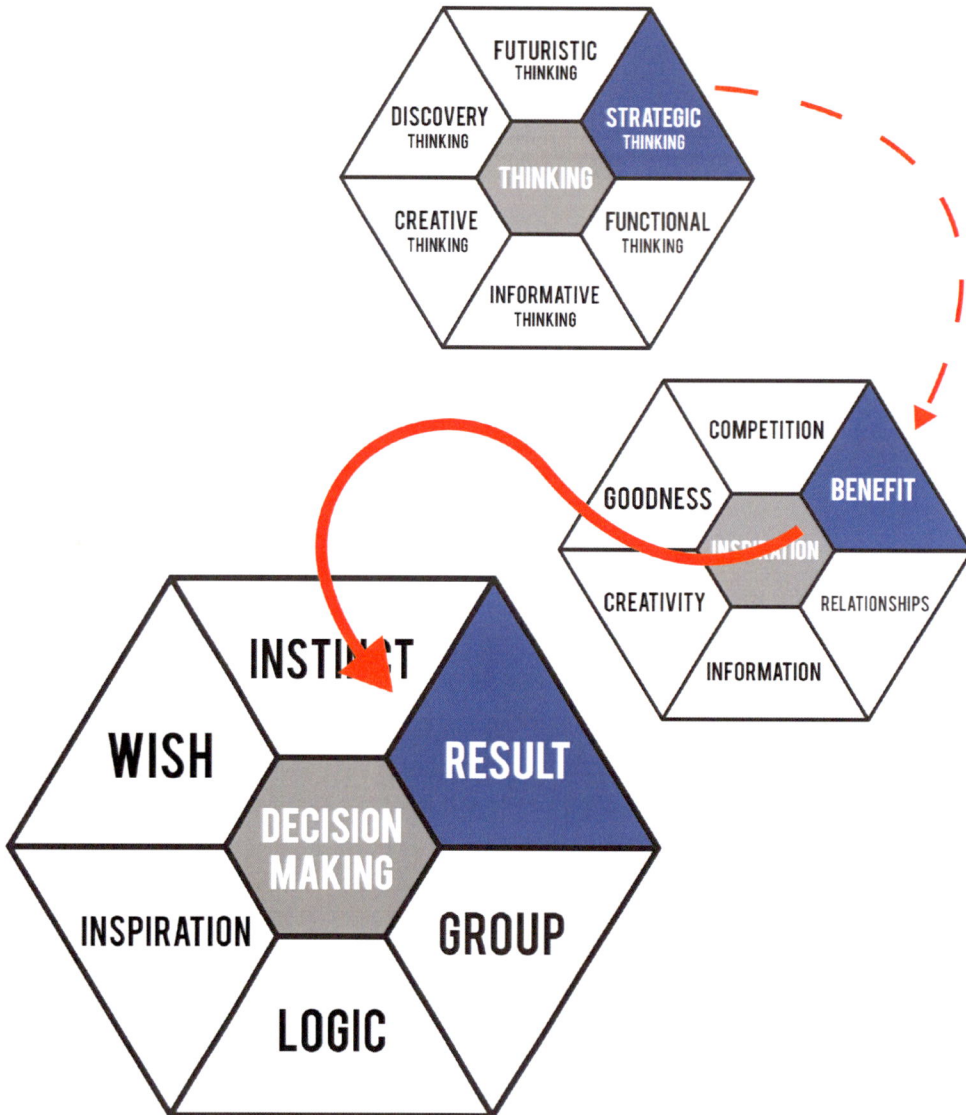

E Decision by Result

Decision by *Result*

2. Result First (Making decisions based on clear answers)

Entrepreneurs always make decisions by looking at the expected outcome of their planned action. They tend to prefer to be fairly certain about a result and whether or not it will result in "a profit" or "a loss". They arrive at a decision that is the best answer for them. **E-type** people shy away from making decisions if there are no clear answers to their questions. For example, 'Why must I do this? What am I doing it for? What will I get in return?'

An example might be: Ms. B takes a vacation in Asia where she comes across a new type of footwear that she thinks would sell well in the US. She has no local contacts to mass-produce her shoes, but buys 100 pairs on instinct because the price is so cheap. After talking to the shop owner, she is given the contact details of the supplier and arranges to have five different samples made to order that will earn her more profits. Taking her purchases back to America, she features them on Amazon. com and pretty soon the shoes are sold out.

Application

Making decisions based on instinct, "sellable" becomes the most important point for **E-type** people. Regardless of their circumstances, **Entrepreneurs** look for new products and buying price over selling price. They are willing to take a risk more easily than other people. Although their quick decision-making is based on what they believe is profitable, haste can sometimes result in financial losses, but the risk of losing out on an opportunity drives them to act first.

Advice: Think about an outcome that may harm partners

Apart from acting on instinct, **Entrepreneurs** need to be mindful of their partners' investments – if they have any – for acting alone can cause distrust.

Decision by Assembly

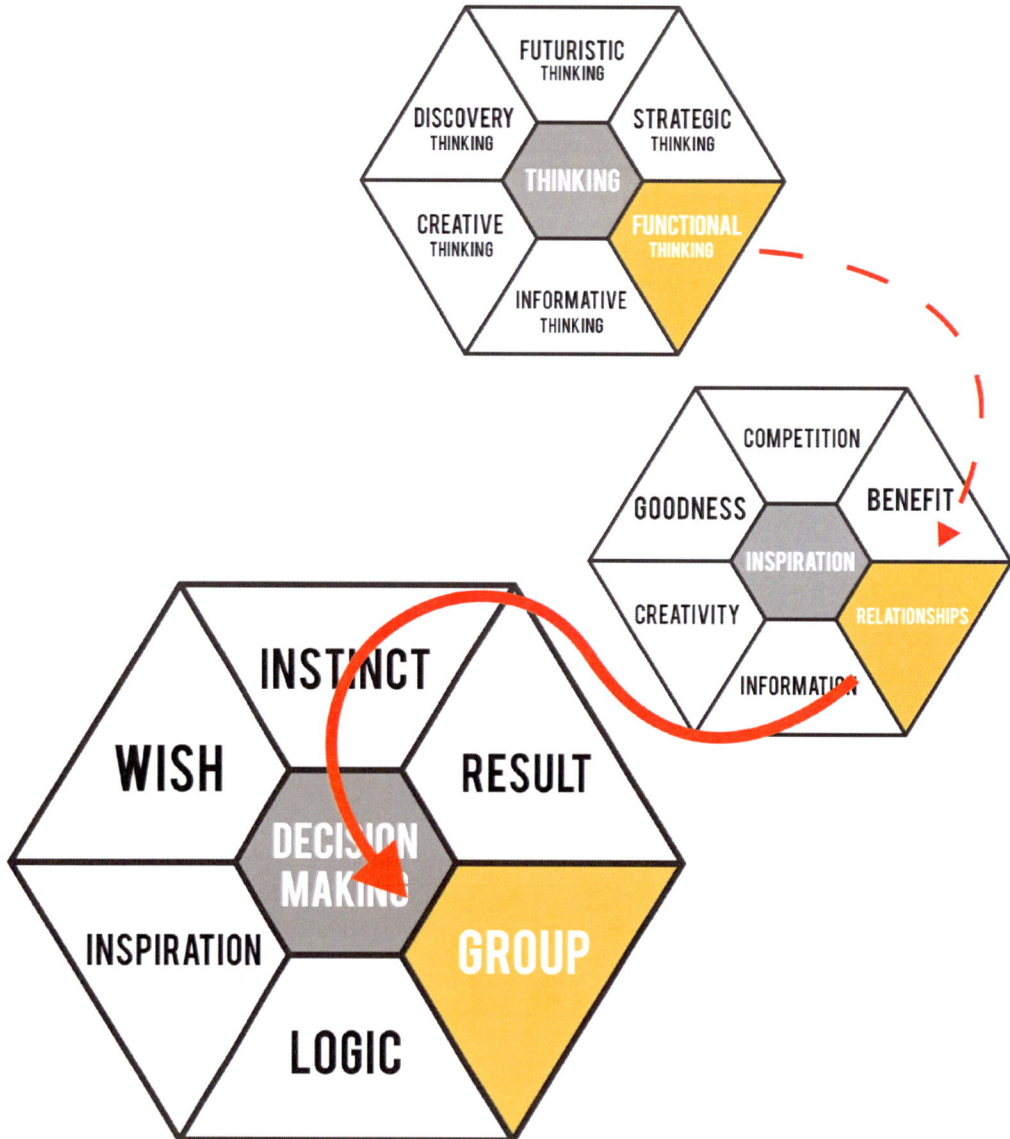

FUTURISTIC THINKING

DISCOVERY THINKING

STRATEGIC THINKING

THINKING

CREATIVE THINKING

FUNCTIONAL THINKING

INFORMATIVE THINKING

COMPETITION

GOODNESS

BENEFIT

INSPIRATION

CREATIVITY

RELATIONSHIPS

INFORMATION

INSTINCT

WISH

RESULT

DECISION MAKING

INSPIRATION

GROUP

LOGIC

Decision by *Assembly*

3. Assembly Decision (To follow the decision of the group)

Networkers make decisions by gathering ideas and opinions from a wide range of people in order to arrive at a solution that upholds common values. Using this approach permits all voices to be heard and often gives rise to better communal understanding. If it is not agreed and accepted by a majority of the group, voting can be used to reach a consensus that supports a decision.

For example, Miss C is the manager of a condominium and has invited co-owners to help make a decision about which business she should invite to open a store in her building. There are three interested parties; a launderette, a fast food outlet and a convenience store. She organises a co-owners meeting to seek group opinion on which shop should be awarded a contract. The majority of the group rejects the first two options and votes for the convenience store. Taking all options into account, she awards the contract to the convenience store, thus satisfying the group.

Application

The Decision by Assembly is the most effective method when a group has diverse ideas. **N-type** people have interpersonal skills that make it easy for them to obtain the right decision. By following the majority's choice **Networkers** seek to bring different opinions together for the greater good.

Advice: Listen to your heart
Listening to other people's opinions always helps in decision-making. However, by not siding with the majority, **Networkers** risk alienating themselves and causing division among their group.

Decision by Logic

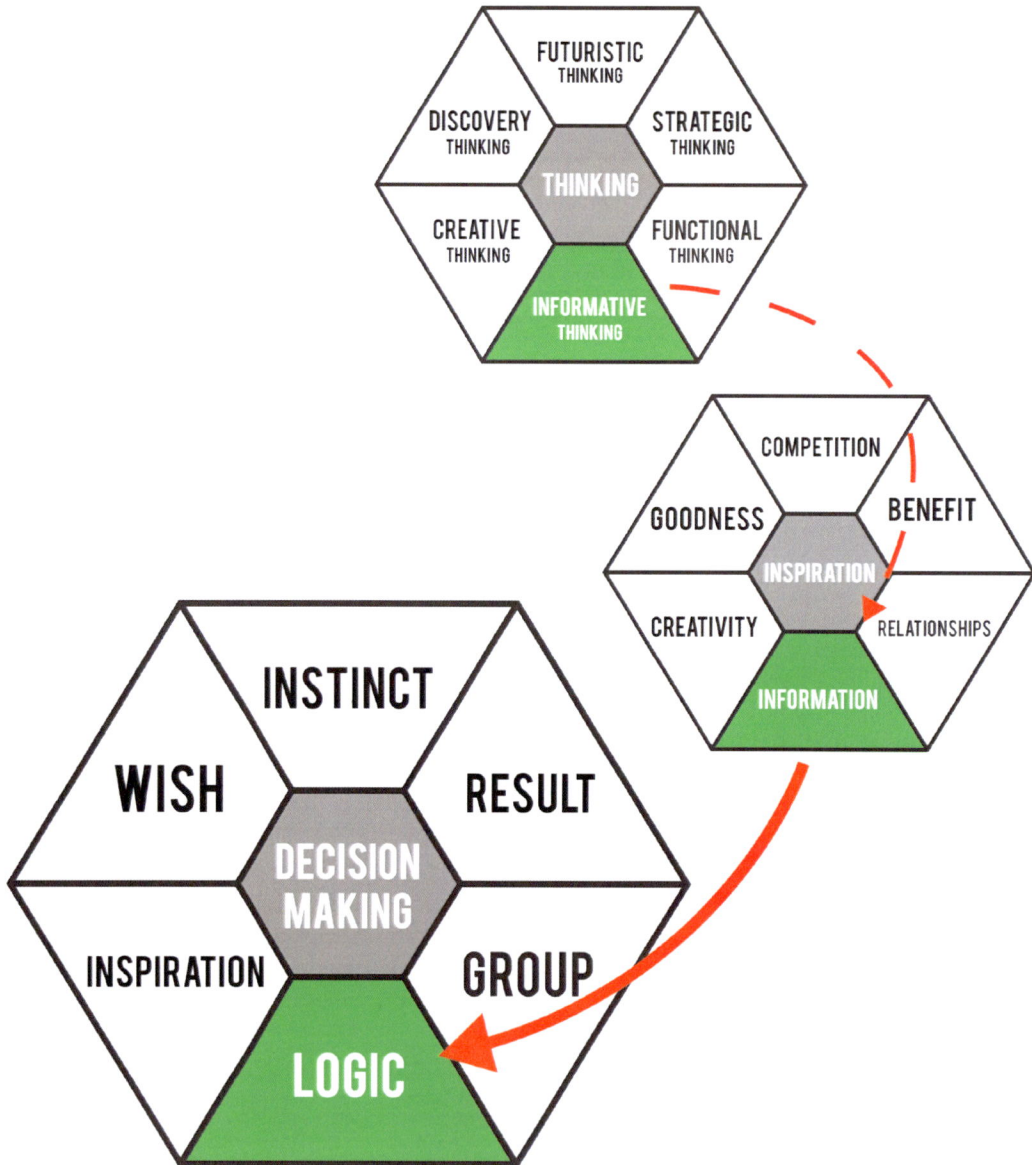

Decision by *Logic*

4. Logical Decision

Informationists usually make decisions based on logic which they have honed over a number of years. Logic dictates that decisions are made based on processing all available information to determine the outcome of an event. **I-type** people will also make comparisons to assess any risk factors. This decision-making method is very systematic and follows pre-defined steps.

For example, Mr. D lives in the suburbs and is interested in buying a new car, but he is aware of the introduction of the Ultra Low Emission Zone (ULEZ) now in force in London. He contemplates buying a hybrid car, an electric car or saving the money and using public transport. After carefully researching his options, he decides to buy a hybrid car to meet his personal needs and to stay within the ULEZ law.

Application

Decision by Logic is most effective when you have ample information at hand and are able to compare different scenarios to form the best decision with the least risk. Although Decision by Logic is a careful and thorough method, it requires time to research and analyse all the available facts to support such a decision.

Advice: Break the mold by diverting from the rules

Although Decision by Logic is viewed as reliable and the safest route to making the right choice, you should always be prepared to look at alternative options. Applying fresh reasoning instead of using what you're used to can sometimes result in unexpected success.

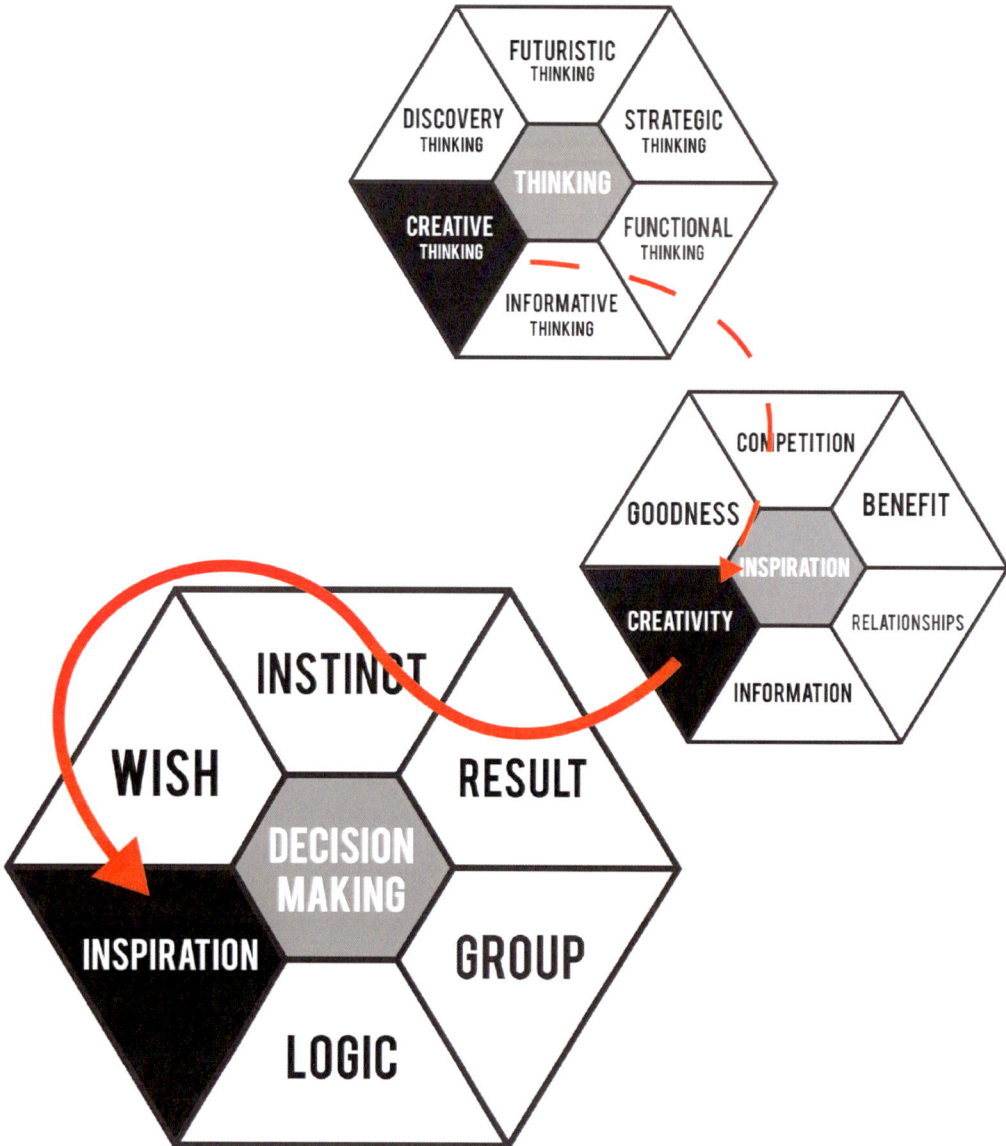

Decision by Inspiration

Decision by *Inspiration*

5. Inspiration

Unique people rely on inspiration to drive their decisions. They can take inspiration from virtually anything such as other people they see, an image on a train or words in a book (like this one). Inspirational decision-making does not adhere to any principle or reason, rather it is drawn from emotion, feelings and impressions. Decision by Inspiration often occurs quickly in **I-type** people and comes from pure feelings of the mind.

A good example is Mr. A, who after watching a television programme about stray animals decides he wants to become a volunteer at his local animal centre. As a retiree, Mr. A has plenty of free time and finds caring for unwanted animals to be a very theraputic experience. Each day he is assigned small duties such as washing and cleaning stray cats and dogs. His love for animals outweighs his need for recognition or reward.

Application

Decision by Inspiration will be most effective when **U-type** people have total freedom of thought; no rules or limitations. Whenever they find inspiration, they are ready to decide and quickly move forward. If they fail to find the necessary inspiration, they will postpone their decision until the feeling is right.

Advice: Find a goal

When faced with a lack of inspiration, **Unique** people's decision-making can be seriously affected. Therefore, the solution is to break the impasse and think of the long-term goal. This allows **U-type** people to make hard decisions easily.

U
N
I
Q
U
E

Decision by Desire

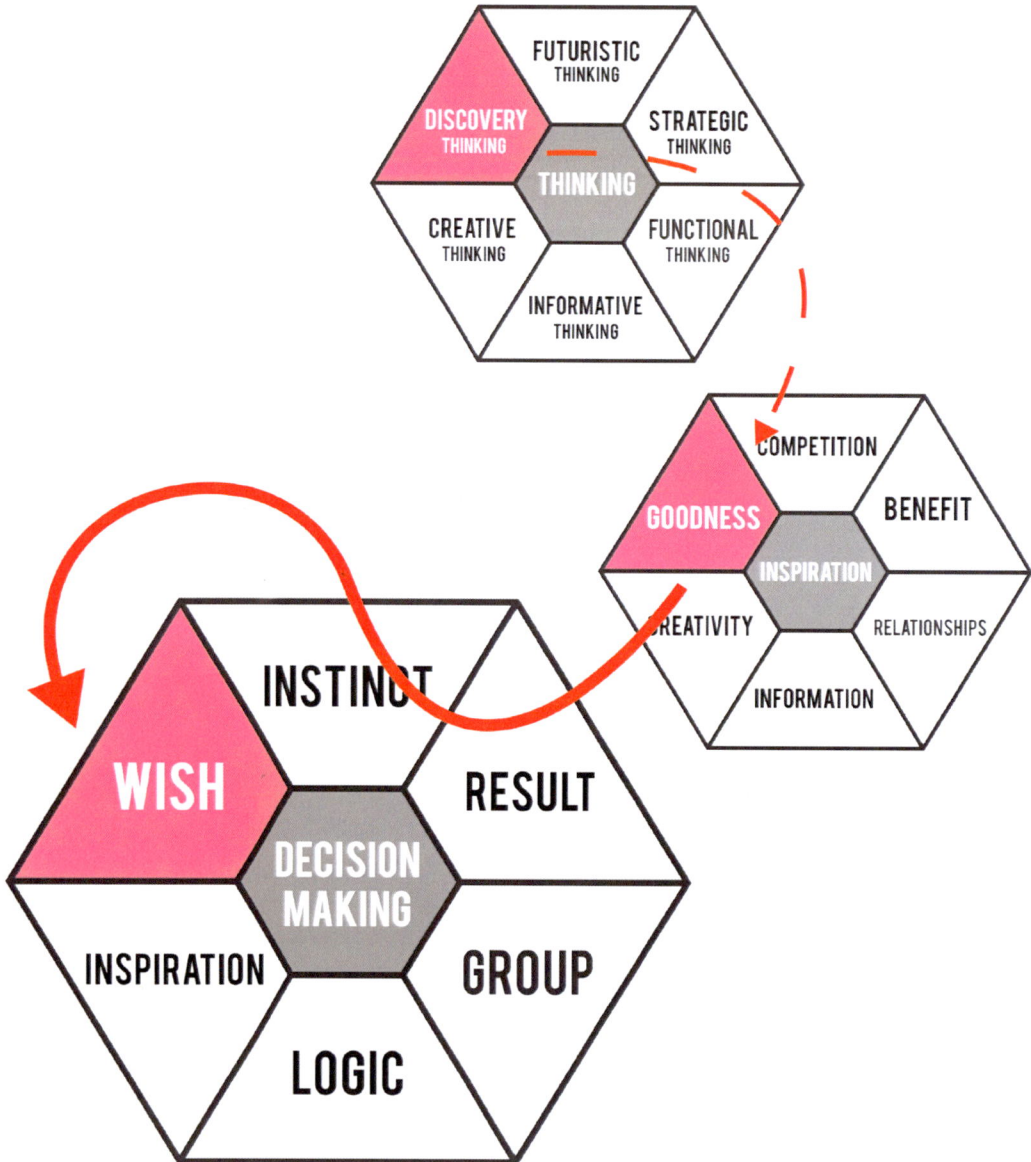

Decision by *Desire*

6. Desire

Sharing people always make decisions based on their personal desires which are driven from their heart. Nothing can compare to the dedication of **S-type** people who use their life experience to do something wholeheartedly and with every fibre they possess. What **Sharing** people want is to make society kinder and more equal. In an office environment, **Sharers** are always the first people those with problems turn to for advice, while in the wider world, natural disasters are the calling card for **S-type** people. They don't do what they do for money or reputation, they do it because of their inner drive or "what their heart wants."

For example, Mrs. H has just retired from her full-time job and feels her spare time should be spent helping others less fortunate in society. She visits old people's homes and homeless shelters to see if her company can be of help to anyone in distress or simply other people who crave personal contact. Mrs. H doesn't do this for fame or money, she does it purely to satisfy her true desires.

Application

S-type people are sympathetic to those in need and will go out of their way to give as much help as humanly possible. Spending their money or time in the company of others is the least of their worries and if they can leave a person feeling slightly happier, then their function has been fulfilled.

Advice: Sufficiency brings happiness

In real life, we cannot always base our decisions on personal desires or requirements. So, try to make decisions by considering all the facts, this way it is possible to prevent any unwanted problems.

Did you know?

When we feel tired and go to bed,
we usually go through four stages
of sleep; stage 1, 2, 3
and REM (rapid eye movement).
The first complete sleep cycle
can last up to two hours,
but later in the night as each
sleep cycle gets longer
our deep sleep time increases.
However, if you are not getting
enough sleep,
it's hardly surprising
how dull, upset and sleepy
you will feel even
after being in bed all night.

Chapter 6

GeniusX
Management

"Management" is a measured combination of planning, organisation, direction and control. In the digital era, it is not possible to use managerial trial and error. With the GeniusX method, I've focused on managerial and organisational cognition and define management as "a set of processes to achieve the highest efficiency in the shortest time possible." Therefore, modern management must not only be suitable for, and in line with, business or industrial structures, but it must also be consistent with corporate cultures and administration approaches of the management team.

Management is a set of five basic skills that are gradually improved over the course of a person's managerial career. As people have different and diverse thoughts, so administration and management processes can differ significantly.

1. Planning: The majority of business leaders are competent planners with strategies used from small companies to global corporations. However, there are some owners who prefer to rely on their instincts when planning.

2. Authority: Game Changers are good at giving orders to their subordinates, while Entrepreneurs are more likely to want other people to see them as a role model.

3. Confidence in teamwork: Meanwhile, N, I, U and S-type people are confident in their teams and are good at maintaining a strong team. They choose team members who share the same opinions and give their total support.

4. Clarity: A successful administrator is always clear about their intended goals and will explain why achieving such goals should be important to the team.

5. Result: An administrator who continues to measure their team's performance will be more successful than an administrator who fails to monitor their team.

G-Management
(Directive Management)

G

G-Management or Directive Management

G-type people prefer to work fast and want to see quick results as they can be quite impetuous. Therefore, the Directive Management approach of giving orders is appropriate for **Game Changers.** Directive Management is the easiest method to understand; a direct order from the boss does not need questioning. Simply doing as requested by a **G-type** boss is enough.

This management method has the following advantages:

1. High work performance.
2. Clarity of orders and direction.
3. Easy to perform evaluation.
4. High possibility of success.
5. Mainly dedicated to the work environment.

The approach defines expectations and allows for the corporate direction to be followed as closely as possible. In a working environment, it is essential that every directive is understood, transparent and clear in its objectives so that staff members can yield higher production. With clear commands and communication, even if a crisis occurs, work stability will not be adversely affected.

This method works well when:
A) The leader has gained the trust of their workers and shows consistency.
B) Workers possess specialised skills and can work under pressure.

G-MANAGEMENT
DIRECTIVE MANAGEMENT

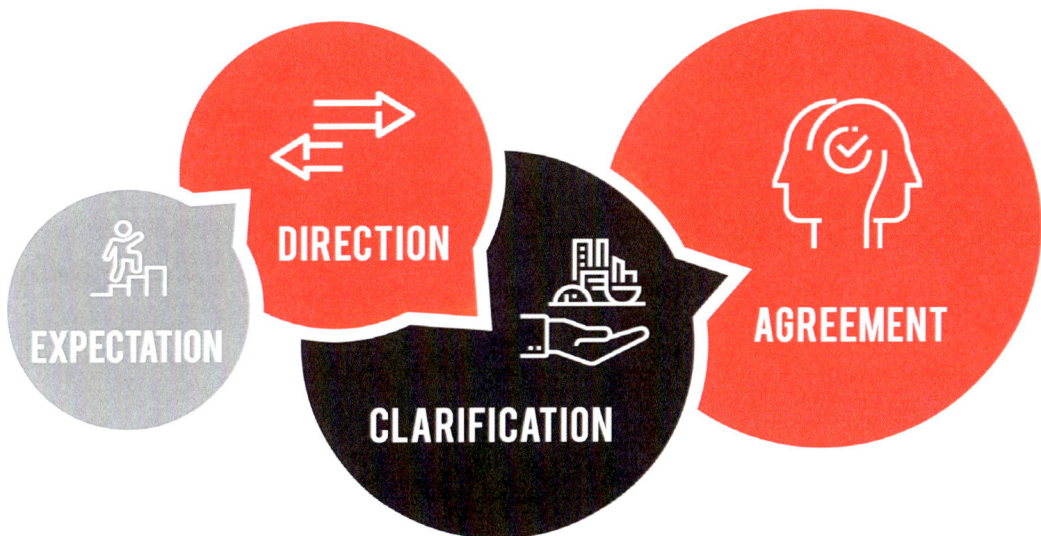

EXPECTATION

DIRECTION

CLARIFICATION

AGREEMENT

Caution
1) If any employee has limited capabilities or lacks certain skills and thus requires constant working directions, Directive Management will not achieve its maximum benefits.

2) Trust from employees is an important factor in Directive Management. Therefore, any leader who wishes to use this method must be absolutely certain that they have the ability to gain 100% trust and confidence from their staff in what they are doing. If a leader is not able to gain the confidence of their staff, Directive Management will not function properly.

E-Management
(High Standard Management)

High Standards need to be applicable to one's self where you are seen as a Role Model and other people act the same way.

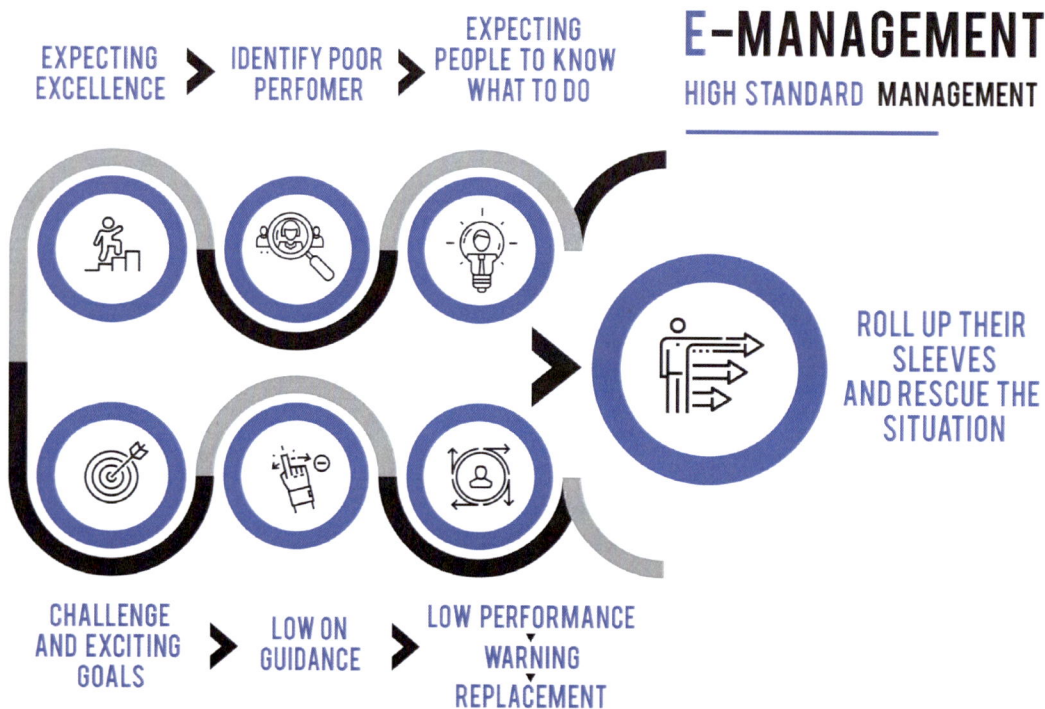

EXPECTING EXCELLENCE > IDENTIFY POOR PERFOMER > EXPECTING PEOPLE TO KNOW WHAT TO DO

E-MANAGEMENT
HIGH STANDARD MANAGEMENT

ROLL UP THEIR SLEEVES AND RESCUE THE SITUATION

CHALLENGE AND EXCITING GOALS > LOW ON GUIDANCE > LOW PERFORMANCE WARNING REPLACEMENT

Over a period of 2 years, a businessman opens 30 branches of a convenience store and creates a step-by-step, month-to-month, year-to-year performance evaluation plan and a month-to-month, year-to-year profit measurement standard for his franchisees to follow. By sticking to the highest principles and being seen as a successful role model, continual success is not only possible, it is virtually guaranteed.

E-Management or "High Standard Management"

Entrepreneurs tend to use High Standard Management to portray themselves as a role model and standard-bearer. They do not like weak links or those who do not follow orders. If necessary, an **E-type** person will jump in, roll up their sleeves and do a job themselves so workers can see and act accordingly.

Advantages of E-Management

1. High-quality work output.
2. Dedicated to the workforce.
3. Easy to perform evaluations.
4. Assessments can be made when needed.
5. Suitable for employees who like a competitive working environment.

The approach is two-fold in that is puts pressure on the workforce and permits control over the workflow by setting goals and expecting improved output from employees. If staff cannot achieve set goals, **E-type** administrators are required to step in to achieve the intended goals. **Entrepreneurs** are likely to point out problems and instruct staff to improve. If problems cannot be rectified, **E-type** people will simply find new staff to do the work.

This method works well when:

A) Employees or the team are competent at their tasks.
B) Employees or the team are stimulated to compete.

Caution

1) This may cause stress to both administrators and workers.

2) If this method is used for the long-term, it will often yield lower productivity. Also, problems may occur when some staff perform better than others. This divide might cause bigger problems if not addressed in a timely manner.

3) When assistance from other departments or external parties is required to complete set goals, cooperation from existing staff may not be forthcoming.

4) This method makes it difficult for some staff to accept new processes and can lead to restrained human resource development.

N-Management
(Affiliative Management)

N-Management
or Affiliative Management

Networkers believe that harmony and unity within a team makes for limitless possibilities. Employees will dedicate their efforts and spirit to the organisation and there will be fewer problems among fellow employees. Both internal and external coordination is unlikely to be an issue. Therefore, administration by **N-type** people is in the form of "Affiliative Management" or "People, first... Task, second."

Advantages of the N-Management
or Affiliative Management

1. There is unity; fewer conflicts.
2. Coordination is highly effective.
3. Less stress within the organisation.
4. Workers willingly do their assigned jobs.
5. High productivity over the long-term.

While the majority of owners care for their workers, N-type people fear losing the love and respect of their staff and often refused to point out their mistakes to the extent that they are afraid of enforcing punishment for violating the rules. Networkers would rather promote love and unity in the workforce. However, this does not always result in improved staff performance.

The administration method of N-Management

Affiliative Management focuses on team building to reach an understanding before setting targets. Time is spent on voluntarily understanding of assigned duties and in the case of conflicts, rectification will be made with mutual understanding.

This method works well when:

A) It is a repetitive and routine task.
B) Instructions and assistance are always offered.
C) Workers are responsible for their own duties.

N-MANAGEMENT
AFFILIATIVE MANAGEMENT

HARMONY
IN WORK GROUP

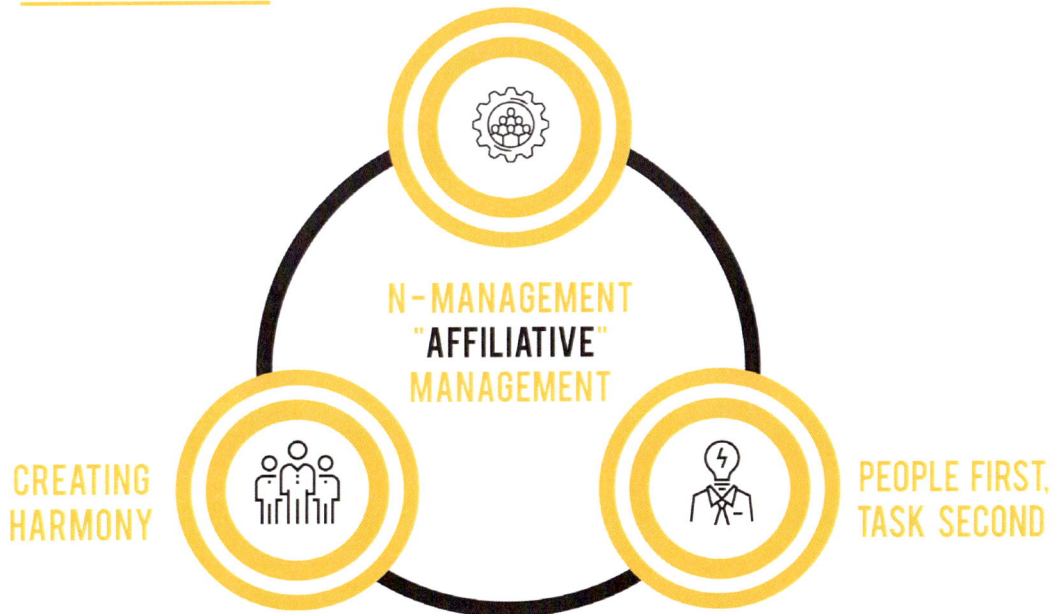

N-MANAGEMENT
"AFFILIATIVE"
MANAGEMENT

CREATING
HARMONY

PEOPLE FIRST,
TASK SECOND

Caution

1) Productivity may not meet expectations.
2) When there is a crisis it may be hard to find a solution.

I

I-Management
(Participative Management)

I-Management or Participative Management

I-Management or Participative Management is suitable for **I-type** people in that it focuses on information as a basis for decision-making. Sharing preliminary information and establishing cooperation opens the door to analysis and evaluation where solutions can be found for all types of issues. This style leads to determined decision-making among members.

Advantages of the I-Management method application

1. Less conflicts at work.
2. Having a clear standard.
3. Low stress and pressure.
4. Efficient work performance.
5. Mutual decision-making based on rational information.

The approach helps gather information from various sources and establishes concepts and ideas in order to zoom in on the correct solution. It makes forming decisions easier as the analysed information acts as a solid foundation.

When an I-type person is placed in a supervisory position, staff will receive positive training because Informationists are detail-oriented, meticulous and strict workers. All relevant facts must be in order and to the point. Informationists are dedicated followers of corporate rules and regulations and nothing passes without scrutiny. Working under an I-type person gives lower ranking staff a crucial insight into how they should carry themselves in a company and thus opens the door to future promotion.

This method works well when:

A) Employees work together.

B) The team has experience and credibility.

C) There is a stable working environment.

I-MANAGEMENT
PARTICIPATIVE MANAGEMENT

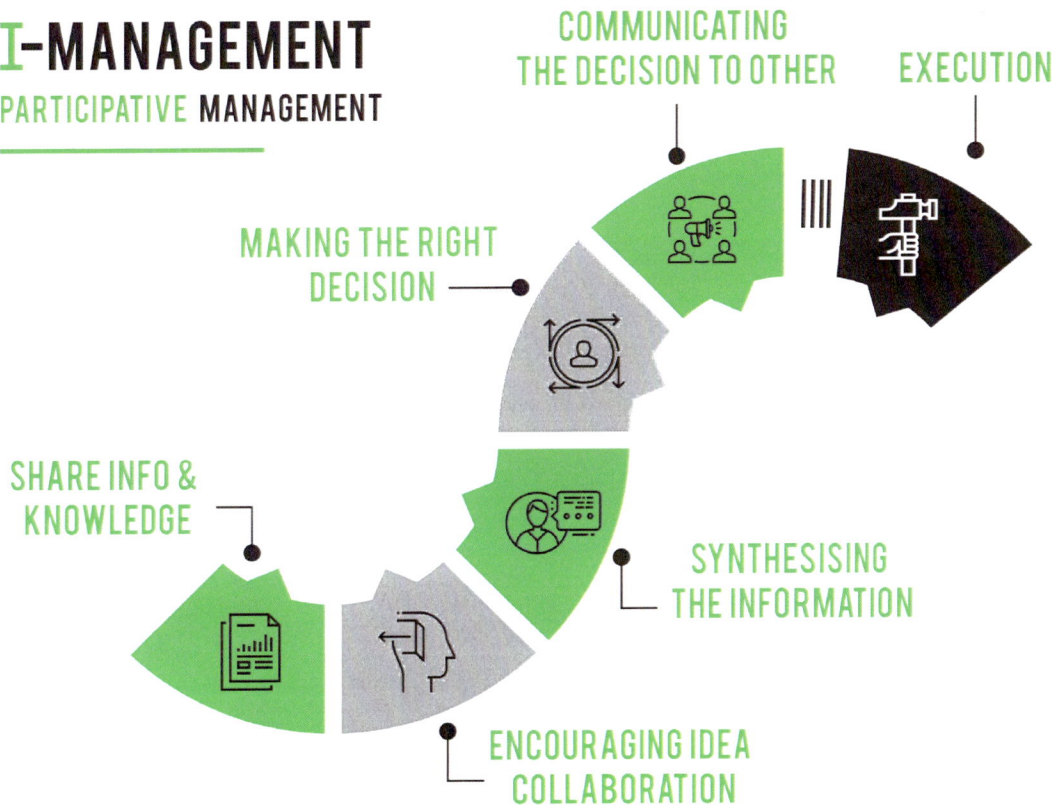

COMMUNICATING THE DECISION TO OTHER

EXECUTION

MAKING THE RIGHT DECISION

SHARE INFO & KNOWLEDGE

SYNTHESISING THE INFORMATION

ENCOURAGING IDEA COLLABORATION

INFORMATION

Caution

1) When a crisis unfolds, there is no wiggle room.

2) This method should not be employed in emergencies.

3) It can sometimes create a lack of competitiveness.

4) Causes delays in administrative processes.

U

U–Management
(Visionary Management)

U–Management or Visionary Management is administration by sharing visions.

U–Management means establishing a companywide vision in order to maintain direction and to take corrective action when necessary. Although this method sounds simple, it requires all staff sharing the same vision so that production is maintained and orders are fulfilled. Of the six types of personalities, this management method is most suitable for **U–type** people.

Advantages of the application of U–Management or Visionary Management

1. It requires less communication while working.
2. Clear understanding of a mutual goal.
3. Faster work.
4. Firm work output.
5. Staff can work together efficiently.

The approach of Visionary Management

In order to implement this method, the leader's vision must be clearly established and then shared with the workforce to reach an understanding of the company's direction. Once staff are all reading from the same page, it is possible to introduce more defined or abstract tasks.

This method works well when:

A) The leader has a precise vision.

B) Workers understand the abstract concept and can interpret and visualise it.

C) Workers possess skills for multiple tasks.

U-MANAGEMENT
VISIONARY MANAGEMENT

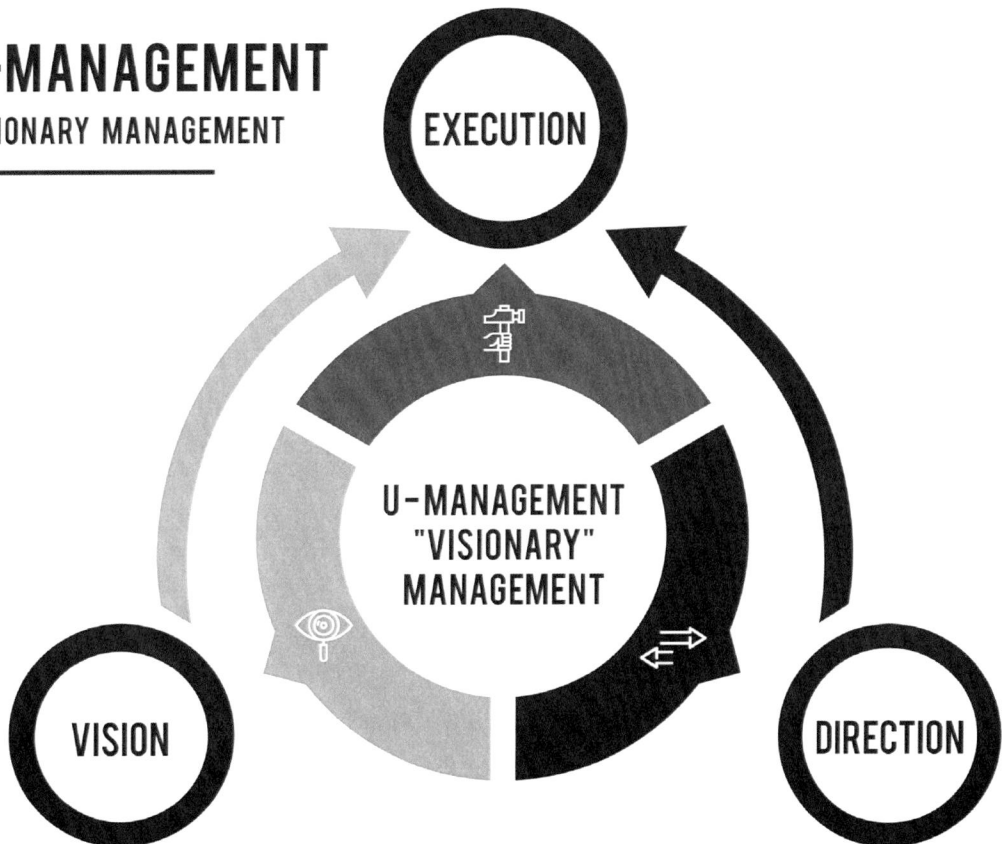

EXECUTION

U-MANAGEMENT
"VISIONARY"
MANAGEMENT

VISION

DIRECTION

Caution

1) When staff do not have a clear direction, their work output will suffer and their attitude will vary from department to department.

2) A vague vision can lead to confusing scenarios as each worker interprets the vision differently.

3) A lack of productivity is very likely as there is no stimulation for staff to cling to and this ultimately will damage corporate turnover.

S-Management
(Coaching Management)

S-Management or Coaching Management

Coaching Management applies guidance and encouragement by providing resources that make the workplace more harmonious. This management method is suitable for **S-type** people who have a good understanding of people and gives them the chance to see the hidden potential in personnel.

Advantages of applying S-Management or Coaching Management

1. It can provide long-term personnel development.
2. It yields positive outcomes both within and outside the company.
3. It creates a stronger organisation.
4. Employees' skills can be consistently developed.
5. There is no limitation to the workforce's capabilities.

The approach of Coaching Management

It is to set a long-term working target and to understand each worker and their abilities in order to guide them in such a way that they are able to develop to his or her full potential.

This method works well when:

A) The leader is passionate about personnel development.

B) Employees happily accept detailed training.

S-MANAGEMENT
COACHING MANAGEMENT

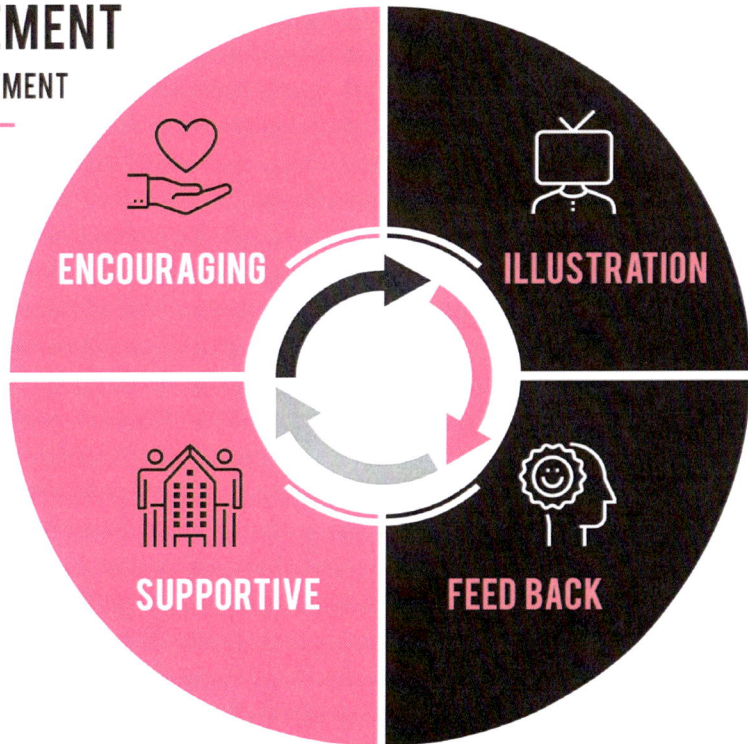

ENCOURAGING

ILLUSTRATION

SUPPORTIVE

FEED BACK

Caution

1) A leader who is not passionate about staff training and development may inadvertently approve the wrong training and as a consequence workers may not develop effectively. People-management is key to success.

2) In situations where many unqualified personnel are employed there is always the chance of bad workmanship. Because the leader has ignored vital training, they can hardly blame the workforce for poor work performance.

Our lives

feature

a series of

personal stories;

some good and some bad.

The matters of our mind and our thoughts,

teach us that both sets of stories

will continue from the past to the future.

The key to balancing our thoughts

so that we enjoy our lives

is

to adhere to the right principles

which in turn will lead us

to follow the correct path in life.

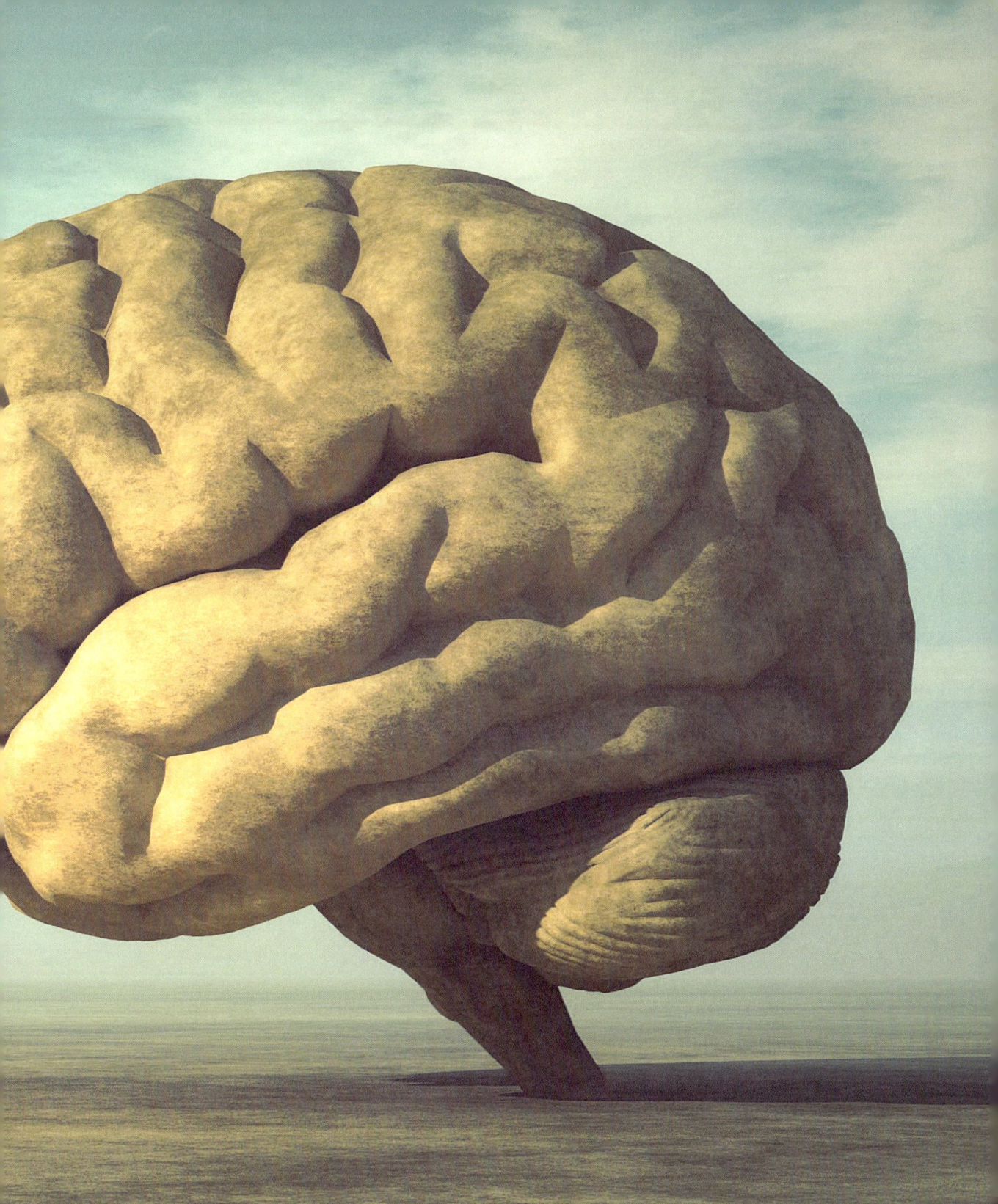

Chapter 7

GeniusX EQ

EQ Model Management
EQ Model Management is a method for
dealing with different emotions and is suitable
for the six characteristics we've discussed so far.
Every person has changeable emotions
and I believe we are all capable of managing
our emotions effectively so that we create
a calming balance in our lives.

Emotional Quotient or EQ is the capability to recognise one's own – and other people's – emotions and feelings and to manage those emotions regardless of the circumstances. There are five key elements to emotional quotient, which are:

1. **Self-awareness** – the ability to recognise, perceive and understand your own feelings and emotions and how your mood can affect other people. Leaders who are self-aware have a clear direction and are able to make honest decisions.

2. **Self-regulation** – the ability to manage one's own emotions appropriately in difficult situations while adapting to changes in life. By keeping your emotions in check, making rational decisions and staying in control, you will have a better life.

3. **Motivation** – the ability to keep working towards your life goals regardless of the obstacles you face. Controlling personal desires and empowering yourself to solve problems without compromising your standards.

4. **Empathy** – the ability to perceive and understand other people's emotions through their facial expressions and body gestures or by putting yourself in their position. Empathy is vital for leaders who want to be successful.

5. **Handling Relationships** – the ability to foster relationships and effectively diminish conflicts with other people via communication.

Take a Break
you deserve it!

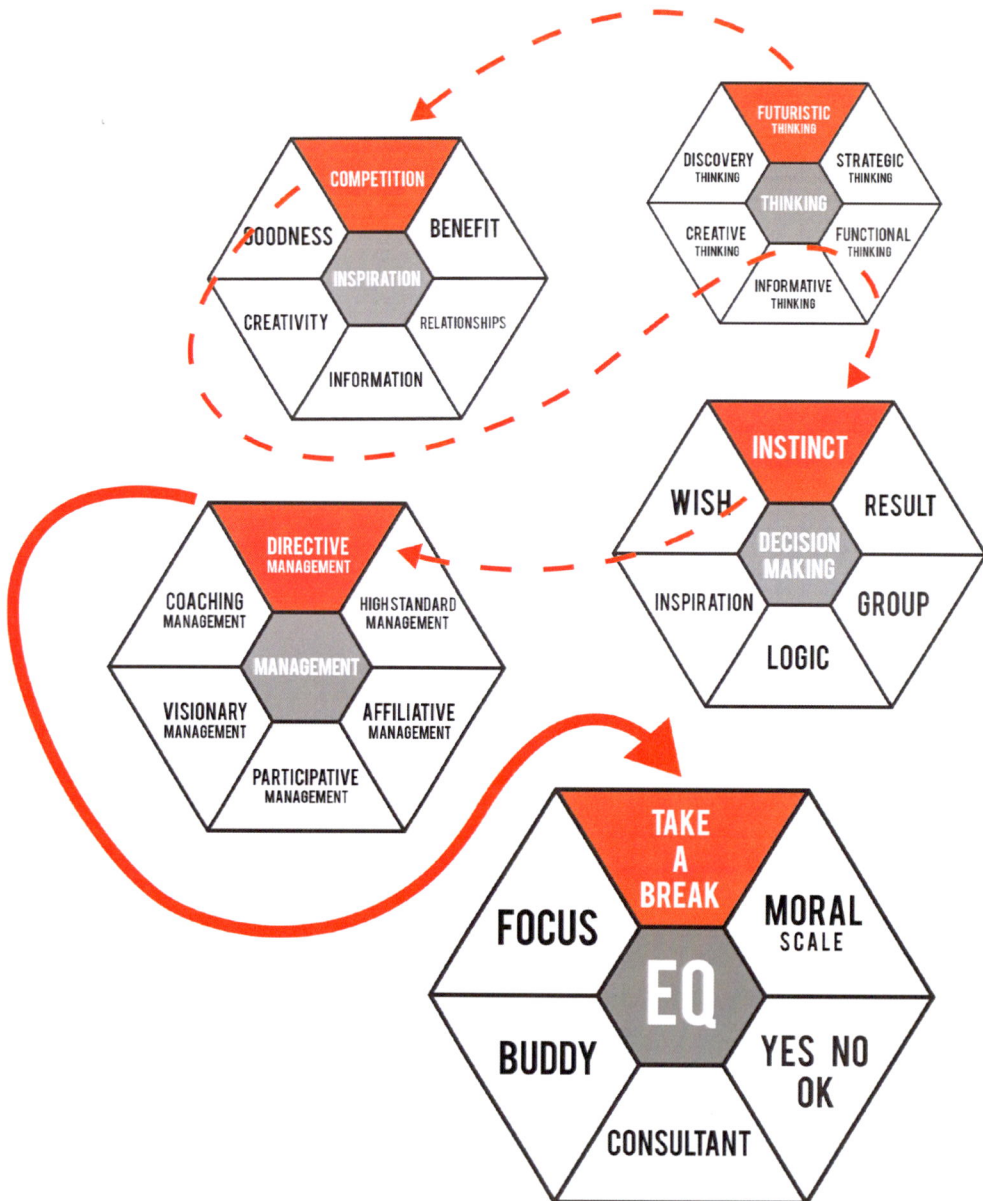

Take a Break – take time to stop thinking

When we are consumed by thought it is always good to be able to turn off for a period of time. Spending time doing something totally different helps the mind relax and reorganise before being rebooted. Try watching a movie, listening to your favourite music or simply go for a walk or drive in the countryside in order to give the mind a rest.

This is especially true for **Game Changers** who can become easily obsessed with new challenges in their lives. **G-type** people are driven by being the first to reach their goal or to become successful and so need to give their minds time to relax before moving on to the next challenge.

Being so focused on what they are doing, when G-type people encounter problems they become trapped, as if lost in a labyrinth. Due to the fact they are impetuous, it is very easy for them to let their emotions and desires overwhelm rational thought. Game Changers tend to use their emotions to solve problems instead of looking at the issue logically. Consequently, they go round and round in circles, trapped in their emotional maze unable to find a solution.

To let go and free themselves from burdening issues in order to feel relaxed, **Game Changers** need to use emotional management. This method aligns with the EQ's element of **Self-awareness** as it helps them realise their true desires and enables them to use self-control (Managing Emotion).

This method is suitable for **G-type** people who are impatient as it allows them to calm their emotions and take control of difficult situations.

Moral Scale
be true to yourself

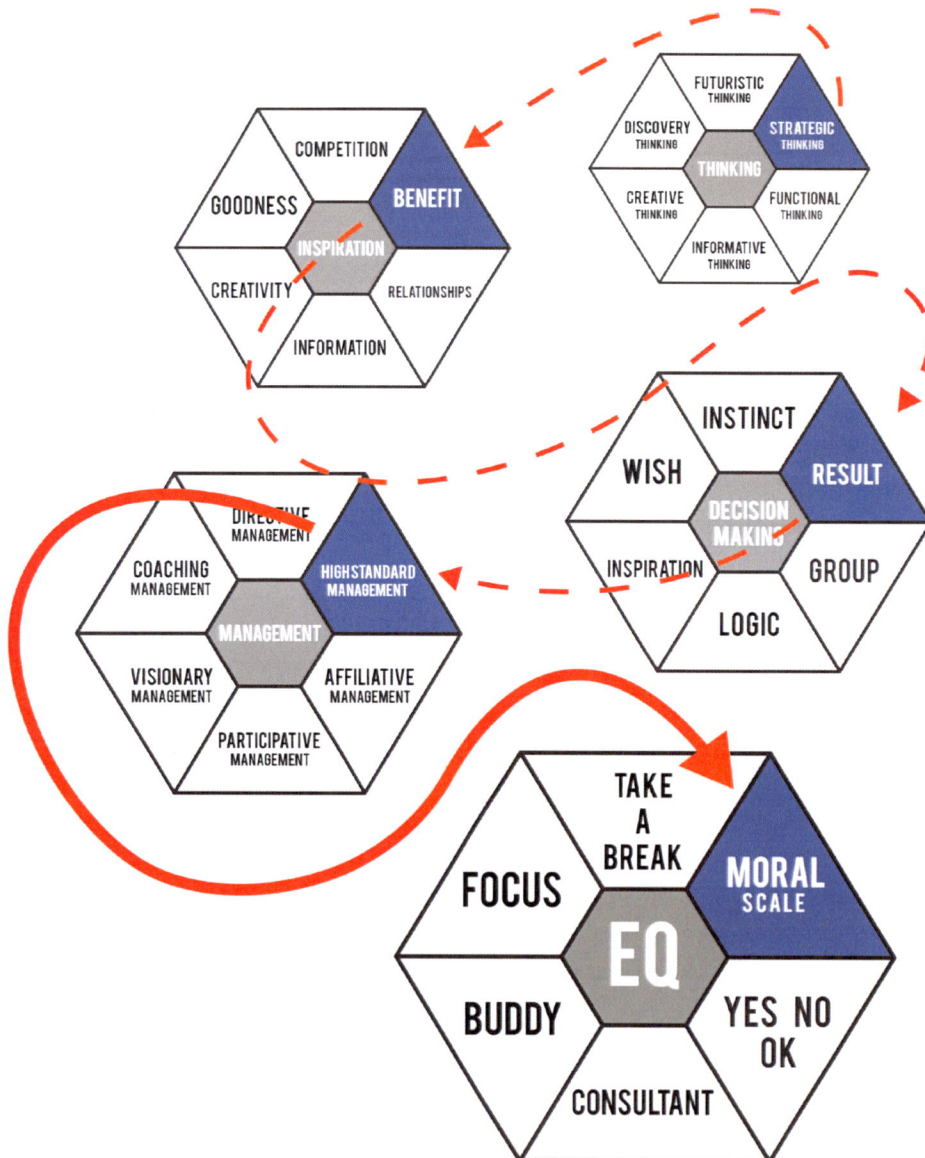

Moral Scale — following the correct path

This means holding true to your virtues, morals and ethics which act as a personal guide for your actions — a moral compass if you like. In Buddhism, **Dharma** is a kind of cosmic law and order that guides you along the path of life.

There are times when **E-type** people have an idea or a strong desire to do something, but the first thing they think about is 'What will benefit me by doing this?' At this point, **Entrepreneurs** usually cease to be aware of other people's feelings and opt to follow their own instincts regardless if they are right or wrong. Therefore, a moral compass helps to create a balance between desires and principles.

Emotional management when used correctly by **E-type** people aligns their EQ elements of **Empathy** and **Handling Relationships.** In order to prevent excessive self-obsession that may hurt other people's feelings, **Entrepreneurs** need to show their associates that they really do care.

This method is suitable for **E-type** people who are mainly interested in benefits or what they expect to get. If **Entrepreneurs** employ this method it will help enhance their empathy and make people admire them more.

Triple Choice

(Yes / No / OK)

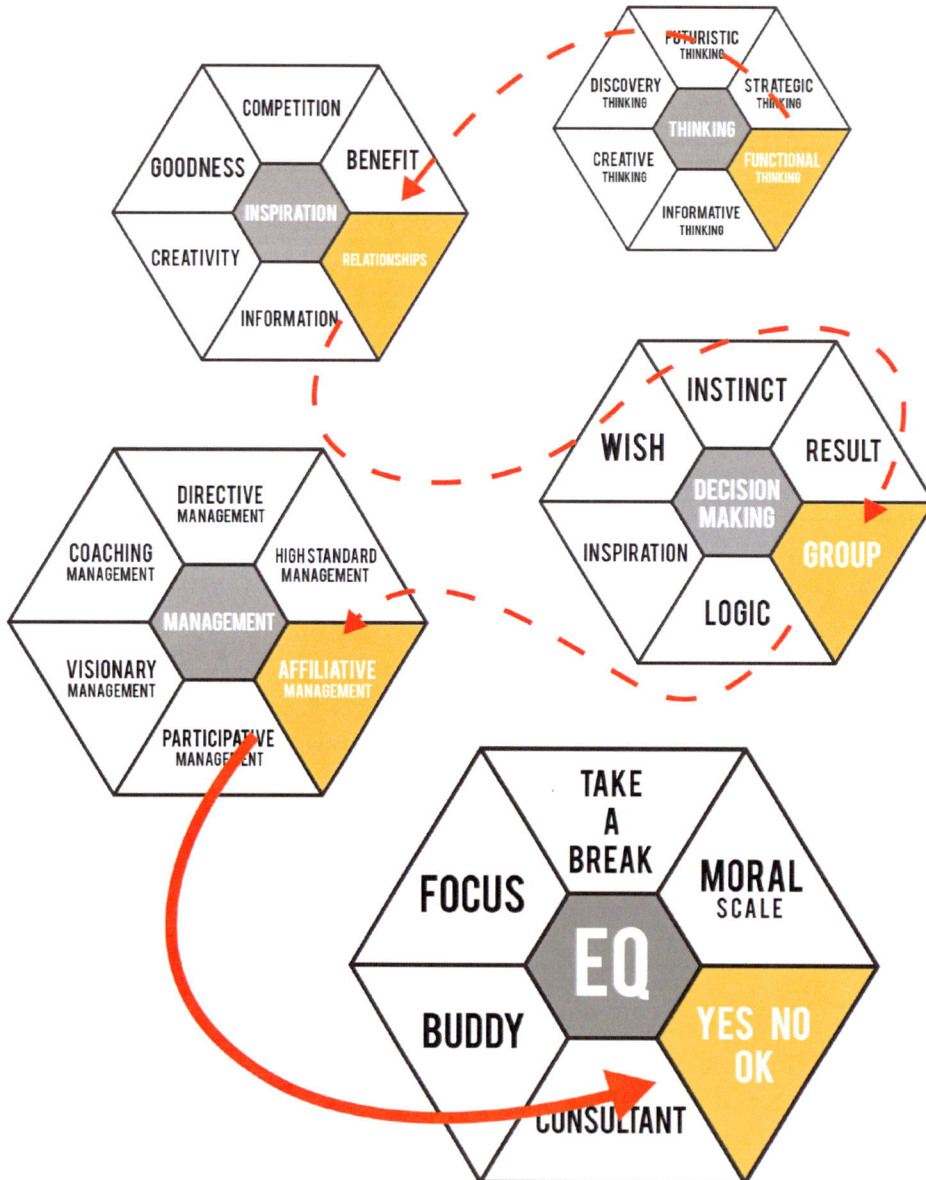

Yes / No / OK – Triple Choice

By thinking carefully and exploring various outcomes to find the right answers, **N-type** people will be better at decision-making. When answers are found they should be acceptable and not make people feel uncomfortable or troubled. The Triple Choice method can be used in situations where a choice must be made or consideration must be reached based on rational principles.

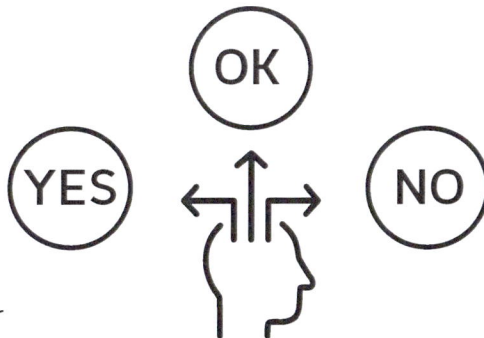

Throughout life, **Networkers** often do what other people want in order to keep them happy. Although what they end up doing may not actually be what they want, their personality trait of understanding and sympathising with others makes it hard for **N-type** people to deny their friends' requests. Therefore, the solution for this matter is a **"new thinking method"** with three choices to be used in all situations – **Yes / No / OK.** For example:
1) If the answer is Yes...what will the result be?
2) If the answer is No...what will the result be?
3) If the answer is OK...what will the result be?

This emotional management method sits perfectly with **Networkers'** EQ element of **Self-awareness.** Whenever a person's thoughts are swayed by persuasion, turning to the Triple Choice option to arrive at an answer will help recognise one's own desires. This in turn will boost confidence when faced with making tricky decisions. This method is most suitable for **N-type** people.

There is nothing too hard in life. Sometimes when the answer is 'No', try to explain its reasons to your friends or try using the above thinking method with other choices. This should make your associates understand and you need not feel uncomfortable or troubled.

Consultant

giving advice when needed

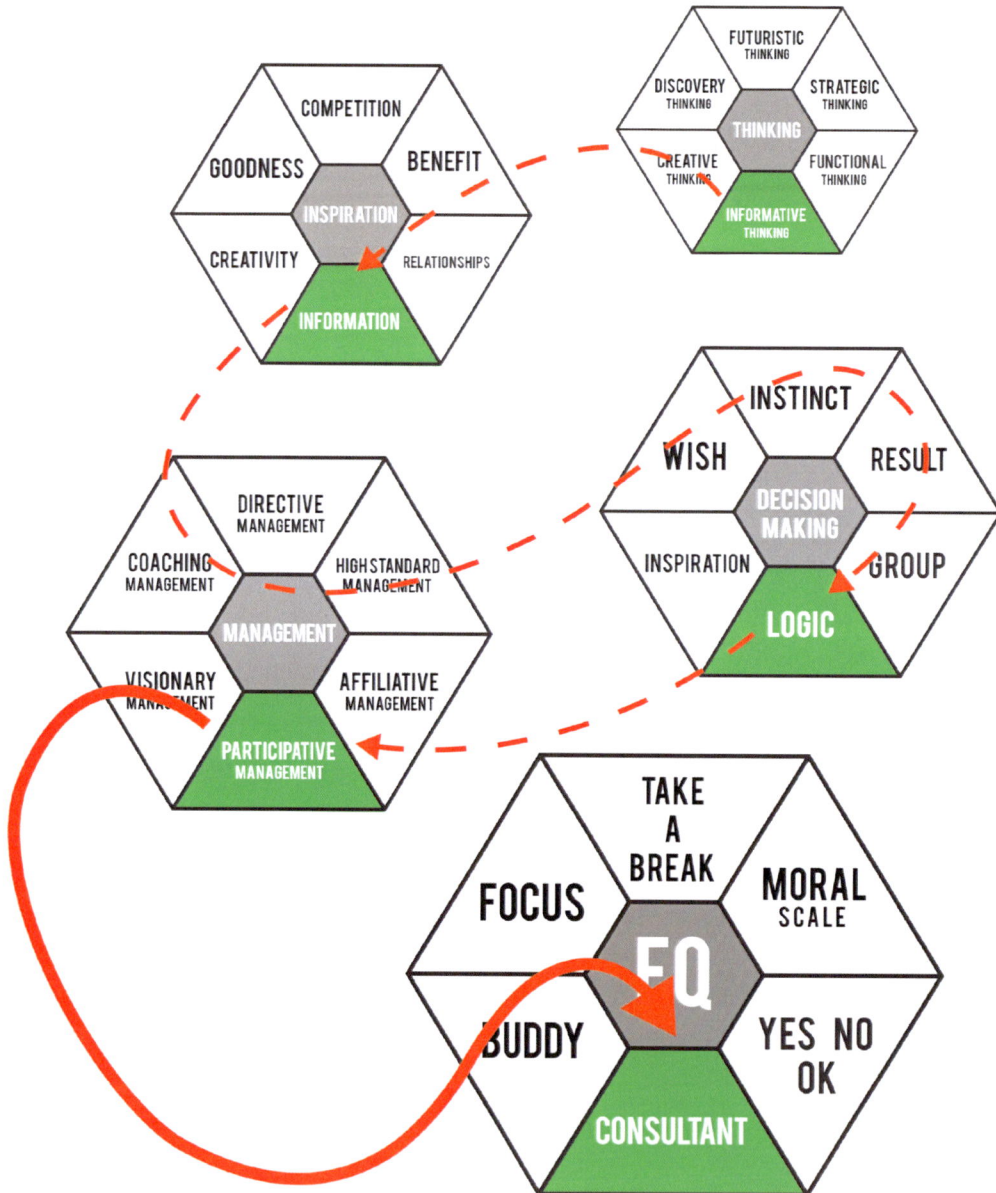

COMPETITION

GOODNESS BENEFIT

INSPIRATION

CREATIVITY RELATIONSHIPS

INFORMATION

FUTURISTIC THINKING

DISCOVERY THINKING STRATEGIC THINKING

THINKING

CREATIVE THINKING FUNCTIONAL THINKING

INFORMATIVE THINKING

DIRECTIVE MANAGEMENT

COACHING MANAGEMENT HIGH STANDARD MANAGEMENT

MANAGEMENT

VISIONARY MANAGEMENT AFFILIATIVE MANAGEMENT

PARTICIPATIVE MANAGEMENT

INSTINCT

WISH RESULT

DECISION MAKING

INSPIRATION GROUP

LOGIC

TAKE A BREAK

FOCUS MORAL SCALE

EQ

BUDDY YES NO OK

CONSULTANT

Consultant - expert advice from the heart

Looking for new or alternative knowledge that goes beyond their own sphere or sharing their problems with other people to arrive at a solution is part of the makeup of **Informationists.** This is because they are often wrapped up in their own little world and do not notice their mistakes, they rely on close associates to point out their shortcomings. Leaders who are capable of listening to their team, earning the trust of their staff and making informed decisions are true consultants who can bring the best out of people.

Most of the time, **I-type** people are confident in their own thinking methods, the information they have researched and the decisions they have arrived at. If after using their methodology they discover they have made a mistake, **Informationists** are likely to plead for understanding. While we all make mistakes from time to time, **I-type** people believe they have covered all possible outcomes through research. While other personality types might turn to a consultant for advice, **Informationists** also need direction in their emotional management.

Albert Einstein once said; "The definition of insanity is doing the same thing over and over again and expecting different results." Therefore, it is important for **Informationists** to discuss their findings with close associates otherwise they will never be prepared to try new methods.

This emotional management method aligns with an **I-type** person's EQ element of **Motivation,** as words or advice from other people can inspire motivation that drives and empowers them to solve problems. Great leaders always lend an ear to **I-type** people because they understand the personality trait they are dealing with and know how to control the flow of information. If we all listened to and respected ideas from knowledgeable people, our IQ and EQ would no doubt improve significantly.

Find a Buddy

two's company

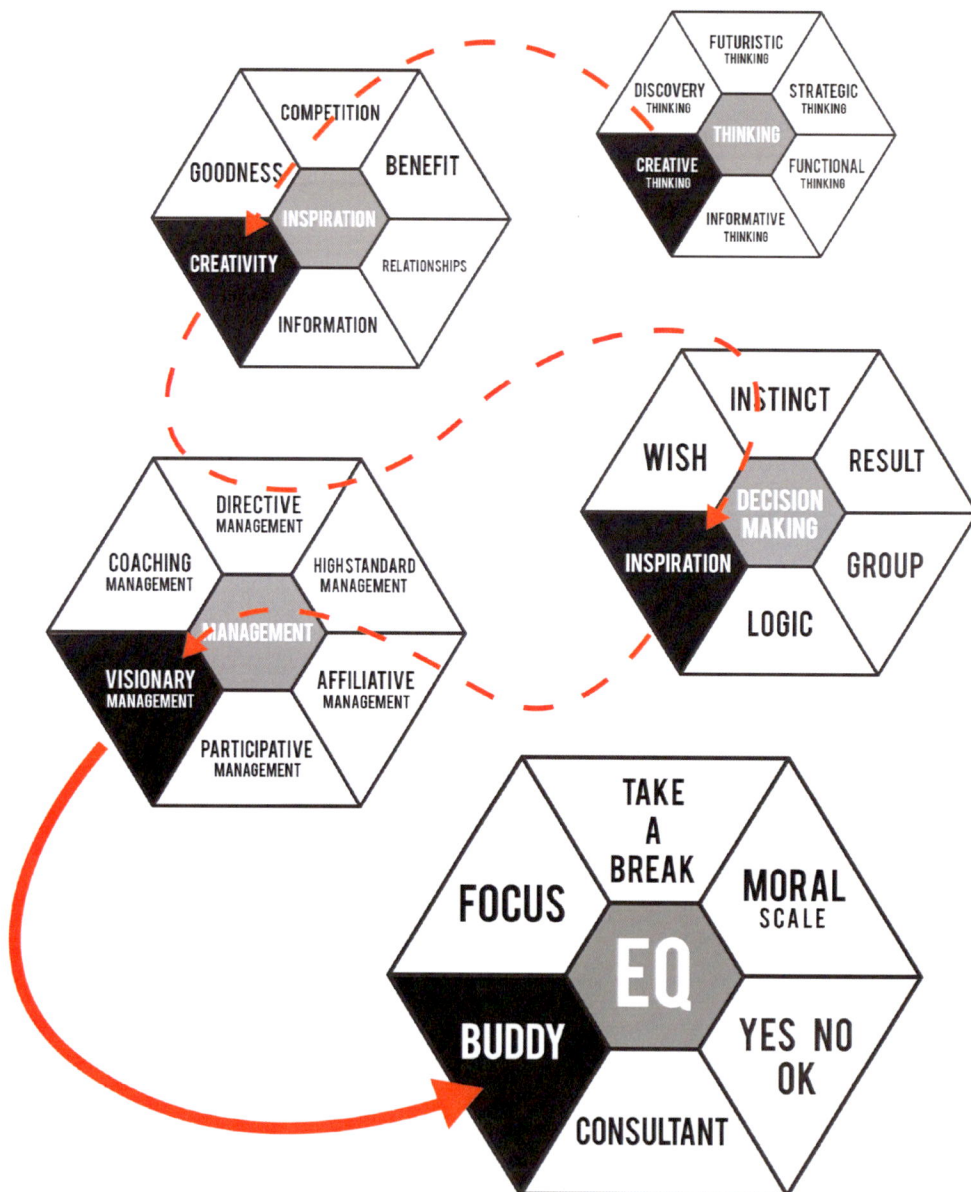

Find a Buddy - never being lonely

This means finding someone who you can trust unreservedly and who will always listen and understand a **U-type** person's emotions and thoughts without being judgmental. This close friend should be the type of person who you can bounce your thoughts off and will give their honest opinion.

With their exceptional characteristics, **Unique** people usually solve problems by escaping from their predicament and retreating to a quiet place where they can be alone to contemplate their position. Most of the time they are unwilling to share their problems with other people for fear of being a burden.

Thus, **U-type** people need a confidant who they can talk to openly. The most outstanding trait **U-type** people have is their brilliant creativity, but they are not the best at dealing with heated situations and will back away from any confrontation. When faced with a serious problem in life, they are quite willing to flee from their surroundings and move elsewhere.

This emotional management method meets **U-type** people's EQ elements of **Self-Awareness, Self-regulation** and **Motivation,** as being able to talk about their intimate feelings will help provide a better understanding of their ideas and feelings, which in turn will help them deal with their emotions. Moreover, this close friend will help boost a **U-type** person's self-esteem.

Psychologically, if you keep a problem to yourself and refuse to share or discuss it with someone else, it could lead to mental issues. So, if **U-type** people cannot solve their problems, they should find a close friend to talk to and openly speak their mind. If you hide your emotions, it only serves to make you afraid of them.

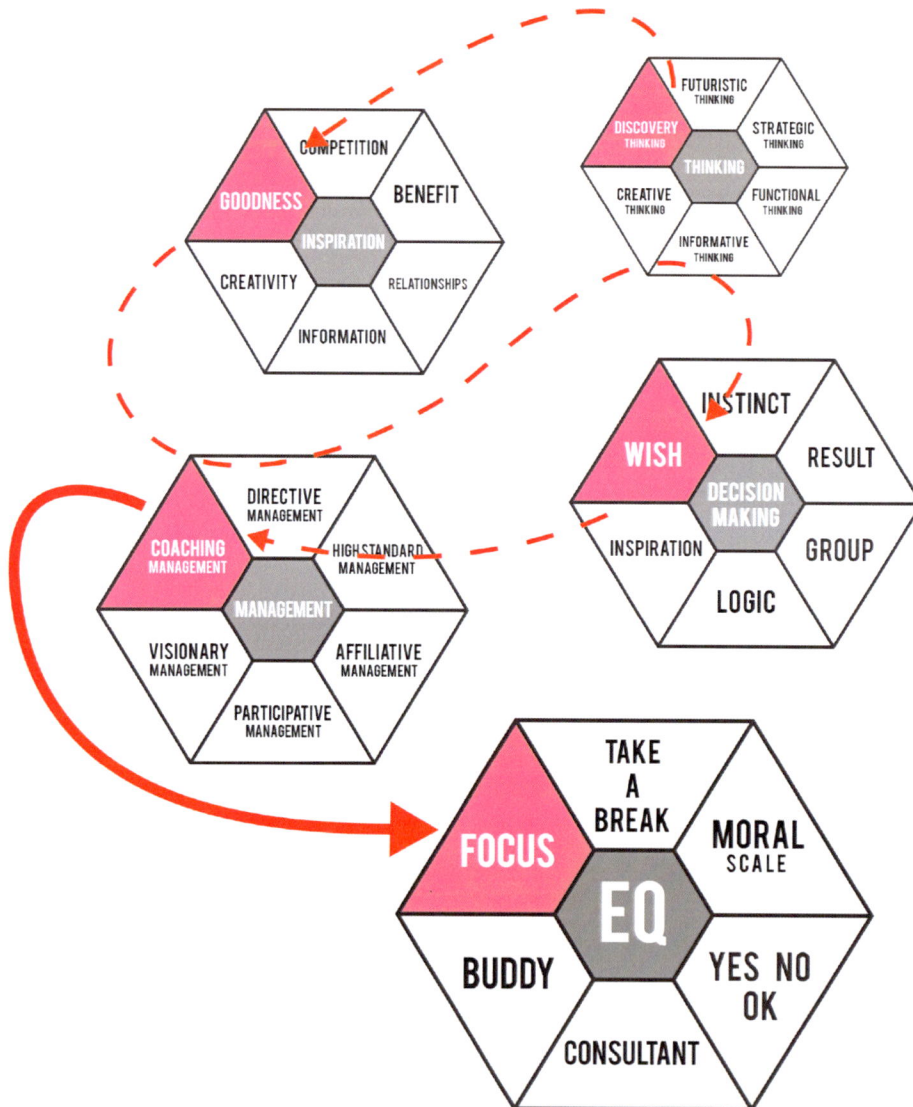

Focus One Thing – aim for your target

While we all have multiple events happening in our daily lives, if we are to achieve our targets (goals), then it is important to prioritise our goals and pursue one at a time. If we try to achieve multiple targets simultaneously we risk not giving 100% effort and thus ruining our chances. Focusing on one thing also applies to problem solving, decision-making and other such fundamentals.

Sharing people are known for being kind, merciful and generous to fellow colleagues, friends and people in general. So, when someone requests help they will offer it without hesitation. However, the downside to being so quick to lend a hand often means **S-type** people bring trouble to their own door. While we all want to help those in need, it is better to target giving rather than worry about not offering help. With so many charities being set up these days, people are inundated with requests for donations and so I think it is best to choose one charity which you think will ultimately do the most good.

Focusing on one thing, be it a personal goal or a company mission, is to dedicate all your efforts to reaching one level at a time. While the buzzword of the late 20th century was multi-tasking, I firmly believe that we should focus on 'mono-tasking' as it allows for total concentration and the least distraction. Most successful people in the world have become so because they focused on one goal until they realised it. Some 90 years ago, John D. Rockefeller said: 'People fail to achieve their goals because they lack concentration.' What's more, they didn't have mobile phones, email and television back then to distract them!

The EQ element for **S-type** people is **Self-Awareness** and the ability to evaluate their capabilities in order to achieve what they are best at. As **Sharers** are always willing to help others, applying this method will help them feel better about helping people while preventing any unnecessary trouble.

SHARING

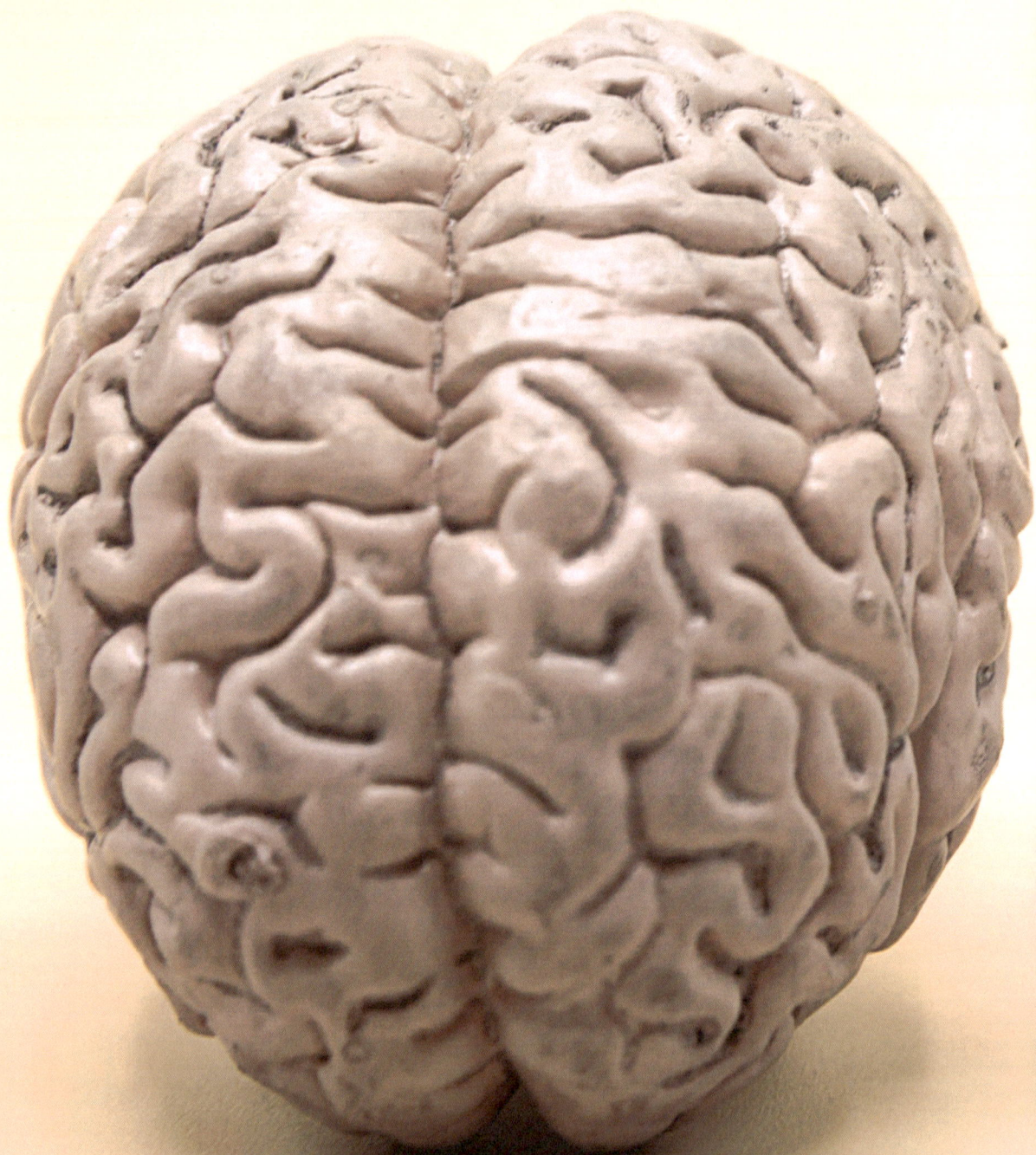

The brains of both genders

are roughly the same weight.
An adult **male's brain** weighs
approximately **1,400 grams,**
while an adult **female's brain**
weighs **1,230 grams.**

However, even though our brain

weighs around 3lbs,

it consumes 20% of the

body's **oxygen supply,**
while approximately
20% of the blood pumped
by the heart goes to the brain
and the 400 miles
of capillaries it contains.

Chapter 8

GeniusX
Negotiation

Investment is committing money or capital to an undertaking with the expectation of receiving an additional income or profit in the short, medium or long-term. Every investment, however, comes with the risk of losing the initial investment of money or capital.

In economics, investment means to purchase a type of product that we may not utilise in the short-term, but is one that we expect will add value and create a return in the future.

In finance, investment means to purchase and possess tools or monetary assets and expect that such assets will increase in value in order to create future returns or profits. "Investment" can be divided into 2 main categories:

1) Investment in concrete assets that yield benefits (Tangible Investment) For example, residential property, land, buildings, gold or precious jewelry; tangible objects that can be quickly realised in to cash.

2) Investment in assets that cannot be seen (Intangible Investment) For example, investments in stocks, bonds, debt securities or consolidated funds, which take time to convert to cash.

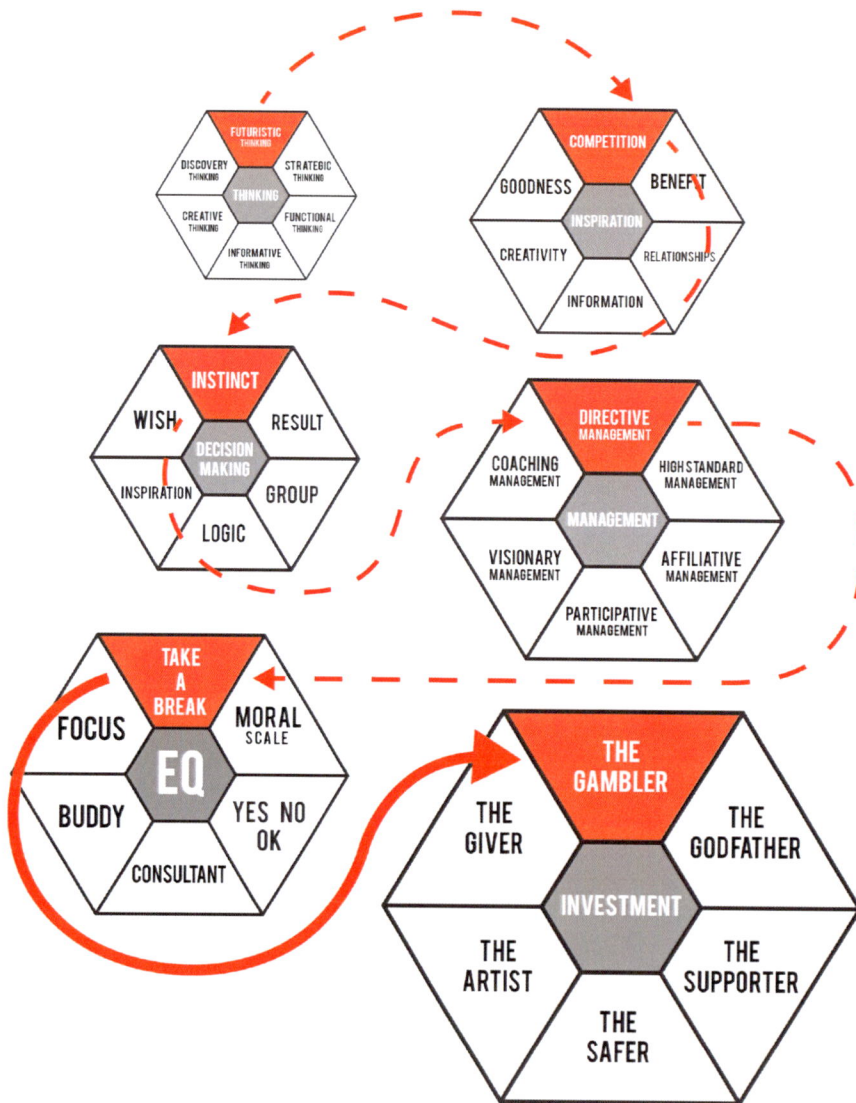

The Gambler

Diagram of interconnected hexagonal models:

- **THINKING**: FUTURISTIC THINKING, DISCOVERY THINKING, STRATEGIC THINKING, CREATIVE THINKING, FUNCTIONAL THINKING, INFORMATIVE THINKING

- **INSPIRATION**: COMPETITION, GOODNESS, BENEFIT, CREATIVITY, RELATIONSHIPS, INFORMATION

- **DECISION MAKING**: INSTINCT, WISH, RESULT, INSPIRATION, GROUP, LOGIC

- **MANAGEMENT**: DIRECTIVE MANAGEMENT, COACHING MANAGEMENT, HIGH STANDARD MANAGEMENT, VISIONARY MANAGEMENT, AFFILIATIVE MANAGEMENT, PARTICIPATIVE MANAGEMENT

- **EQ**: TAKE A BREAK, FOCUS, MORAL SCALE, BUDDY, YES NO OK, CONSULTANT

- **INVESTMENT**: THE GAMBLER, THE GIVER, THE GODFATHER, THE ARTIST, THE SUPPORTER, THE SAFER

To invest like the Gambler

This is the realm of **Game Changers** who are known for their courage, determination and big-hearts. They wait for no one and are willing to fight for their corner without a thought of surrender. These personality traits tend to make **G-type** people some of the most "sporting gamblers" in society.

Each time they invest, the generous **Game Changer** Gambler will "invest all their stakes" – an all-or-nothing bet – in order to achieve the outcome they desire. They are so fearless that they are willing to bet big with the aim of winning big. If they lose, they are sure to regret it, but will not lose sleep over it.

Among the personality types we've looked at, the **G-type** Gambler is the one who is prepared to stake the **"the highest risk investment."** If they hit the jackpot, it's like they knew it would happen, it was only a matter of time until their numbers came up. If they are smart with their winnings, they won't need to restart from zero.

This fearlessness creates high risk and is very dangerous for those who have a responsibility to look after their family or business. **Therefore, the best option to minimise risky investments is for G-type people to befriend a consultant with personality traits that match Entrepreneurs or Informationists.** This will help **G-type** people prioritise their risk while at the same time enhancing their thought process, analysis and comparison skills.

The Godfather

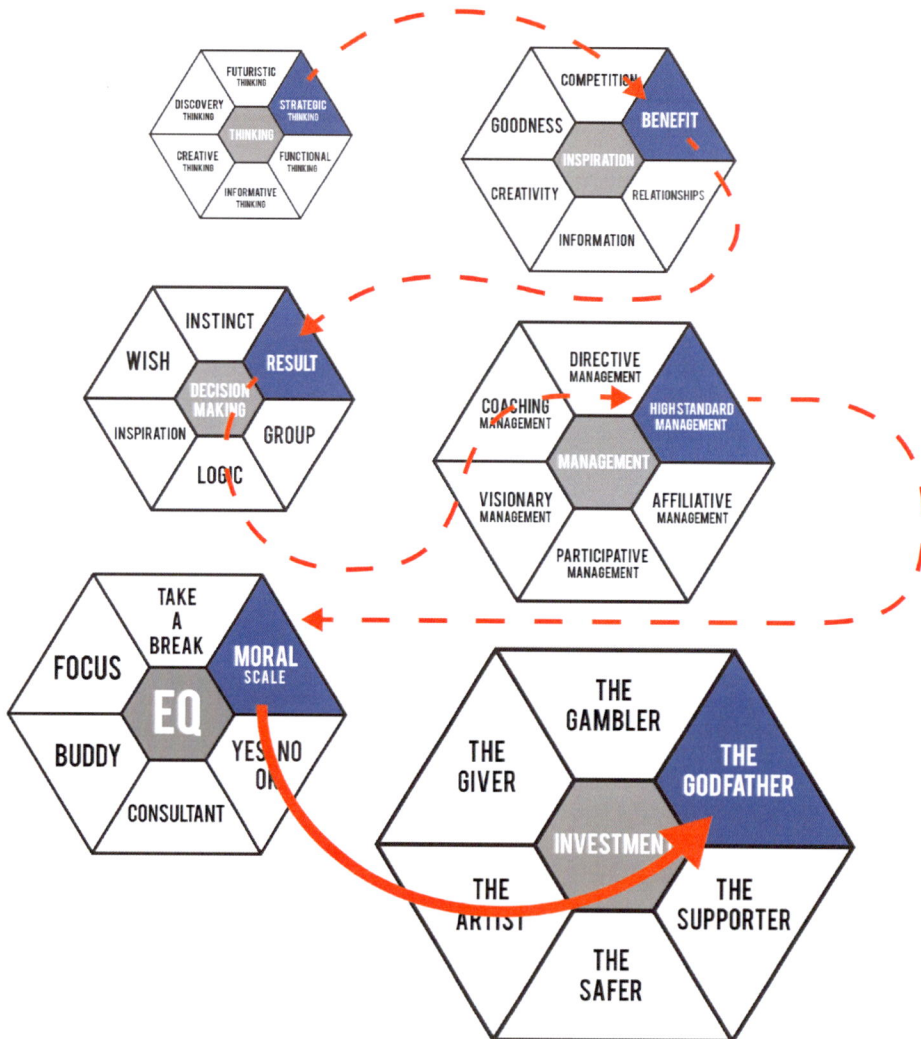

Invest like the Godfather

This is the domain of **Entrepreneurs,** those self-driven people who come across as "super-smart". When they meet new people, **E-type** people will ask about any new ideas so that they can broaden their horizon with more investment opportunities. While most **E-type** people are small investors, they love what they do and will probably not quit until they retire. If they do well they will go on to become a business owner or stockholder of a company they've invested in.

Investors like E-type people like doing all types of trades and love the feel of power of **"ownership".** It is always their goal to have their own successful business where they are in charge. Their natural leadership trait can sometimes make them unyielding. For **Entrepreneurs,** there is no "Whatever you say" policy as every step must be controlled and fit with their strategy.

The **thinking methodology of the Entrepreneur** is to follow the path to wealth, something other personality types do not feel comfortable pursuing. Everything close to **E-type** people is engulfed in their relentless chase for financial success. Even if they are involved in a friend's or relative's business, they will only be interested in one thing: money.

However, if they wish to be a successful investor and minimise the number of people they are sure to upset, **E-type** people should find a consultant, a friend or an assistant who is a **Networker** or a **Sharer** in order to preserve their friendships and business relationships.

The Supporter

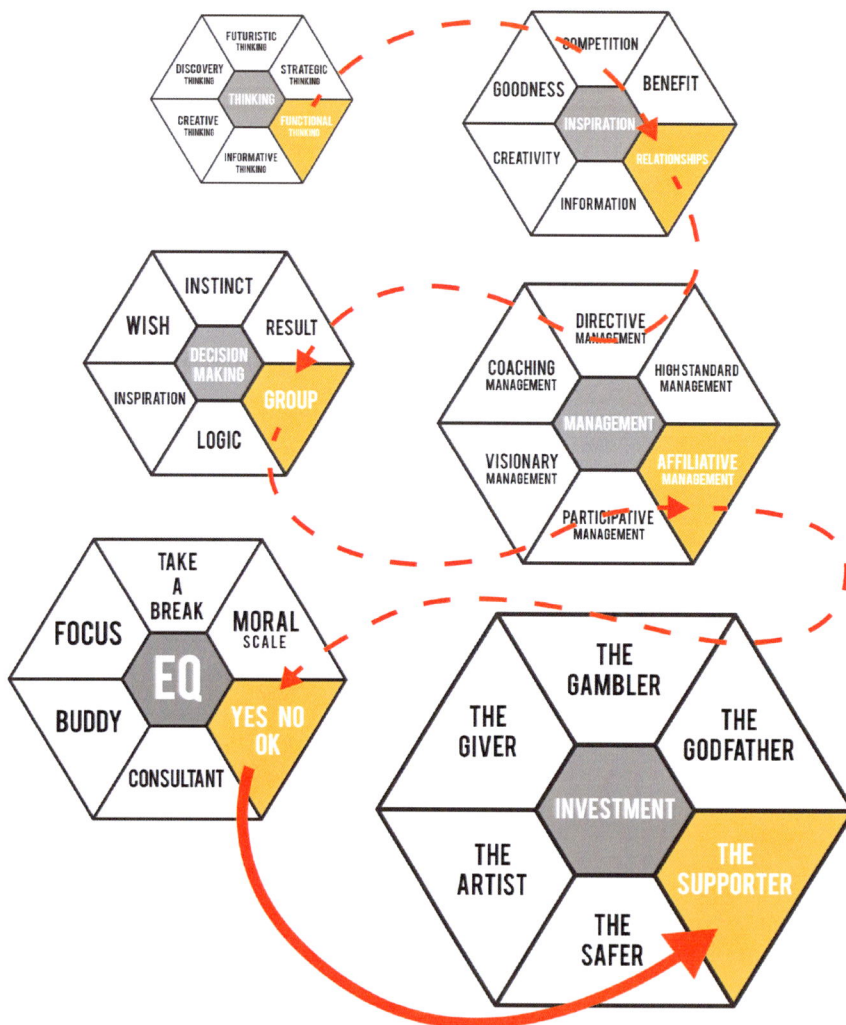

Invest like the Supporter

This refers to **Networkers** who wish to be an investor in a business, but not the actual owner. What makes **N-type** people happy is meeting friends, enjoying social activities and taking part in other types of gatherings. They may want to be involved in a new business, but they do not seek control. A **Networker** would be happy with a small shareholding in a business or would look to invest as a silent partner.

Investors like **N-type** people are not interested in "ownership" because they don't really enjoy wielding power over others. They would rather protect their friendships than fall out over a business gone wrong. A **Networker** would sell his or her share if there were issues with other investors.

The thinking process of **Networkers** is to follow the path of friendship, that's it. Other personality types may not understand why **Networkers** worry so much about building and maintain good relationships, but this is how **N-type** people are wired and they hold true to friendships. Throughout their lives they have always done things for other people, which gives **Networkers** great pleasure. They will go out of their way to avoid conflicts with people. They may even go as far as putting themselves at a disadvantaged to put an end to any trouble.

However, if a **Networker** wishes to decrease their risk and increase their options in an investment, they should find a partner, a friend or a consultant who has an **E-type** or **I-type** personality trait.

The Safety First Investor

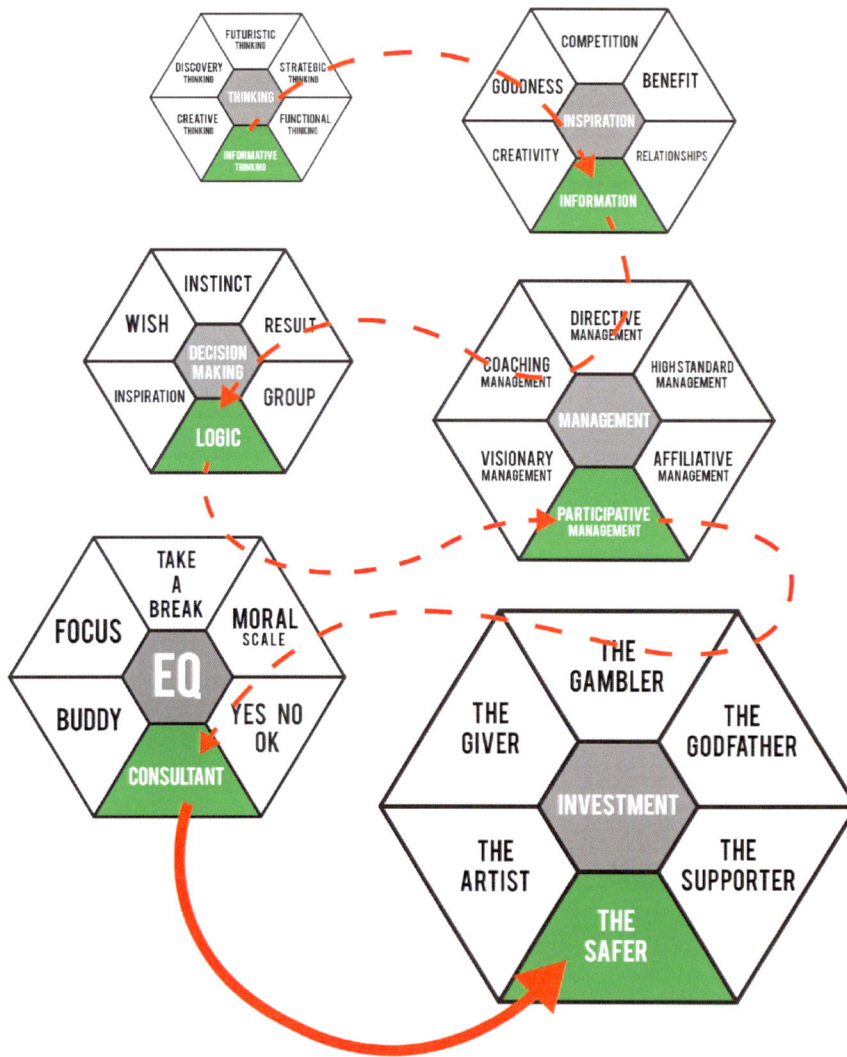

Invest in Safe Ventures

When **Informationists** make an investment they do so not based on feelings or emotions, but on solid evidence.

I-type people apply reasoned comparisons thanks to the information they have researched. If the investment is perceived to be safe, they will inject their money. However, if there is a high risk or moderate risk, they will refuse to invest in any such project. Even in the case of a minimal risk, they will procrastinate about investing.

Investors like **I-type** people pay attention to all the details, especially the three major issues of "income + profit + future". Their investment must carry the least amount of risk as possible while still providing steady returns. **Informationists** are thoughtful by nature and will thoroughly research any investment so as to be able to make a sensible decision, regardless of who tries to persuade them to invest. There is a reason why very few **Informationists** own businesses; they hesitate, think too much and are afraid of taking a risk.

The thinking method of **Informationists** is to always stick to the risk-free path in life. The facts they learn about a subject must give them 100% confidence before they take any action. Sources of all data must be known and clear with no vagueness or hidden agendas. Any situation that worries an **Informationist** will be researched until they are able to verify the information is reliable and trustworthy. **I-type** people are quite happy to let investments pass them by if they feel it is too risky.

If an **Informationist** wanted to be more courageous, increase their prowess and minimise hesitation, they should find a consultant, a friend or an assistant with a **G** or **U-type** personality. Trusting one of these personalities will help enhance the effectiveness of **I-type** people's investment policy.

U

The Artist

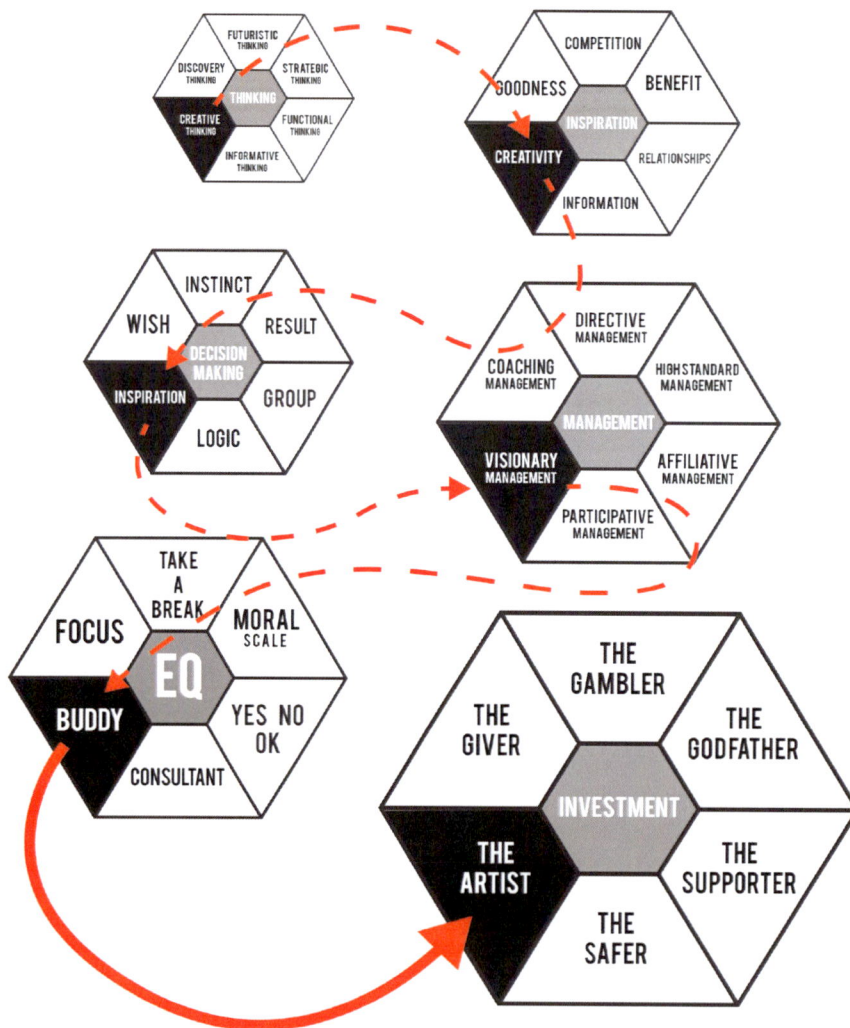

Invest like an Artist

If there is one thing you can count on with **Unique** people it is that they are certain to only invest in a business they love. **U-type** people always do things from the heart even if it makes them different. If they open a coffee shop, the shop will be distinctively decorated and could even feature a resident cat. Any business they participate in is sure to be one they feel attached to.

U-type investors care for "their own preference" above and beyond anything else. If an investment opportunity came their way but they did not immediately fall in love with it, it is very unlikely they could be persuaded to change their mind. In most towns and cities, you can see **U-type** people's stores on the high street, standing out from the corporate brands and charity shops. Unique people are prepared to go it alone with their venture rather than conform to what other people are doing.

The thought process of Unique people is **"to do whatever they like"** and everyone else can just get on and do their own thing. The majority of **U-type** people don't worry about what's going on in the world, whether it's related to economics or politics. They are the last people who you'll see jumping on the bandwagon to follow the latest craze. If they are asked to invest in a spa or a restaurant, unless they could design the interior they would not be interested. But, if it is something they are given free control to put their creative soul in to, they will embrace it 24 hours a day.

If **U-type** people want to invest in a project, they should partner with a friend who has an **I-type** personality. They should also befriend **N-type** people to help grow their group of friends.

The Giver

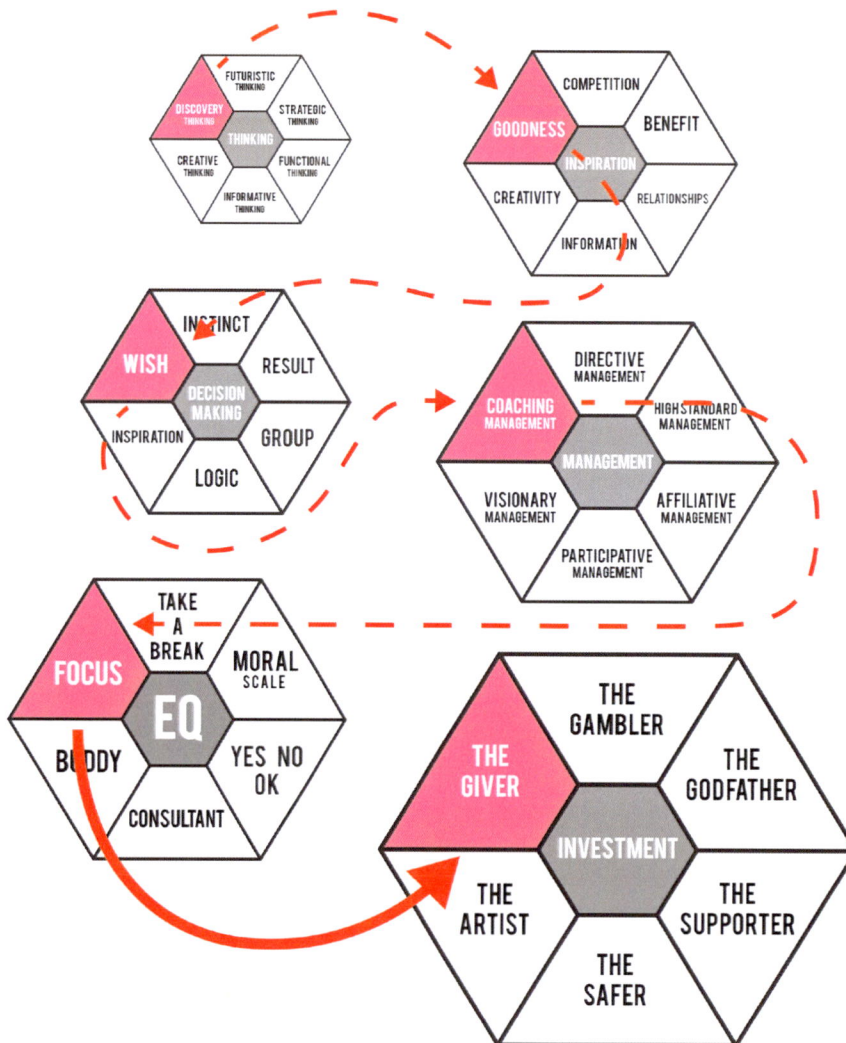

Invest like the Giver

For those **Sharing** people who take the time and make the effort to open their own business, it is sure to be the type of company that takes good care of its employees. **S-type** people shy away from situations that are too difficult or they deem involve chaotic organisation. **Sharers** usually make investments or open a business that mirrors their kind nature and this is often reflected in businesses such as flower shops, cake shops or culinary schools. They prefer to help others with value for money services rather than seeking lots of profit.

S-type investors care about "giving" and many are involved in corporate social responsibility (CSR) programs close their businesses. Keeping the local community happy also results in repeat business, so for **S-type** people it is a win-win situation. As long as their operating expenses are covered, profits are hardly talked about. If they have been successful and earned lots of money, they are likely to donate money to a local charity, hospital or their faith.

S-type people work along the principles of "doing things for other people" without expecting anything in return. They are happy to put others first and are attentive to other people's thoughts and troubles. They care about the world we live in and have even offered their homes to strangers such as in Europe during the mass migration from Syria as well as after natural disasters in the Caribbean, Japan and the USA.

If **S-type** people do not want to invite problems to their business they should consult with an **E-type** personality who will help them protect their interests or partner with a **G-type** person to learn about taking advantage of an opportunity.

There has been a lot of research that has
confirmed the brain functions between men
and women are surprisingly different.

A female uses ten times more white matter
in the cerebrum (rationality)
and the hypothalamus
(emotion and creativity)
while doing activities.
White matter is the neural pathways that connect the brain's processing centres.

On the other hand, a male's brain
has been shown to utilise seven times
more grey matter for activities.
Grey matter areas of the brain are localised
and act as information and processing
centres and often lead to a kind
of tunnel vision in males.

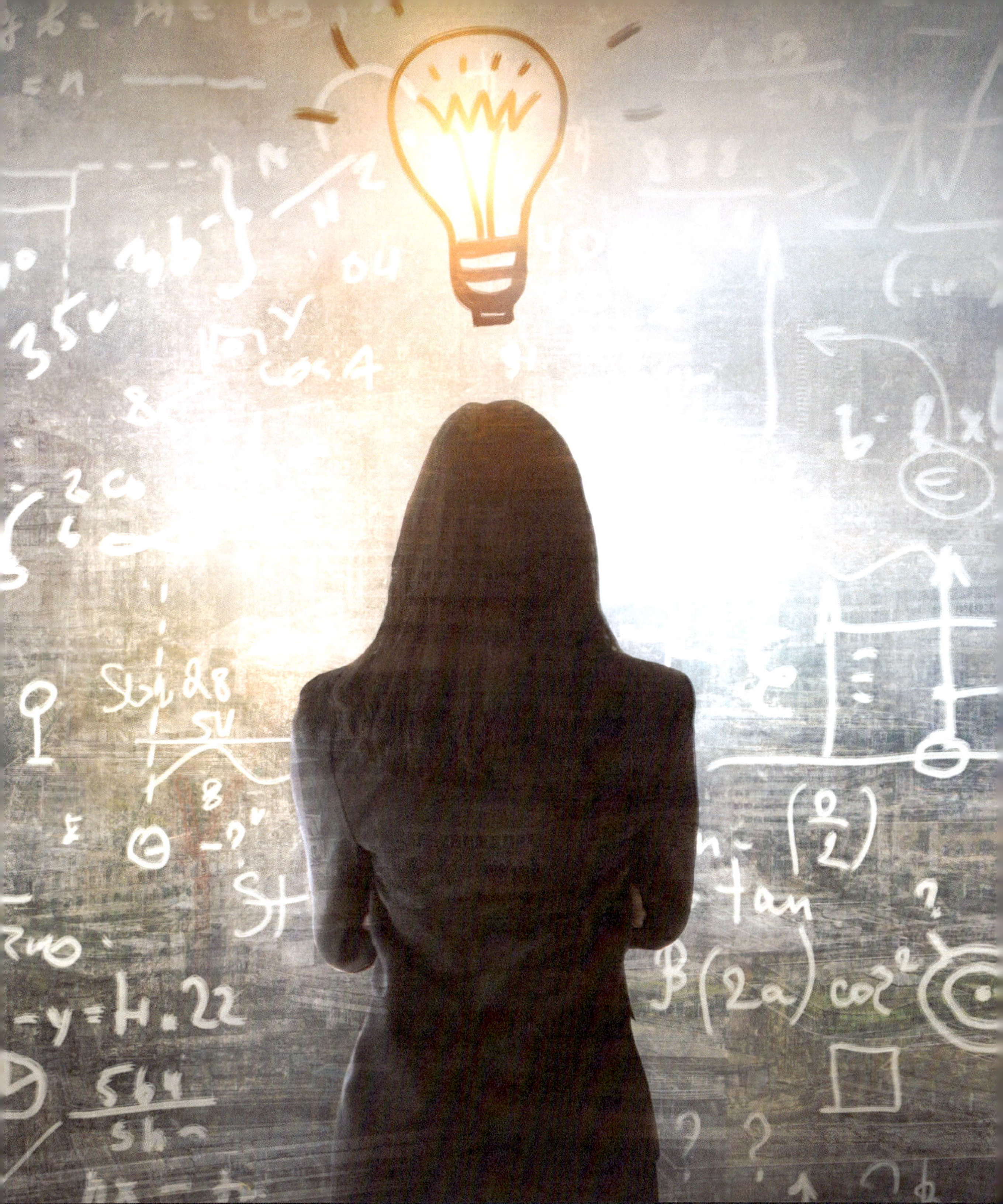

Chapter 9

Methods To Gain Success For Each Personality Type

GeniusX Idea

Two of the main reasons why so many businesspeople fail to experience the sweet taste of success is that even though they may use a similar approach and procedures, they opt for a business strategy that does not match their thinking methodology and they employ the wrong type of people.

For example, Owner #1 chose a proactive strategy as his business plan although he wasn't adventurous and preferred to stay at the office and work with his staff rather than visit clients. Therefore, he really should have selected a network creation strategy to expand his business rather than a proactive strategy and hired a **Game Changer** to be the face of his company.

Hence, if you are contemplating starting a business, you first need to understand that everybody has a **different thinking approach,** which results in diverse behaviours, personalities, working methods and skills. You also need to recognise which type of person you are according to the GeniusX classification so that you can select the best strategy that suits your thinking approach and hire the people that complement your personality. Now you are ready to conquer the business world.

The strategies for success for each personality type are as follows:

1) Game Changer Strategy
2) Entrepreneur Strategy
3) Network Strategy
4) Informationist Strategy
5) Unique Strategy
6) Sharer Strategy

Game Changer Strategy

A Strategy Designed For Game Changers

This is designed for proactive businesspeople who realise they have a good product or service and are willing to go that extra mile or spend that extra $10,000 to achieve their business goal. While **Game Changers** are prepared to take risks here and there, if they are truly smart competitors they will assemble a team or hire the right person who fits with their thinking approach.

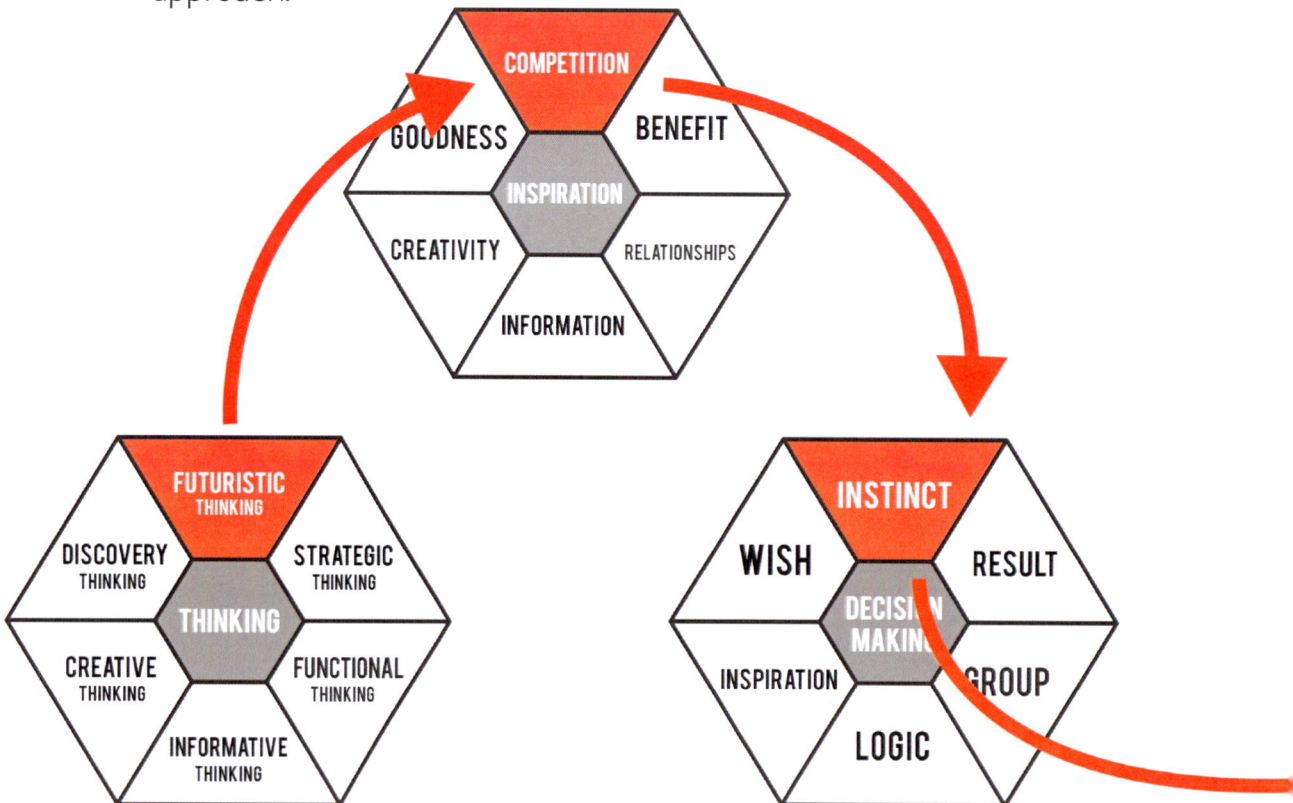

Let's say you hire a new marketing manager who happens to be a G-type person. Now, you must accept there will be great changes in your company's marketing performance because G-type marketers are daring and tend to spend a lot of money to get their brands noticed in the marketplace in a very short period of time.

Dietary supplement and other such businesses typically employ a team of **Game Changer** marketers that use reality TV stars and minor celebrities to endorse their products. They are known to invest heavily in digital marketing so that their targets groups on Facebook, Instagram, YouTube and other social networks will constantly see their products. They utilise Google AdWords to the maximum in order to push their product to as many websites as possible where they know their target audience likes to visit.

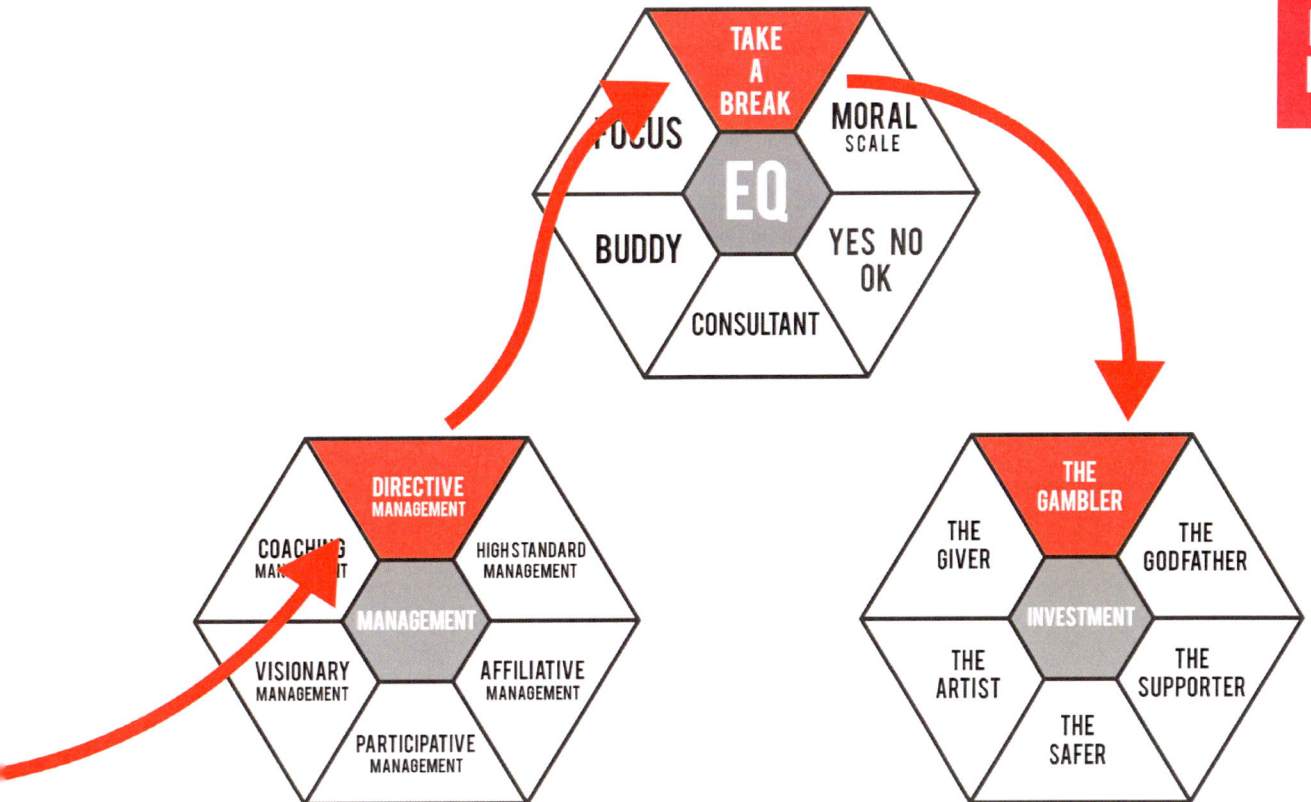

Dietary Supplement Business

Jenny Jones decided to open a dietary supplement business and hired a company to produce a new product with an innovative formula. Jenny has a Master's degree in pharmacy and her personality type is an **Informationist.** She has in-depth knowledge on the types of vitamins, minerals and other ingredients used in the most popular dietary supplements, but she knows very little about marketing. Six months after launching her revolutionary new product her sales have not improved.

So, Jenny hires Gill, a marketing guru and **Game Changer** type personality, to formulate a six-month marketing plan for her company. Gill convinces Jenny to invest $10,000 a month in digital marketing and within two months Jenny's sales have soared by 150%.

Reviewing the marketing plan, Jenny and Gill discuss whether their sales would increase further if they invested more money for marketing. As so often with bold **Game Changers** who believe in what they do, Gill convinces her boss to increase the company's marketing budget from $10,000 to $15,000 a month. Within a month of starting their new marketing campaign, Jenny's sales grow from $200,000 to $300,000 a month. Believing that they are reaching their target audience, they decide to increase the marketing budget to $20,000 a month in the hope of making $500,000 a month in sales.

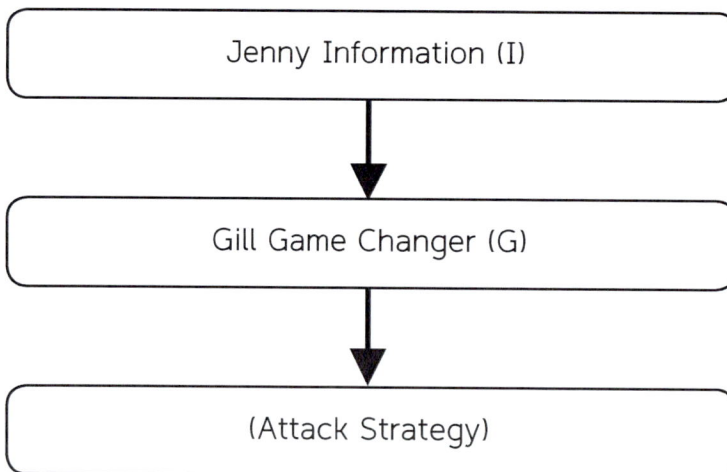

```
┌─────────────────────────────────────┐
│      Jenny Information (I)           │
└─────────────────────────────────────┘
                  │
                  ▼
┌─────────────────────────────────────┐
│      Gill Game Changer (G)          │
└─────────────────────────────────────┘
                  │
                  ▼
┌─────────────────────────────────────┐
│        (Attack Strategy)            │
└─────────────────────────────────────┘
```

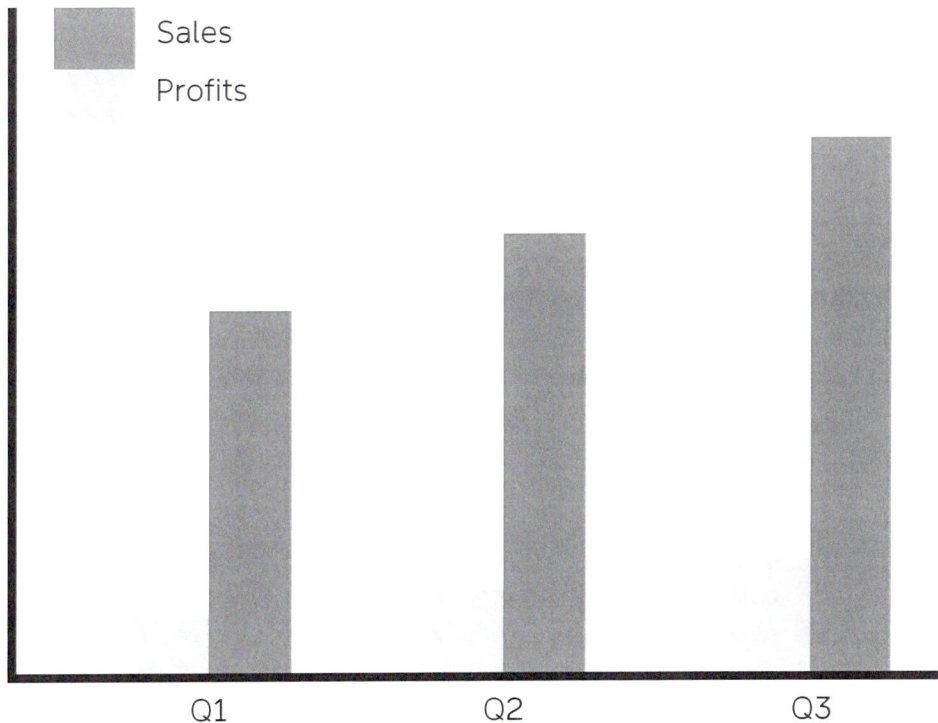

Legend:
- ▮ Sales
- Profits

Bars: Q1, Q2, Q3

A Team of G-type People

If you own a sales-focused business like Jenny and your sales are not growing as you would like, the first thing you must do is review your strategy. If your original strategy has problems or is not effective in generating better sales, you need to find a new strategy and quickly.

In this example, Jenny is an **Informationist** and therefore should not hire a marketer with the same personality type because they will obviously think the same way. **I-type** people are hesitant and take long time to take meaningful action. Therefore, a defensive marketing campaign would be more appropriate for an **I-type** person going it alone. To initiate a proactive marketing (Attack Strategy) campaign, an **I-type** business owner would need to employ a **Game Changer** personality to fully realise their marketing campaign.

E Entrepreneur Strategy

A Strategy Designed For Entrepreneurs

This is designed for brilliant businesspeople who are prepared to grab every possible opportunity that comes their way in order to make money. It's like **Entrepreneurs** have a magic wand with which they can conjure up business opportunities that always make money. We can see examples of this throughout modern history. When the economy booms, **E-type** people make money, but when the bottom falls out of the market and businesses start closing, it seems only **Entrepreneurs** can continue making money. Why is that?

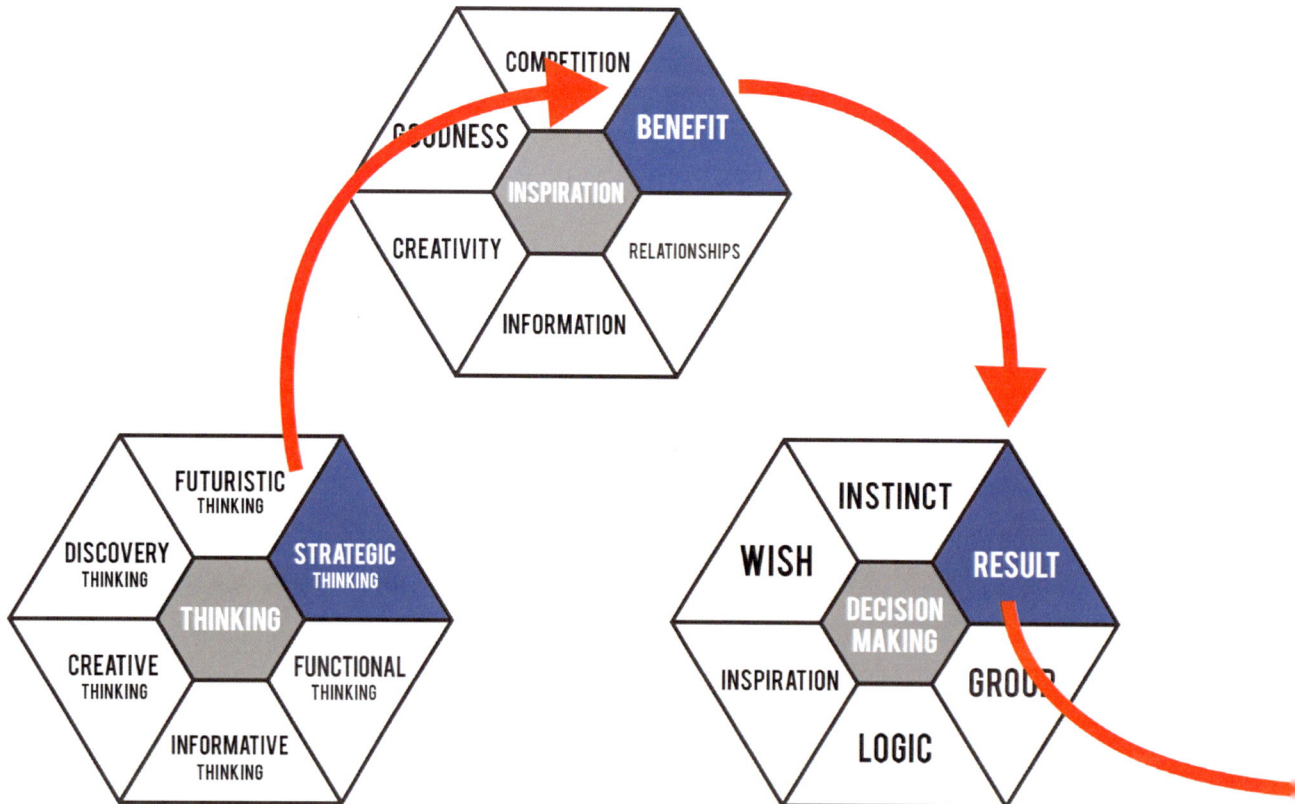

Most people probably have a Chinese friend whose ancestors settled in the city where you live and started a business. These people have a business spirit that flows through their veins and this is partly why almost 90% of those who start a business will achieve great success.

In my home city of Bangkok, on any given day of the week more than one billion Baht – over $30 million – circulates through small businesses that are run by Teochew **Entrepreneurs.** These businesses include family gold shops, clothing manufacturers, stores in Bangkok's biggest markets and traditional Chinese food and medicine shops.

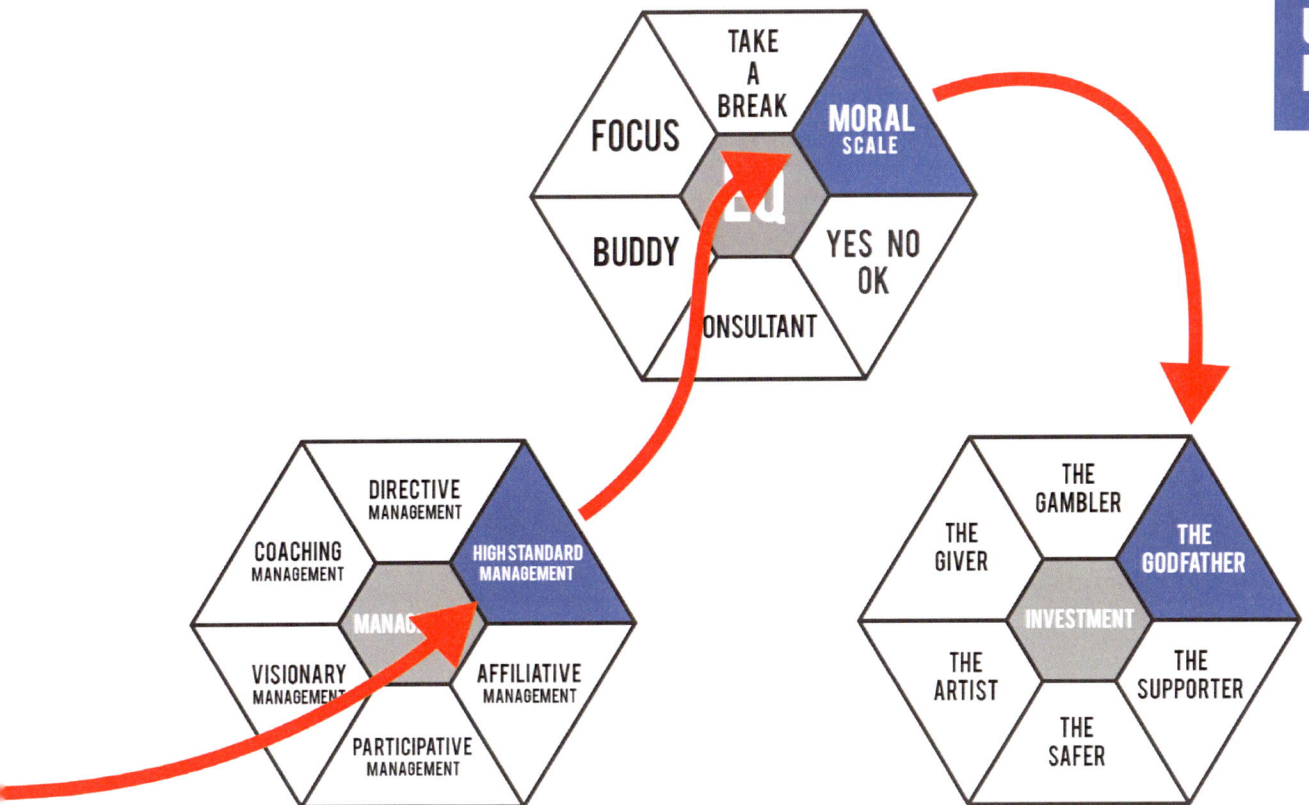

Starting a Business

Li Wei, an **N-type** personality, graduated with a Bachelor's degree in Business Administration (Field of Management). Shortly after graduating, he took a corporate job with a large retail company where he gained a great deal of knowledge and information during the five years he worked there. This, he believed, gave him enough experience and information to start his own company.

Wang Jing, an **E-type** personality with a merchant's spirit in his blood, was on the look out for his next business opportunity when he met Li Wei in a Chinatown teashop. The two men got along very well and decided to go into business together. Li Wei's personality type meant that he had a large network of friends, whereas Wang Jing was used to doing things his way.

Wang Jing, an **E-type** merchant and canny investor, and Li Wei, an **N-type** negotiator, established a company selling water purifiers that they had imported from China. At the start, they depended on the contacts Li Wei had made in his previous job as their product distribution channel. Although business was a little slow, everything was going to plan.

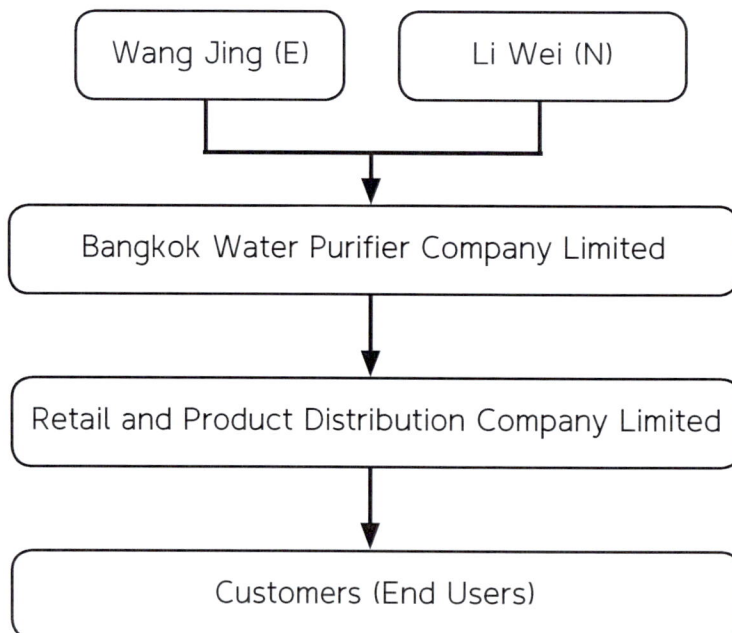

```
┌─────────────────────┐   ┌─────────────────────┐
│   Wang Jing (E)     │   │    Li Wei (N)       │
└─────────────────────┘   └─────────────────────┘
            │                        │
            └───────────┬────────────┘
                        ▼
┌───────────────────────────────────────────────┐
│   Bangkok Water Purifier Company Limited       │
└───────────────────────────────────────────────┘
                        │
                        ▼
┌───────────────────────────────────────────────┐
│  Retail and Product Distribution Company Limited │
└───────────────────────────────────────────────┘
                        │
                        ▼
┌───────────────────────────────────────────────┐
│            Customers (End Users)               │
└───────────────────────────────────────────────┘
```

Expanding The Business

After two years of hard work, their business had turned a profit of more than ten million baht (> $300,000). Wang Jing was then invited to invest in Bangkok's booming real estate business, especially high-end, downtown condominiums. With each condo sale, Wang Jing increased his capital and soon began buying plots of land in a business segment that netted billions of baht a year.

Wang Jing retained his stake in the company with Li Wei and they continued to expand to other Thai cities thus earning more profits. Wang Jing was happy to allow Li Wei to run their business because he wanted to focus on his new real estate business. Such was the growth in Thailand's real estate sector during the 1990s that Wang Jing became a multi-millionaire in just a few short years.

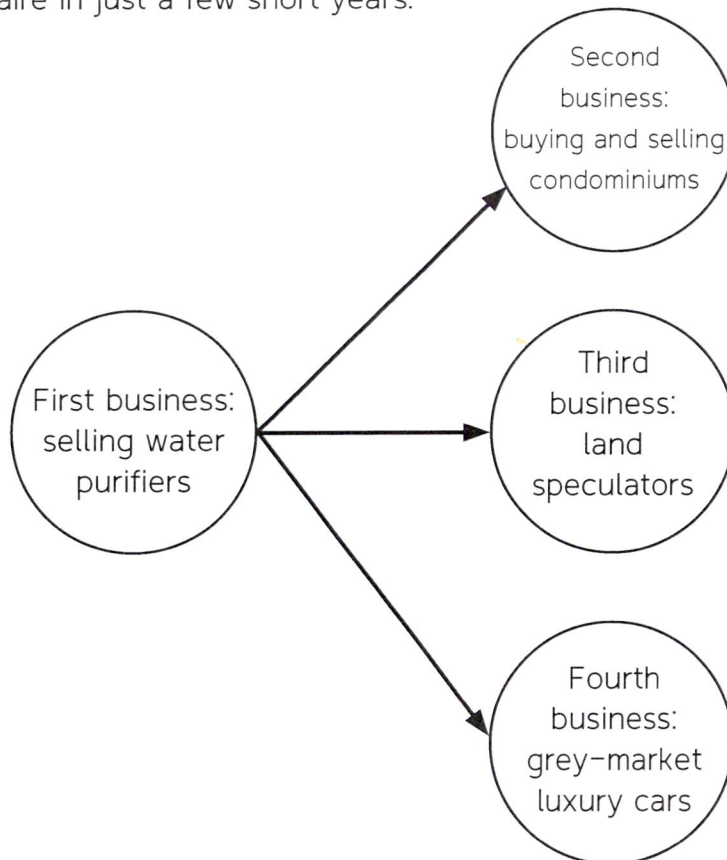

Network Strategy

A Strategy Designed For Networkers

This is designed for **Networkers** who are skilled at making – and keeping – all types of personal connections. **Networkers** might seem really nice people who care more about friendships than money, but in business an **N-type** partner can be worth their weight in gold. By maintaining a wide network of friends, **N-type** people are often some of the first people to hear about exciting new opportunities.

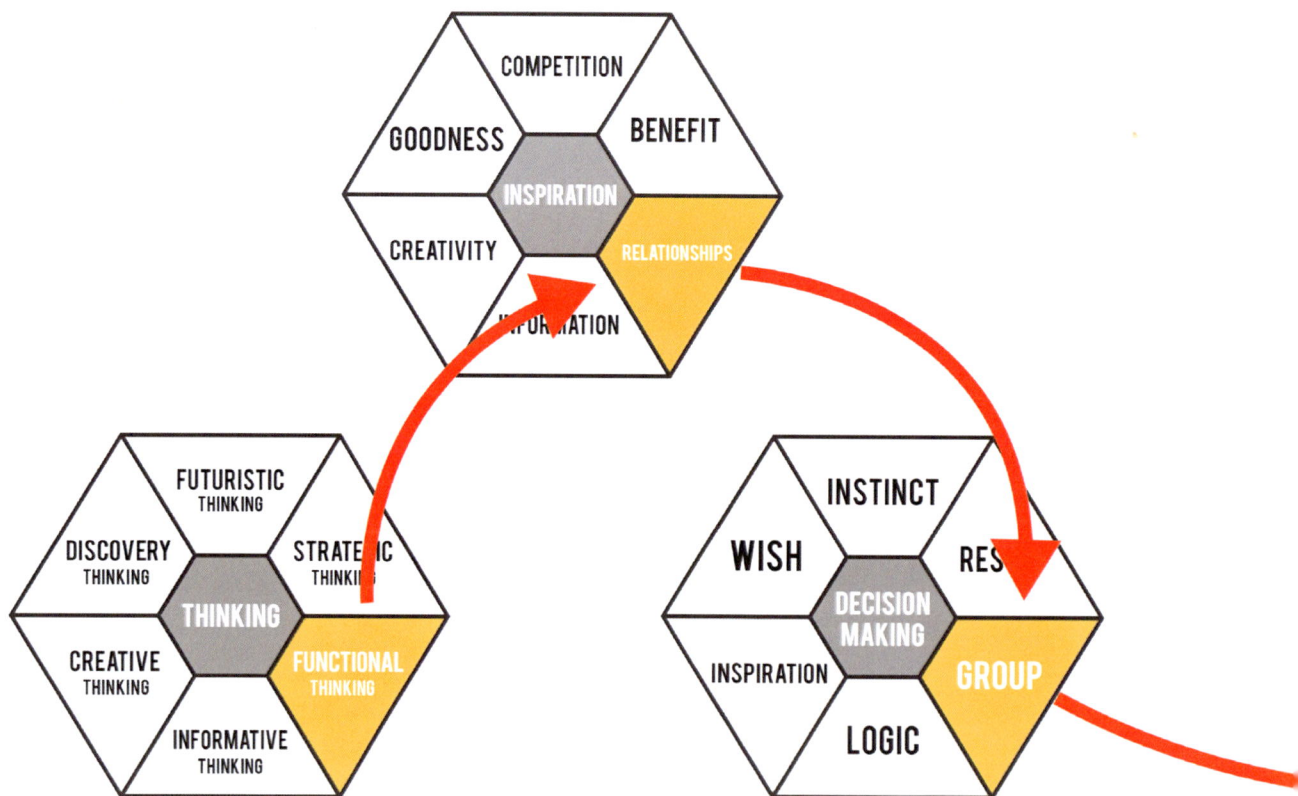

Networkers are the type of people who can get along with every personality type we've reviewed in this book. While a Networker might hesitate to start his or her own business, they are great to have onboard as their connections are invaluable.

N-type people will always put other people first and this can be an important tool in business as taking care of the customer is vital and this comes as second nature to Networkers.

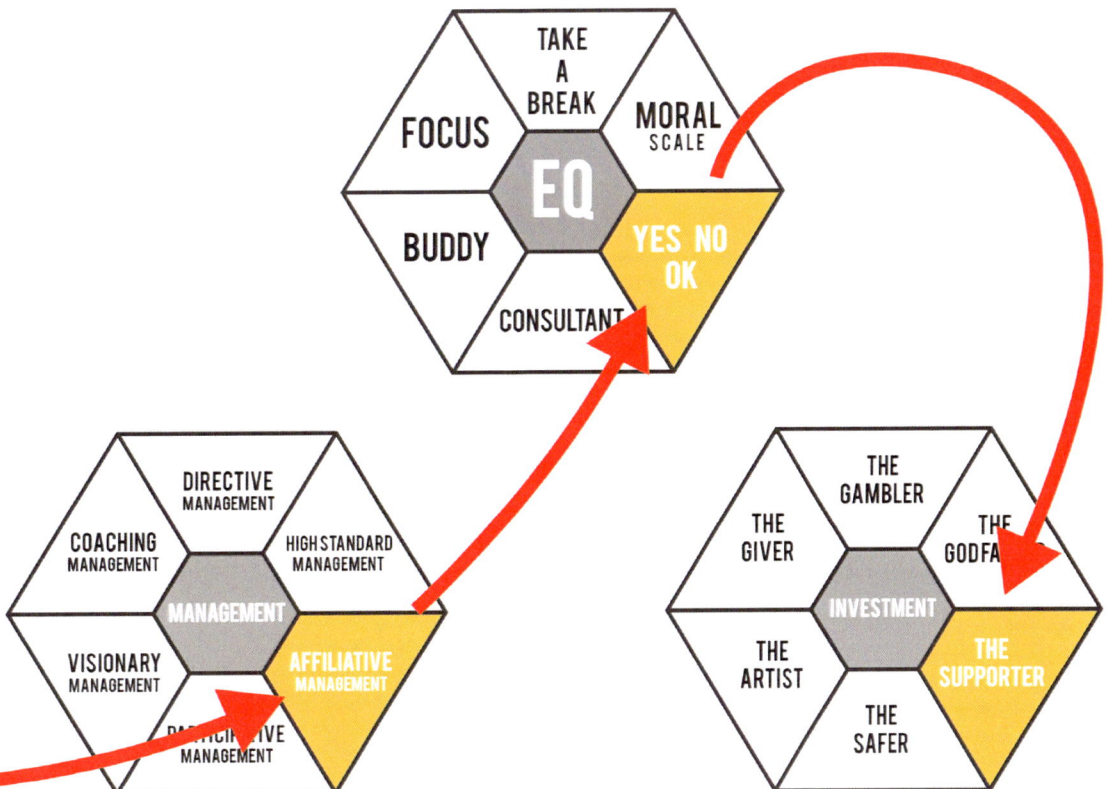

Starting a Business

Matthew, an **N-type** personality, worked for a medium-sized recruitment company where he met lots of people – a job that perfectly suited his personality. During a chance meeting with Peter, an **S-type** person and a friend from another company, they both agreed to quit their jobs and start a new business together. Their idea was to establish a recruitment company providing workers to companies in Arabian Gulf states, where monthly wages are double those in the UK and Europe.

Networkers and **Sharers** are both excellent personality types when it comes to businesses that deal closely with customers and consumers. However, the main drawback here is that both personality types are not so good at giving orders and making tough business decisions. After five years of hard work, Matthew and Peter were looking at filing for bankruptcy, so what caused this to happen?

N-type people are experts in relationships, while **S-type** people are kind-hearted and good at human relations. However, to ensure their business is run successfully they really need to appoint an **E-type** person to act as an office manager. Matthew and Peter failed to do this and appointed **G-type** people as staff, a fatal business mistake. Another area in which they made a mistake was not appointing an **Informationist.** Setting up a business overseas comes with a lot of red tape, so having an employee who knows the laws, processes and documentation that's required is paramount.

In their defence, Matthew and Peter hired **Game Changers** who they believed would drive their business forward if given a financial incentive. But as we know, **G-type** people are impetuous and do things without focusing on the details. When their recruitment business finally failed, Matthew and Peter reflected on the business decisions they had made and agreed they had put the wrong people in the wrong jobs. It is imperative to know your staff's personality type and ensure you have the right balance of how-how and know-who.

In this example, we can clearly see that putting the wrong personality type in the wrong position can be devastating. Both men should have looked at how best to achieve their business goals while at the same time balancing their workflow and office principles. **E-type** and **I-type** people are essential in keeping businesses running in tip-top condition.

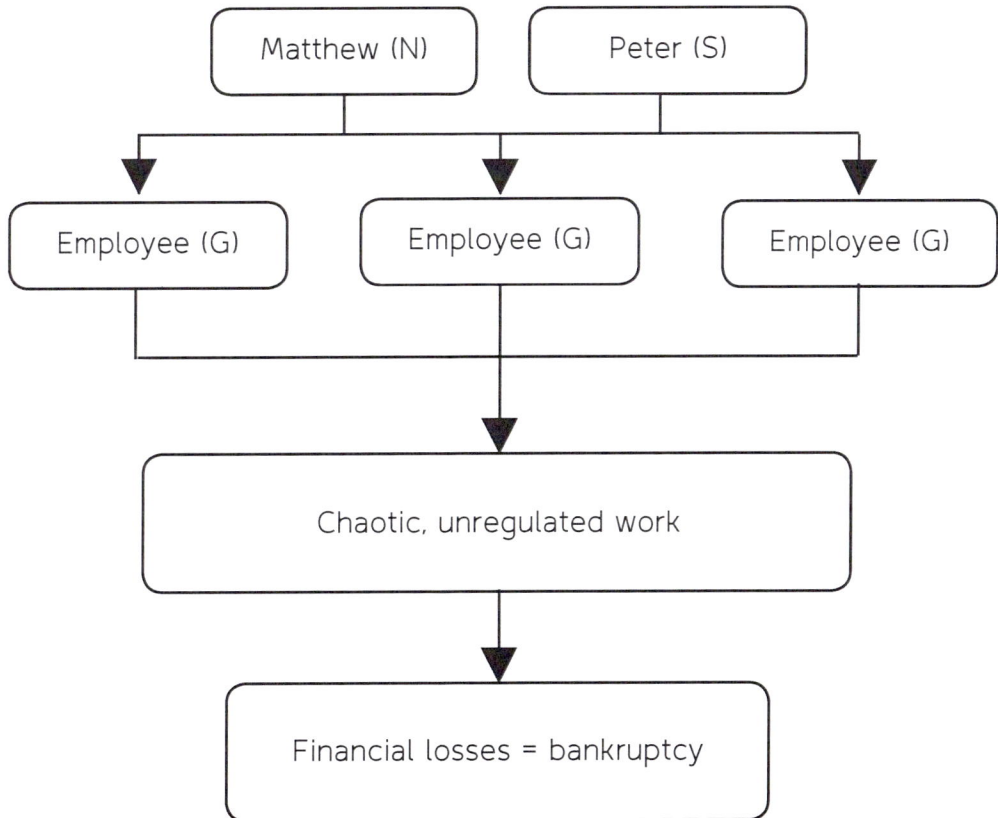

```
┌─────────────────┐        ┌─────────────────┐
│  Matthew (N)    │        │   Peter (S)     │
└─────────────────┘        └─────────────────┘
         │                          │
  ┌──────┴──────┬───────────────────┴──────┐
  ▼             ▼                          ▼
┌──────────┐ ┌──────────────┐ ┌──────────────┐
│Employee  │ │ Employee (G) │ │ Employee (G) │
│   (G)    │ │              │ │              │
└──────────┘ └──────────────┘ └──────────────┘
     └────────────┬──────────────────┘
                  ▼
     ┌────────────────────────────────┐
     │   Chaotic, unregulated work    │
     └────────────────────────────────┘
                  │
                  ▼
     ┌────────────────────────────────┐
     │  Financial losses = bankruptcy │
     └────────────────────────────────┘
```

E-type people will make the frontend work, while **I-type** people are adept at keeping the backend functioning smoothly. **Game Changers** are great too, but you need to ensure they do not run the entire business. Basically, **N-type** and **S-type** people are too easy-going to run a successful business. Unfortunately, most businesses that go bankrupt do so because they hired the wrong personnel type not because their product or service was inferior to their competitors.

Information Strategy

A Strategy For The Informationist

This is designed for knowledgeable men and women who love reading all types of materials such as books, magazines, research papers and web blogs. Gaining information through reading is one of the great joys in life as it allows people to form meaningful judgments based on their knowledge. **Informationists** are always gathering new knowledge even when they are socialising, at work or on holiday. From a business perspective, having an **I-type** personality in a position of authority in your company is advantageous as they bring logic and informative thinking to the table.

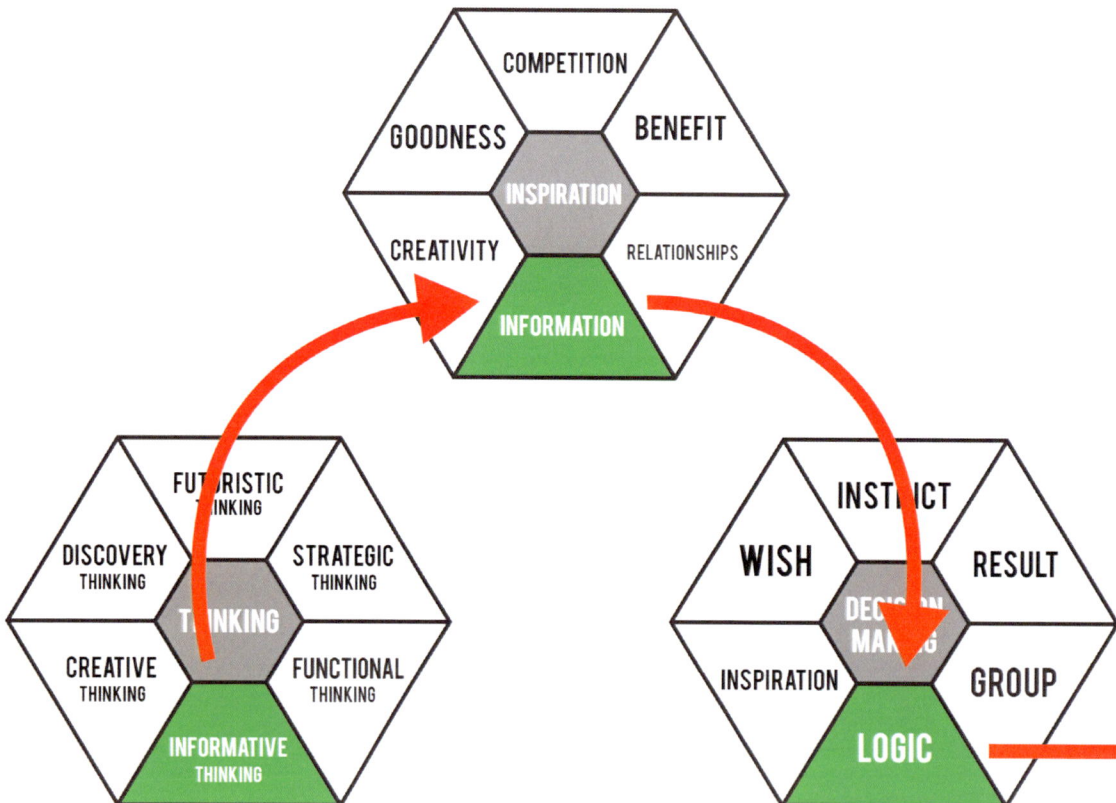

The Informationist is a detailed-oriented individual who carefully examines every request they are given. By strictly adhering to the rules they may not always finish their assignments on time, but the results will be worthwhile.

When they are asked to make an investment, **I-type** people will examine every detail of the company or stock they are investing in. Profit and loss, performance, debt to equity ratio, chances of success, product line up and any other area of interest will all come under the microscope. If you ask an **Informationist** for advice on expanding your business or opening a new product line, you can rest assured you'll be given the best advice.

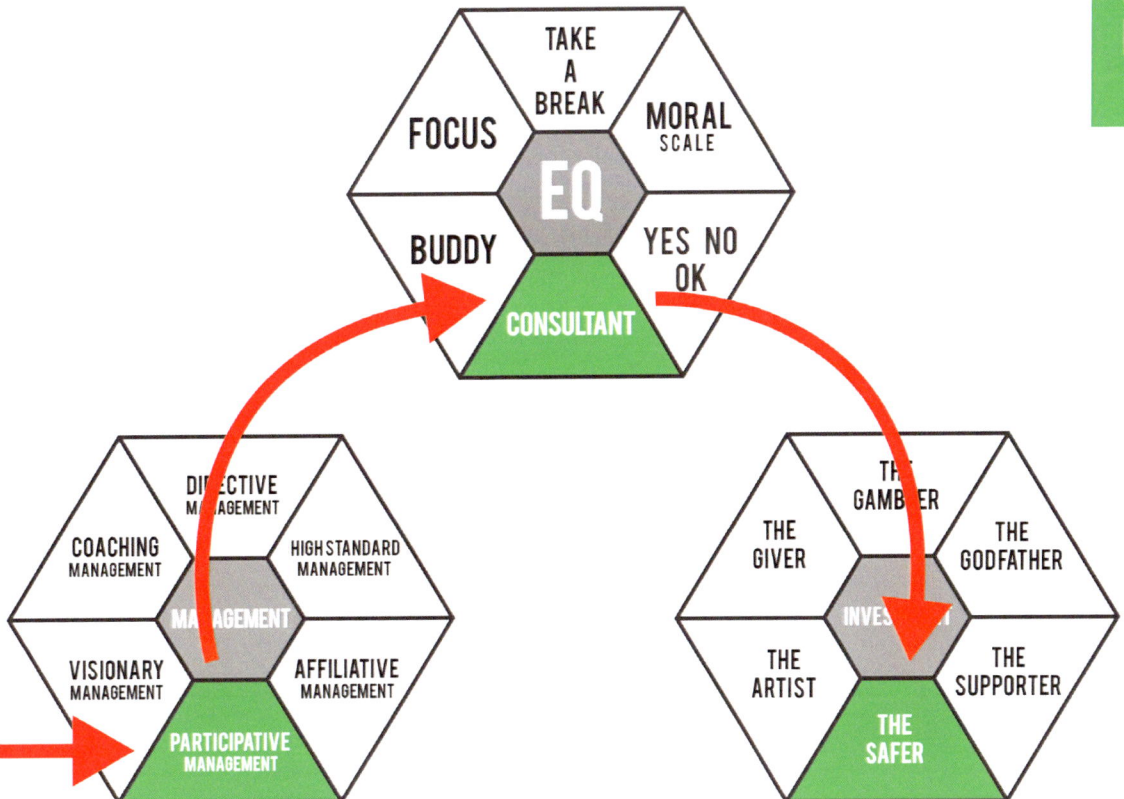

Stepping Up a Business

Tristan Barter, a 45-year-old chief engineer with an **I-type** personality, was extremely proud when his newly formed company was awarded a contract to build a multiplex in Liverpool. The city's Planning Office gave Barter's Building Company a three-year timeframe to complete the construction work before the official handover. Tristan and his team of engineers presented a detailed timetable to city planners and both parties agreed on the timetable.

1st Year	2nd Year	3rd Year
1) Clear the site 2) Begin piling work 3) Lay the foundations 4) Start structural work 5) Bring in health and safety inspectors 6) Complete review of pilings, foundations	7) Reinforce basement 8) Start work on underground car park 9) Erect steel framework 10) Set up cranes for heavy lifting 11) Start laying floors 12) Complete steel framework to 12th floor	13) Outer walls complete 14) Inner floors complete 15) Outer glass installed 16) Interior design 17) Electrical systems 18) Water supply system 19) Drainage system 20) Air conditioning system and thermal system 21) Test all systems

After Tristan's team had been working for 16 months it became clear the project was slipping behind schedule due to months of bad weather and a new request to include a rooftop-viewing platform. Along with his senior engineers, Tristan officially requested a one-year extension to the contract in order avoid to incurring penalties. Having factored in time for delays, Barter's Building Company was confident it could complete the stunning new addition to Liverpool's skyline on time.

However, a bigger problem looming on the horizon was the threat to terminate the contract with Barter's Building Company if the project was not completed in four years. Discussing the matter with his team, it was decided to introduce overtime to all workers to speed up construction. Being an **Informationist,** Tristan drew up a new timetable with all the information now available and concluded the project would be complete in 3 years and 8 months.

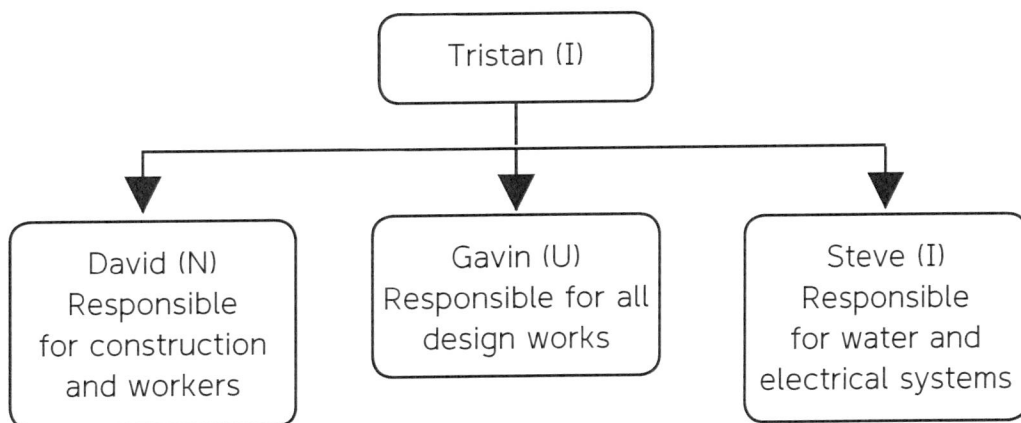

```
                        ┌─────────────────┐
                        │   Tristan (I)   │
                        └─────────────────┘
          ┌──────────────────────┼──────────────────────┐
          ▼                      ▼                      ▼
┌──────────────────┐  ┌──────────────────┐  ┌──────────────────┐
│   David (N)      │  │   Gavin (U)      │  │   Steve (I)      │
│   Responsible    │  │ Responsible for all│  │   Responsible    │
│  for construction│  │   design works   │  │  for water and   │
│   and workers    │  │                  │  │ electrical systems│
└──────────────────┘  └──────────────────┘  └──────────────────┘
```

Thanks to excellent planning, allocation of overtime and hard work, the construction of the multiplex finished four months ahead of schedule, on budget and the opening ceremony went ahead as planned. Tristan's **I-type** personality ensured that little to no risks were involved in the planning and implementation phases and the requested extension was only needed to overcome adverse weather.

1) Tristan did not hire any **G-type** people to work on the project because he knew from experience that **G-type** workers were not detail-oriented.
2) Tristan did not hire any **E-type** people to work on the project because he wanted people who would follow orders and not think out-of-the-box or cause problems.
3) Tristan did not hire any **S-type** people because he already had the skillsets of **N, U** and **I-type** people to work on the project.
4) Understanding your workforce is very important for all businesses.

Unique Strategy

A Strategy For Unique People

This is designed for artisans who cherish their freedom of expression and whose imaginations are seemingly endless. **U-type** people are capable of visualising things they experience in a totally unique way. They gather their emotions and feelings and use these to drive their actions. With obviously different thought processes from other personality types, **U-type** people are essential for companies that need to communicate with their end-users as **Unique** people bring creativity to any project.

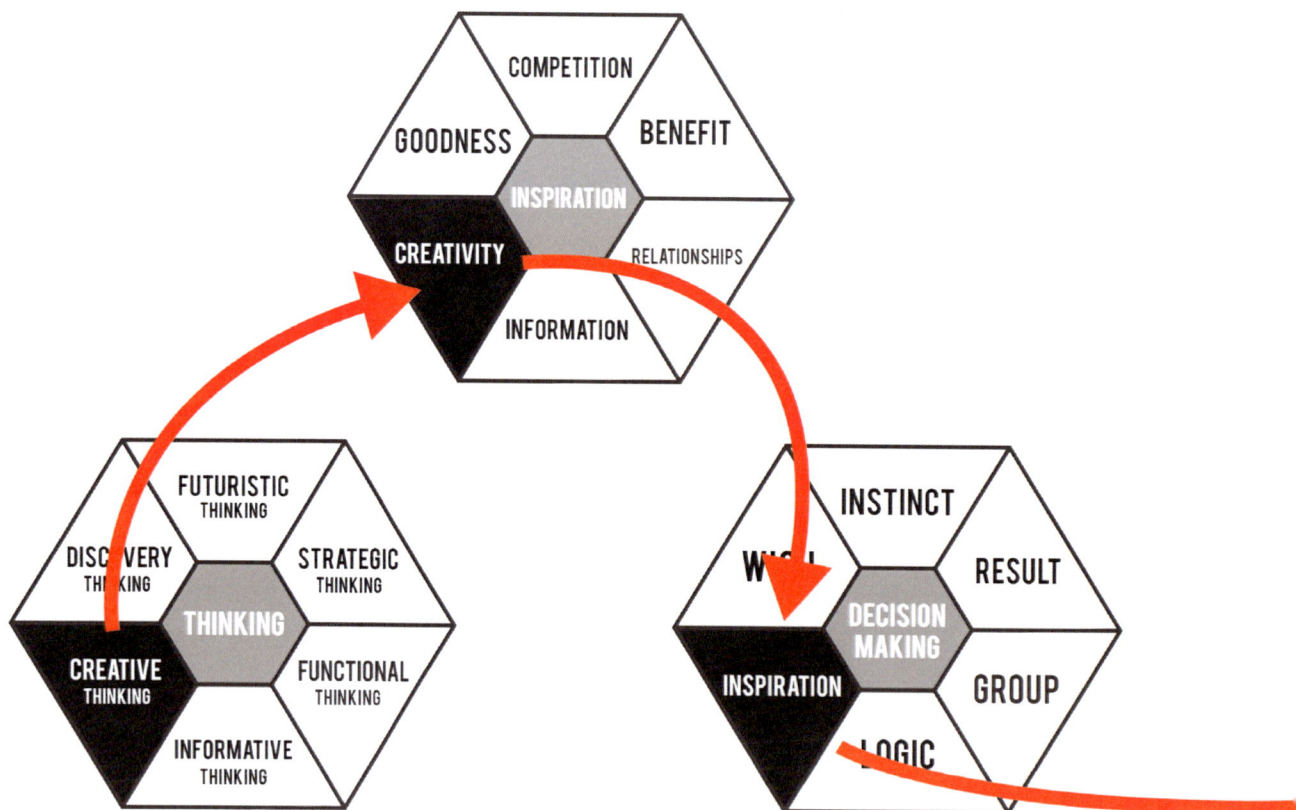

Unique people can be generalised as **artisans who love to express their artistic freedom more than anything else. U–type** people only go in to business when what they are focused on tugs at their heartstrings. They either create huge masterpieces straight off the bat or gradually build up a piece of art bit by bit. If they are asked to invest in a profitable business, they would only commit themselves to a company if it appealed to their artistic nature. For **Unique** people, **"passion"** is **ALWAYS** their first priority.

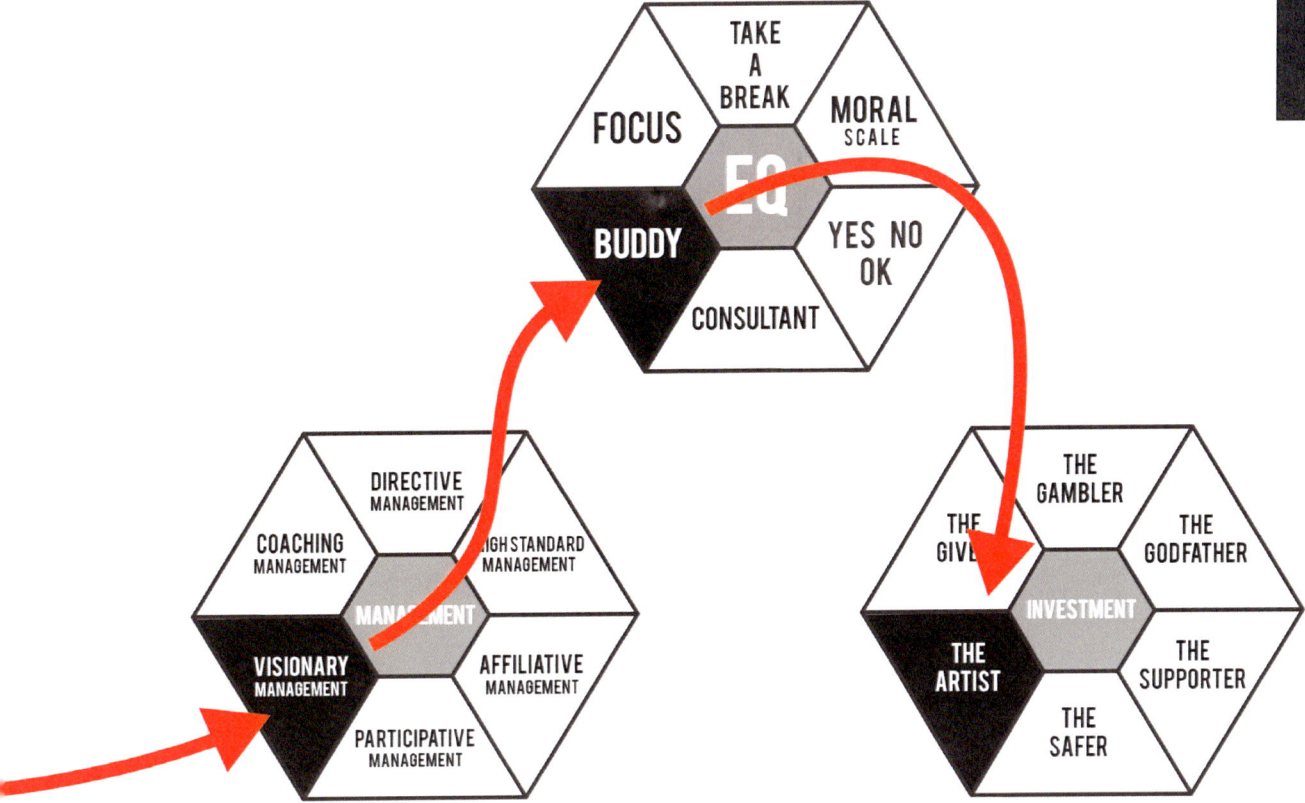

Sculpting a Business

Robert O'Neill, a **U-type** personality, has been a sculptor for 30 years and many of his more popular works have been exhibited in the United States, Italy, Spain and France. Because of his renowned artistic skills, Robert was selected as the chief artist for a new project in Central London that would see the installation of 20 statues of ancient Greek and Roman Gods measuring 2.50 metres in height.

Robert approached the project by spending almost two months looking for an ideal space in the vicinity of Oxford Street. Creative thinking was second nature to Robert as he'd pursued an artistic career all his life. He now wanted to find the perfect location that would help distinguish his work from the many other sculptures located around Piccadilly Circus, Mayfair, Covent Garden and Leicester Square.

Robert decided he needed to find some colleagues who had **Game Changer** and **Unique** personalities because he wanted above everything else for his modern artwork to be more outstanding than any other in the area. As a **U-type** person, Robert realised he also needed an **Informationist** who could help pull together all the information they required to complete the huge art installation.

Hence, Robert allocated all work assignments using his formidable experience to categorise his team's individual skills based on his own creativity and the project's requirements.

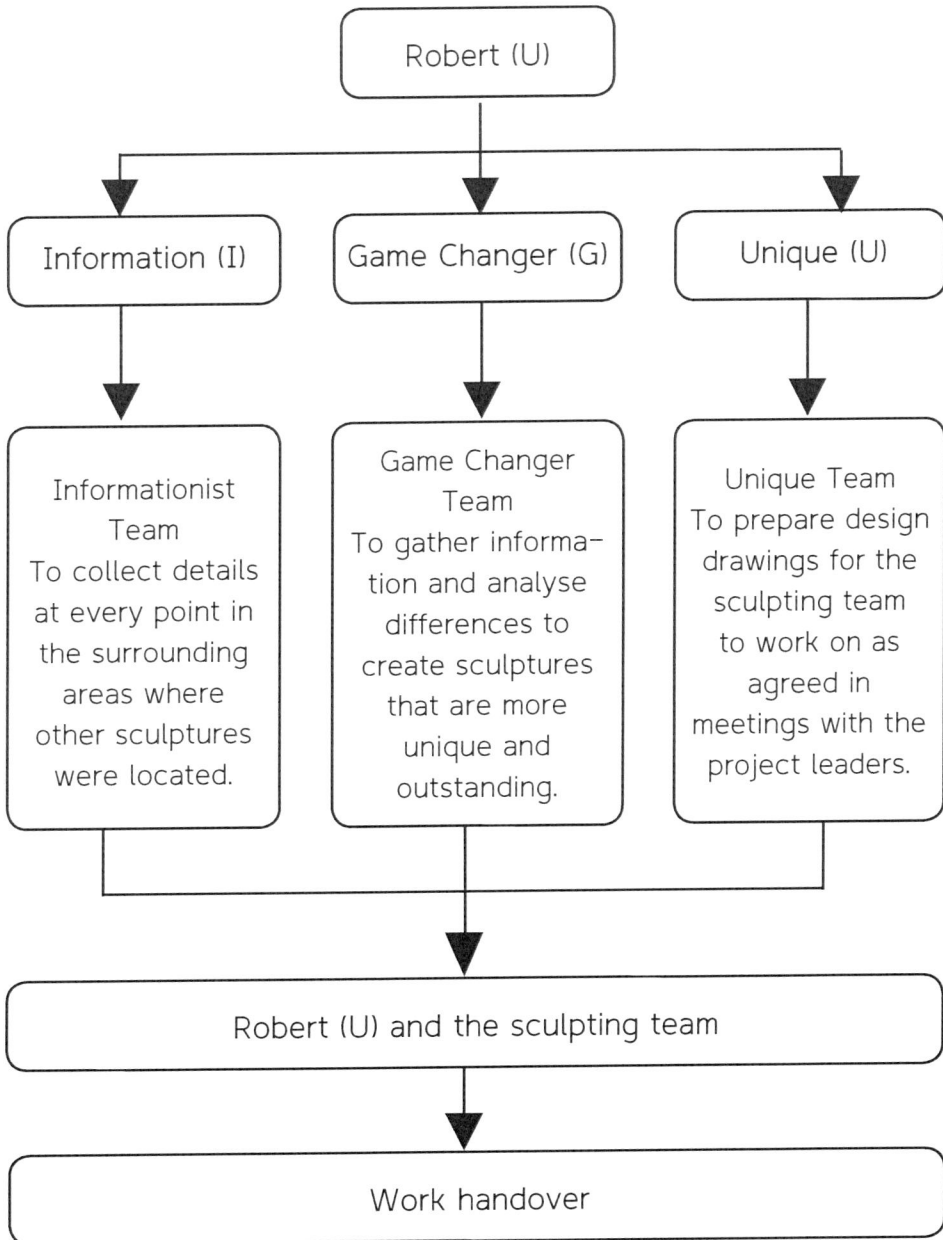

S

Sharing Strategy

A Strategy For Sharers

This is designed for kind-hearted people who although thought of as being gentle and merciful towards other people are key individuals and important to any company that wants to achieve success. **S-type** people are givers who do not expect anything in return for their kindness. Always optimistic, **Sharers** see the goodness in everyone and everything they encounter.

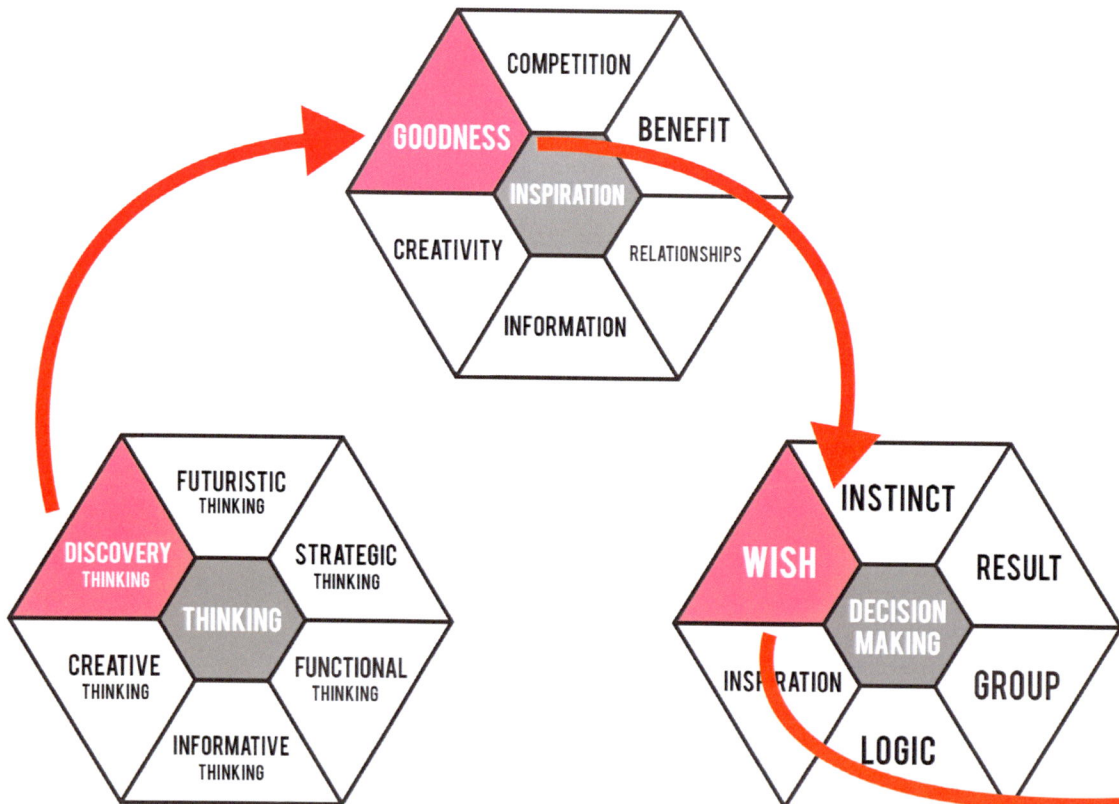

The main strategy of Sharers is to do something that truly appeals to their inner beliefs. At their core is a principle that says doing something ought to be beneficial and provide a measure of happiness to the people receiving it. If by chance what they do also benefits society and the environment, then everyone is a winner. S-type people are known to fully dedicated every ounce of their strength and effort to achieve what they set out to do without expecting any profit, benefit or thanks in return.

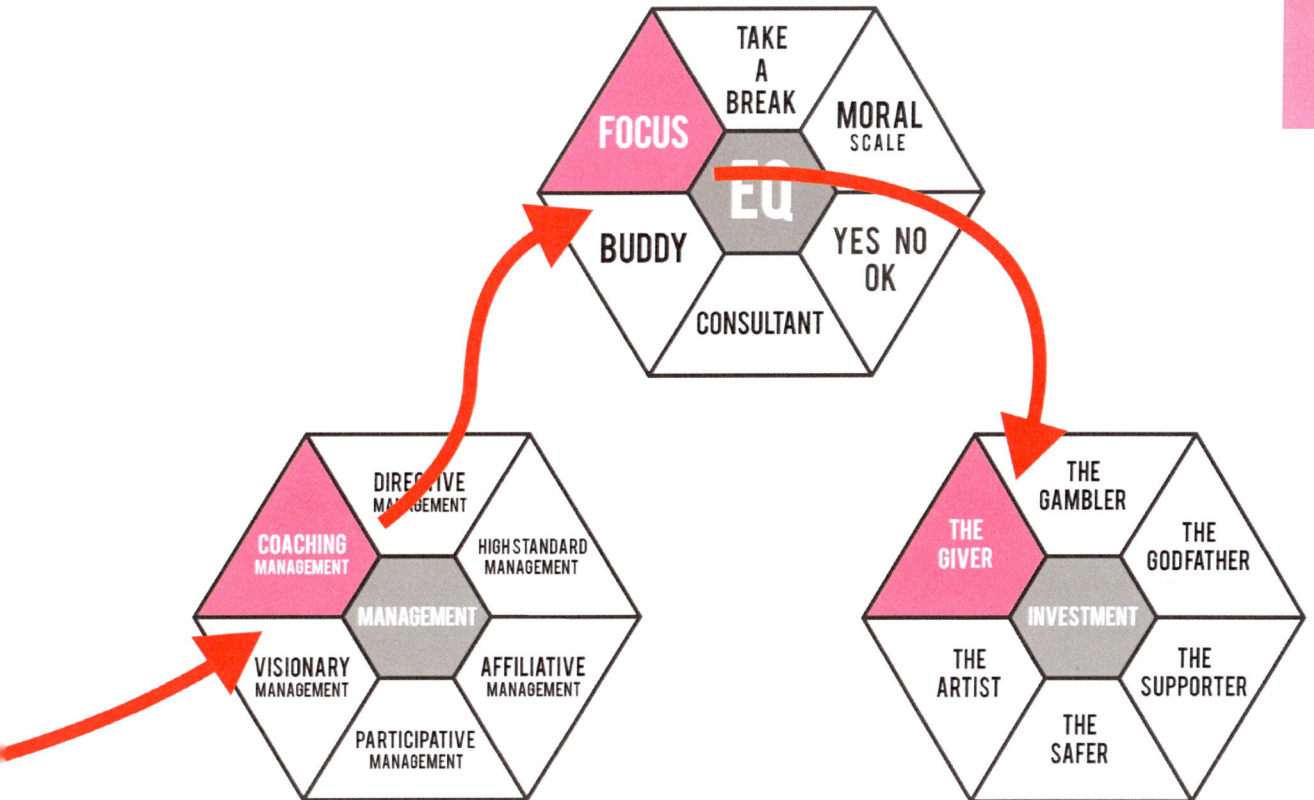

Starting a Foundation

Kathy Burleigh, an **S-type** personality, was a famous actress who spent more than a decade at the top of the entertainment world before realising her true calling was to dedicate her time and energy to the helpless in society. After her final movie, she took the decision to quit and pursue a life more fulfilling as an ambassador of several charitable foundations. However, she decided it would be more helpful if she used her immense wealth to establish her own foundation that would assist destitute people.

Initially, Kathy intended to establish and manage her foundation alone, but she soon realised she would be unable to control the entire foundation and asked her old friend Valerie Clifford, an **N-type** personality, to join her. Together, the two friends announced the foundation and invited their friends to come and help. Kathy's mother, an **I-type** personality, helped by preparing important documents requesting permission to establish the foundation and Kathy's boyfriend, a **G-type** personality, also gave his morale support and helped boost Kathy's spirit whenever she felt desperate.

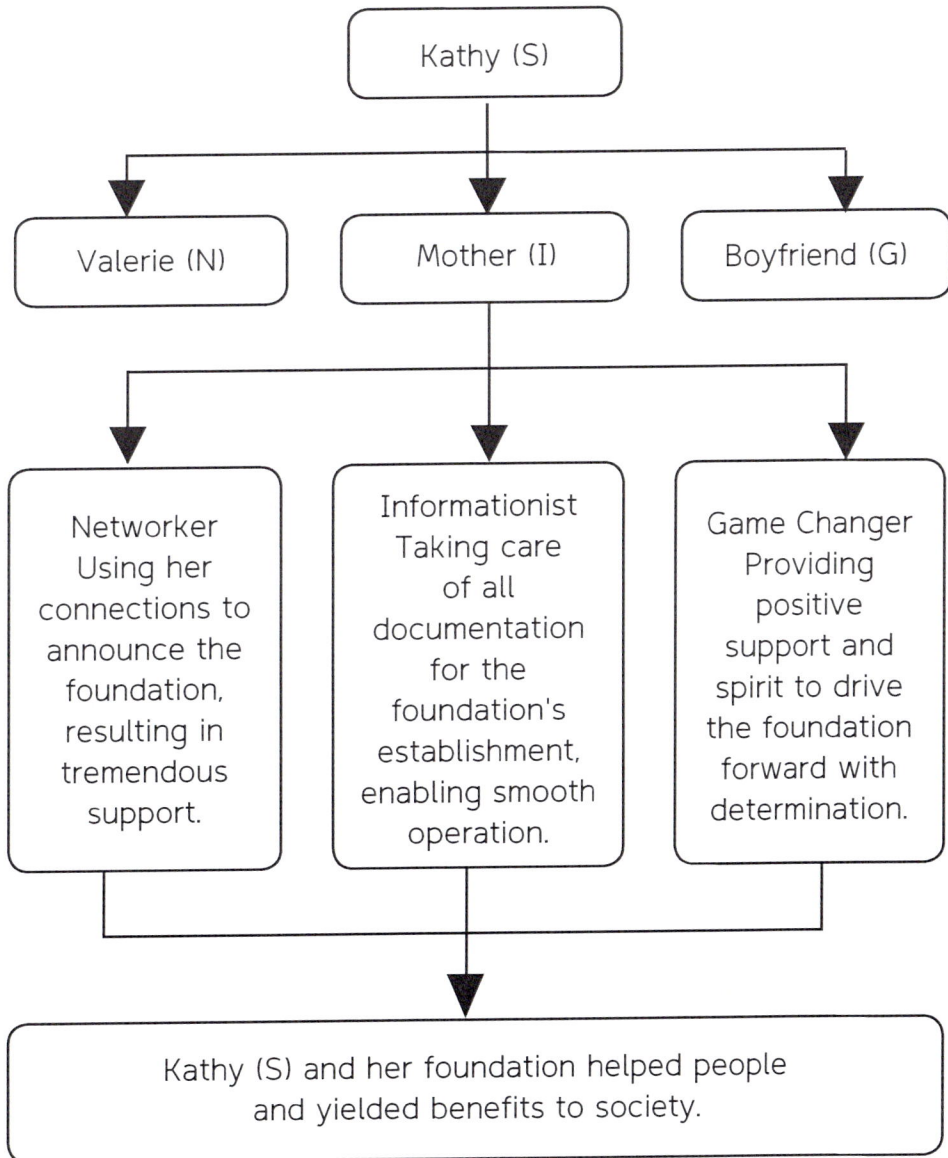

Kathy (S)

Valerie (N) Mother (I) Boyfriend (G)

Networker Using her connections to announce the foundation, resulting in tremendous support.

Informationist Taking care of all documentation for the foundation's establishment, enabling smooth operation.

Game Changer Providing positive support and spirit to drive the foundation forward with determination.

Kathy (S) and her foundation helped people and yielded benefits to society.

From birth, our brain grows at an amazing
rate and at certain stages of development
more than 250,000 neurons are added
almost every minute. By the time
we reach our second birthday,
our brain has reached 80% of its full size.

But does this mean we are intelligent or
does intelligence only come with age?

Although there are roughly 86–100 billion
neurons in the human brain, the brain cannot
keep expanding and so uses glial cells to
keep growing. The billions of glial cells in our brain
divide and multiply throughout our entire life.

Intelligence is very difficult to measure
but many scientists believe it is related
to the brain's **density and** the amount
of synapses that remain active.
This is because **synapses** are established
only **when we learn new things** or **do new activities,**
such as studying new languages or
learning to walk again after a serious accident.

Therefore, the secret to a long life
is to remain active; exercising the body
and the brain in equal measure.

Chapter 10

GeniusX
Business Strategies
Conclusion

From the Industrial Age to the Information Age, a timespan of roughly 250 years, administrators, academics, psychologists and researchers have developed many different strategies. Some strategies are related and complement each other, while other strategies offer conflicting conclusions. Consequently, modern managers can sometimes be confused by the application of so many strategies. Thus, more than 90% of all executives encounter failure every year because no one starts from an understanding of "one's own thinking" and "one's own way of life." They may learn about everything, but most do not learn about who they are.

What these business managers learned and what was instilled in them during their Bachelor's and Master Degree courses comes from a method known as Outside-In.

But in this book, I have described a method for the application of Inside-Out strategy that can help complete the business life by understanding the six personality types, their thoughts, behaviours and actions.

A genuine strategy must come from the "self" so that it has enough power to destroy any obstacle in front of it. If the wrong strategy is used, it is like asking a boxer to dance or a swimmer to climb a mountain. This approach is not likely to benefit either party, plus it may cause adverse effects that destroy the will of those who attempt to do something outside their area of expertise.

The Inside-Out strategy of GeniusX consists of:
1. Self-awareness
2. Attitude
3. Thinking
4. Behaviour
5. Result

Of all the people who start a business, less than 10% will taste success. A few have enjoyed success since day 1 and all it cost them was starting with a deep understanding of their self (Self-awareness). Once they mastered their own 'self' they could use their preferred strategy to overcome any obstruction and thus achieve their goals.

G

Game Changer

The beginning

Game Changers are always eager to get things going – at school, at college and at work. They rise to challenges and thrive on overcoming new encounters that none of their peers has ever attempted before. Winning is the name of the game for **G-type** people and many will go to great lengths to make sure they win. But beware. If a **Game Changer** is faced with an easy challenge, something they deem boring, they will surely look for challenges elsewhere.

Thinking principle

Game Changers love achieving what they set out to do quickly and loathe waiting for things to happen. They give priority to swift actions rather than spending too much time making a plan, then not knowing when to start it.

Way of life

Game Changers like new experiences every day of their life and dislike routine and repetitive tasks. Fun and challenges drive their life forward.

Problem-solving

Game Changers are ready to tackle any problem head on regardless of its size or severity. They don't always know how to solve problems, but they are willing to get stuck in and close the issue.

Relationship

Game Changers are known to ignore relationships because they prefer to keep busy and focused on what they are doing. So long as they can do what they want and go where they want to go they will dedicate themselves to it and a relationship will have to wait until they are finished.

Outcome

Every moment of a **Gamer Changers** life is filled with uncertainty as they contemplate if they are doing the right thing and going in the right direction. While their life may look flamboyant and entertaining, **G-type** people need to be constantly challenged to be happy.

E

Entrepreneur

The beginning

There is nothing more important to an **Entrepreneur** than getting involved in a project that will be financially beneficial to them. When they see a golden opportunity where they can take a chance and turn their idea into reality, they will not hesitate to act immediately.

Thinking principle

Entrepreneurs always evaluate a situation by asking themselves: 'What am I doing this for?', 'How long should this take?', 'How will I be rewarded for this?' and 'Is this really worth the effort?'

Way of life

Entrepreneurs pay attention to all aspects of financial matters, especially what they will get in return. If they anticipate it's a worthwhile venture, they'll promptly commit to it. They are true negotiators and will go over every item no matter how big or small.

Problem-solving

Entrepreneurs will look at a problem confronting them and ask whether it is hard or easy to solve and what benefit they would gain by solving it. If they think it's in their interests, they will set about solving it, but otherwise they'll just leave it alone and come back to it at a later date.

Relationship

Entrepreneurs never reveal their weaknesses in case someone uses it against them. This lack of openness often makes others think they are insincere and this often leads to problems with their associates. **E-type** people cling to positive results and success so much that other people feel uncomfortable, although an **Entrepreneur** may sometimes do anything to make others accept them.

Outcome

Their preference and strong expectation of positive outcomes after they have committed themselves to a project has both advantages and disadvantages. One advantage is that what they do is definitely seen as not being a waste of time. Disadvantages include not understanding all the risks involved, easy to be deceived and focusing on a project that they neglect business alliances, friendships and even personal relationships. Most **Entrepreneurs** have lost good friends, colleagues and even loved ones chasing their dreams.

N

Networkers

The beginning

Networkers generally get hooked in to doing something after having meetings or conversations with their friends. They very rarely start something of their own accord, preferring to have close associates nearby all the time. If they are in agreement with ideas put forward by people close to them, they are likely to put themselves in the frame and participate. The majority of their actions are based on trusting relationships.

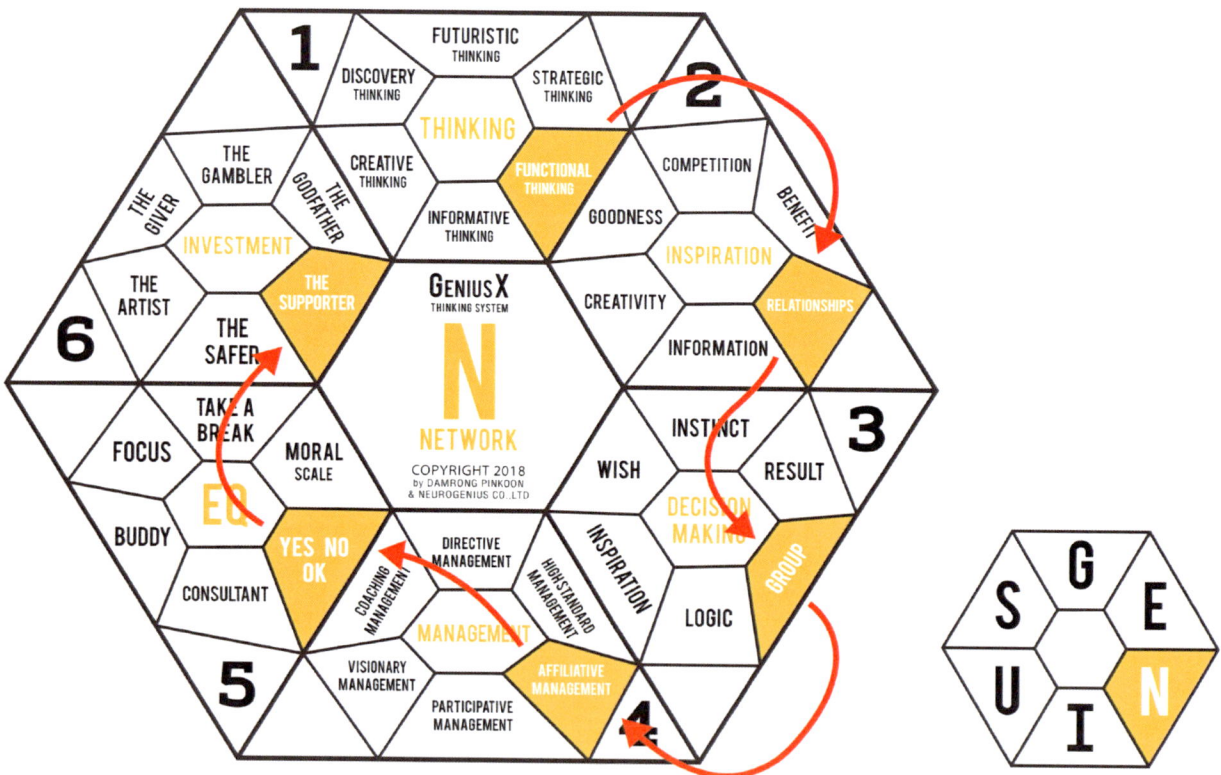

Thinking principle

Networkers believe that people need to socialise. The overriding factor for them is the preservation of good relations with people. If they are loved and accepted by the people around them, they will happily go along with everyone.

Way of life

Networkers would rather be among their friends than be alone. They are willing to spend their time with people they trust and who are on the same wavelength. **N-type** people are creatures of habit and would prefer to stand tall in a crowd than stand alone.

Problem-solving

Networkers do not like trouble or conflict and will go out of their way to avoid confrontation. If a problem cannot be avoided, they will fall back on their motto that "two heads are better than one" and ask a friend to intervene. If a **Networker** is unable to walk away from a problem, they will seek out advice from their close friends.

Relationship

N-type people are talented socialisers and possess excellent human relations. They are adaptable to new situations and new groups and make acquaintances at the drop of a hat. **Networkers** attract other people by being open and honest.

Outcome

Networkers are prone to loneliness and so prefer to spend as much time as possible socialising. If they are asked to join a venture, they will consult people they trust before making a decision. Personal relationships are at the centre of life for **N-type** people and close cooperation and trust are the hallmarks of their personality.

Informationist

The beginning

Informationists always look at the world from an analytical standpoint, where information, principles and reasoning are the foundations that everything else is built upon. Emotions and feelings are separated from decision-making with information being the only thing that matters. **I-type** people will always have a backup to cover the risk of any unforeseen problems.

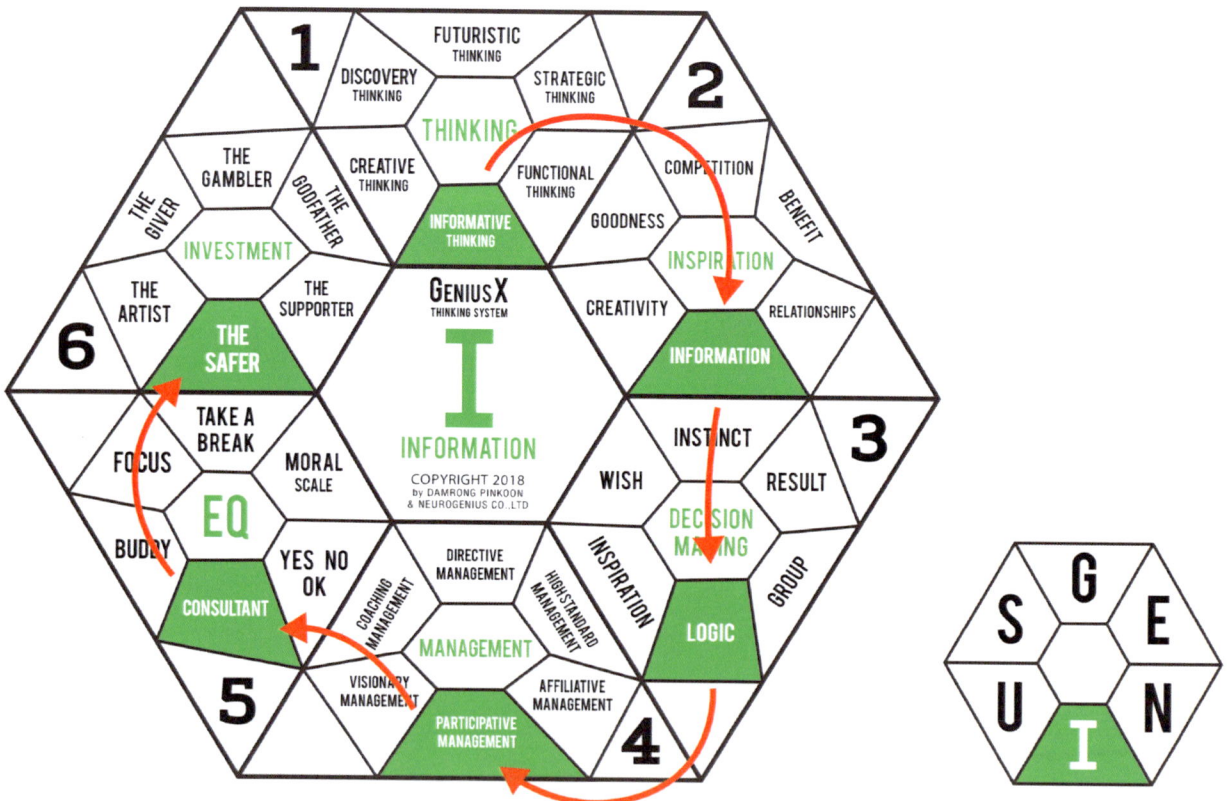

Thinking principle

Informationists usually make decisions by taking into account relevant information, logic, reasoning and, if necessary scientific evidence. They do everything by the book, follow procedures and keep a checklist. **I-type** people are rarely put off their work and will not take any risk of shortcut that would compromise their task at hand.

Way of life

A simple, stable and safe life is a dream for the **Informationist.** They don't need excitement or challenges as they are always focused on long-term planning. This is why **I-type** people avoid risky situations and shy away from mindless competitions.

Problem-solving

I-type people never "shut the stable door after the horse has bolted", their stable door is always tightly locked. They are always prepared to cope with the unpredictable and when they encounter a problem they tend to find a solution pretty quickly. By being 100% focused on what they have been tasked with, **I-type** people remain calm when all around them is chaotic. With an analytical mind, **Informationists** are able to compare both sides of a coin to arrive at a conclusion to solve a pressing issue.

Relationship

Informationists are happy in their solitude and rarely reveal their inner self to new people. Trust is just not given to people, it has to be earned. Although they are fair-minded souls who give others a chance to prove themselves, they can be known to be critical when needed. **I-type** people will always protect themselves and those they work for from being deceived or betrayed by others.

Outcome

Due to the fact that **Informationists** spend most of their time thinking, searching for information and devising strategies, they have very little time left to take action. This means they are not good at making important decisions quickly as they are afraid of taking unnecessary risks and making mistakes.

U

Unique

The beginning

Unique people possess the traits of an artist who appreciates their independence. As a result, all their goals stem purely from their genuine passion and inspiration. For **U-type** people, reasons and rules are pointless because if they are blessed with a good idea they will follow it through regardless. However, the opposite is also true and if they are asked to do something they are not passionate about they will flatly refuse. **Unique** people do not always crave money and fame, their ultimate desire is to be free to do what they love.

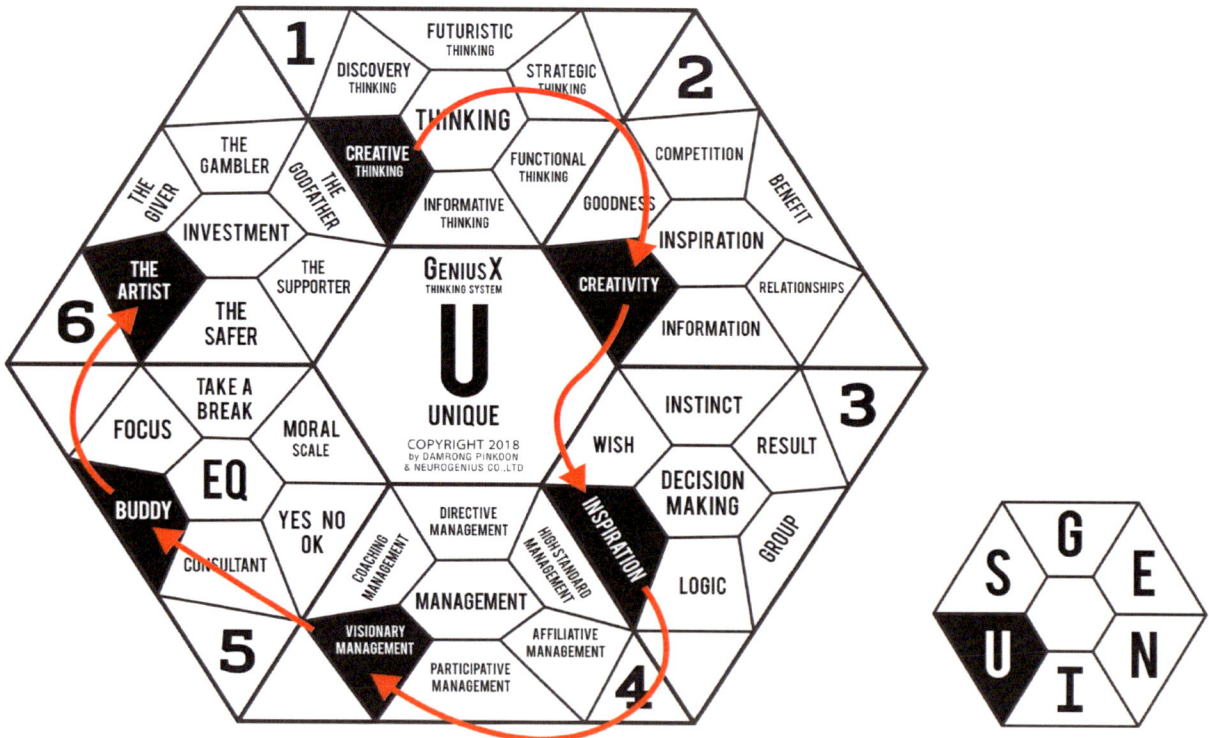

Thinking principle

Throughout life we are trained to follow the rules, stick to a routine and do repetitive activities. **Unique** people hate these confinements and believe in creativity. They dislike being controlled and will always move to do what they like thanks to their strict principles of freedom of expression.

Way of life

Unique people follow their dreams and are happy to live an independent life. They will fiercely protect their privacy so they are able to spend time with their thoughts and imagination. **U-type** people have profound and sensitive emotions towards animals, nature and art.

Problem-solving

Unique people always find a way to avoid problems. It is not because they are afraid they won't be able to solve it, but because they don't like to be distressed. Although deep down they may feel troubled and angry, they choose to hide these emotions. Because they are deeply impacted by emotion, profound feelings and sensitivity, they are prone to be emotionally sensitive.

Relationship

Unique people usually isolate themselves and do not like being among large groups of people. They are quite happy in their own world and prefer their own company to that of others. Some **U-type** people struggle to communicate or express their feelings and this leaves them vulnerable to being hurt. **U-type** people do not have many friends and only open their heart to those they trust.

Outcome

Due to the fact **Unique** people always lead their life based on their heart and feelings, anything they do must be something they love. They may unintentionally lead an excessively flexible life and because they are sort of reclusive means they are never with the 'in' crowd. They prefer to concentrate their mind on art and create happiness rather than conflict.

U N I Q U E

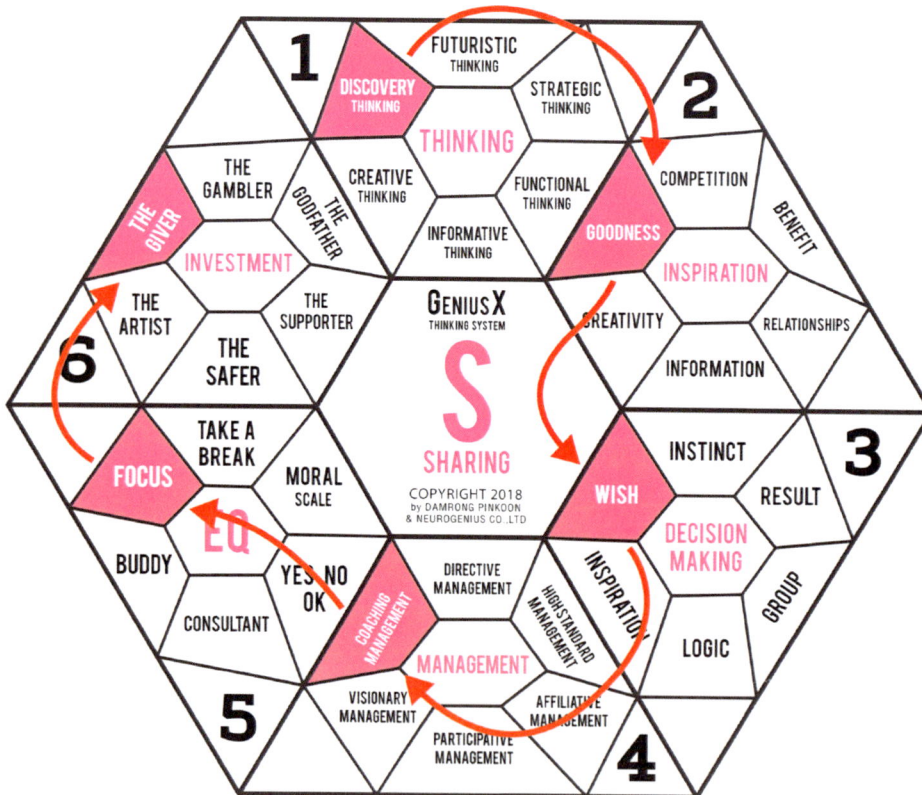

S

Sharers

The beginning

Sharers' beginning stems from their love, generosity, mercy, sympathy and the ability to offer a helping hand to other people. They are born to give and sacrifice themselves without expecting anything in return, whether it is reputation, money or praise. They simply get happiness from doing things for other people. Although others may not understand their thoughts and actions, with their confidence and faith in goodness, nothing can stop **Sharing** people from helping other people.

Thinking principle

S-type people focus on giving happiness through good deeds. Everything in their life is based on destiny and the spiritual principle of cause and effect (Karma). If they think well and do well, their life will go in the right direction.

Way of life

A life of helping other people and giving to the public in good faith is the utmost intention of **Sharers.** They love making merit and carrying out good deeds as often as possible. They do not hurt people, animals or any living being and lack the malicious intentions given to other people. They try to avoid doing anything that goes against their principles because they believe a positive force drives everything forward in peace.

Problem-solving

Most **Sharers** do not face serious problem in life since they are optimistic and do not consider such things as a problem. Even if they encountered a really serious problem, they would use it as a test or a proof of their virtue. So, they cope with problems by letting go or abandoning worldly objects to eliminate their misery.

Relationship

S-type people dislike conflicts with other people and will give way to ensure peace of mind. It is said **Sharers** actually love other people more than they love themselves and they are willing to sacrifice their own happiness to create benefits for society. Therefore, they find it hard to form long lasting, loving relationships. This is the spirit of **Sharing** people.

Outcome

Happiness for **Sharing** people comes from seeing others being happy. They are not known to change their mind easily about what they are doing. Such is their dedication, they may overlook their own health. From a business perspective, **Sharers** are good to have in a company but not in a position of authority as they trust people too easily.

The human brain is a feat of pure magic.
Although we all develop pretty much along
the same path when we reach our teens
we process information with the Amygdala:
the emotional part of our brain.

It is only when we reach adulthood
that we start to think with the prefrontal
Cortex: the brain's rational part. This is
the part of the brain that responds to
situations with good judgment and
an awareness of long-term consequences.

So, whether in business, in life
or in a relationship, use your brain to the best
of its ability and become the GeniusX
you've always known you could be.

Bibliography

Bates, B., *The Little Book of Big Coaching Models.* (Harlow; Pearson, 2015).

Bauer, T., Freundt, T., Gordon, J., Perrey, J., & Spillecke, D., *Marketing Performance.* (Chichester, West Sussex; John Wiley & Sons, 2016).

BRAINOLOGY. (Kingston upon Thames, Surrey; Canbury Press, 2013).

Filochowski, J. *Too Good to Fail.* (Harlow; Pearson, 2013).

Guilford, J.P. *Is Some Creative Thinking Irrational.* (*Journal of Creative Behavior,* 1982).

John, T.C. & Louise, C, H. *Brain Activation While Thinking About The Self from Another Person's Perspective After Traumatic Brain Injury in Adolescents Trends.* (Cognitive Science, 2009).

Landa, R. *Build Your Own Brand.* (Cincinnati, Ohio; HOW Books, 2013).

Light, L. & Kiddon, J., *Six Rules for Brand Revitalization.* (Harlow; Pearson, 2016).

Marry, R.N, et at., *Brain Activation While Thinking About The Self from Another Person's Perspective After Traumatic Brain injury in Adolescents Trends.* (Neuropsychology, 2010).

McGee, P. *How to Succeed With People.* (Harlow; Pearson, 2013).

McGrath, J. & Bates, B. *The Little Book of Big Management Theories.* (Harlow; Pearson, 2013).

Mootee, I. *60-Minute Brand Strategist.* (Hoboken, New Jersey; John Wiley & Sons, 2013).

Nancy, K.,& Janet, M. *An OT and SLP Team Approach; Sensory and Communication Strategies That Work.* (Las Vegas; Sensory Resource, 2002).

Onartheim, B., & Friis-Olivarius, M. *Applying The Neuroscience of Creativity to Creativity Training.* (Frontiers in Human Neuroscience, 2013).

Purves, M., *Brains: How They Seem to Work.* (Financial Times, NJ; Press, 2010).

Roberts, R. & Kraynak, J. *Walk Like A Giant, Sell Like A Madam.* (Hoboken, New Jersey; John Wiley & Sons, 2008).

Salzman, C. & Stefano, F. *Emotion, Cognition, and Mental State Representation in Amygdala and Prefrontal Cortex.* (2010).

Swinscoe, A. *How to Wow.* (Harlow; Pearson, 2016).

Thompson, H. *Who Stole My Customer?* (Harlow; Pearson, 2015).

Torrance, E.P., *Guiding Creative Talent.* (Englewood Cliffs, NJ; Prentice Hall, 1966).

Watkinson, M. *The Ten Principles Behind Great Customer Experiences.* (Harlow; Pearson, 2013).

Wolfsont, C. *Behavioral Skills And Level of Understanding in Adults; A Brief Method Integrating Dennison's Brain Gym Balance With Piaget's Reflective Process,* (Journal of Adult Development, 2002).

References

Chaipat Chunharas et al., *Basic and Clinical Neuroscience* (Bangkok: Chulalongkorn University, 2012), Vol 4, 1st Edition.

Nat Pasutarnchat, Chaipat Chunharas and Nitsri Channarong, *Basic and Clinical Neuroscience* (Bangkok: Chulalongkorn University, 2013), Vol 3, 2nd Edition.

Deepak Chopra, M.D. and Rudolph E. Tanzi, Ph.D. *Super Genes.* (Bangkok: Amarin Book Center, 2018), 1st Edition.

Nantawat Sittirak et al, *Psychiatry, Siriraj* (Bangkok: Mahidol University, 2016), 3rd Edition.

Asst. Prof. Dr. Termsak Katawanit, *General Psychology* (Bangkok: SE-EDUCATION, 2003).

Manot Lortrakul, Tanita Tantrarungroj and Nida Limsuwan, *Book of Medical Behavioral Sciences.* (Bangkok: Mahidol University, 2016), 2nd Edition.

Assoc. Prof. Dr. Kingkaew Wattanasermkij et al, *Biology of Animals* (Bangkok: POSN Foundation, 2017), Vol 1, 13th Edition.

www.ingramcontent.com/pod-product-compliance
Lightning Source LLC
Chambersburg PA
CBRC101142030426
42336CB00007B/68